A COMPLETE GUIDE TO DOMAIN INVESTING: BUY, SELL & PROFIT

A Step-by-Step Guide to Identifying, Acquiring, and Monetizing Valuable Domains

Rajender Kumar

For more information, contact: support@JambaAcademy.com.

Published by:
Jamba Academy

Printed in the United States of America
First Printing Edition, 2025

DISCLAIMER

The content of any of our books, website, newsletters, videos, or podcast is for informational and educational purpose only, we have taken every effort to ensure the accuracy of data, fact, products or services and their ability to enhance your life. However, we didn't provide any guarantee that any of our books, tools, websites, videos, or any content will help you to get any results. All content is information of general nature and doesn't constitute a financial, legal, psychological, medical and/or professional advice. Any success or failure depend on a lot of factors such as individual's knowledge about the subject, experience, dedication, network, investment, market, time, place, financial situation, decision etc. All these factors are different from person to person, so we can't and don't guarantee any success, financial gain, profit or ability to generate any income. You alone are responsible for evaluating the risks and advantages associated with any of our content and your actions and its consequences in your life and profession. Any forward-looking statements on our website, blogs or in this book are simply our opinion and you are free to take it or not. We are making it clear here that by law, we make no liability or guarantee for any possible results, performances, claims or damages arising from any decision you make based on our ideas, models or contents in this book, or any other platforms and we offer no professional legal, medical, psychological or financial advice. The information and facts covered here are for informational and educational purpose only.

Found Typos & Broken Link

We apologize in advance for any typos or broken link that you may find in this book. We take pride in the quality of our content and strive to provide accurate and useful information to our readers. Please let us know where you found the typos and broken links (if any) so that we can fix them as soon as possible. Again, thank you very much in advance for bringing this to our attention and for your patience.

If you found any typos and broken links in this book, please feel free to email us.

support@JambaAcademy.com

Support

We would love to hear your thoughts and feedback! Could you please take a moment to write a review or share your thoughts on the book? Your feedback helps other readers discover the books and helps authors to improve their work. Thank you for your time and for sharing your thoughts with us!

If there is anything you want to discuss or you have a question about any topic of the book, you can always reach out to us, and we will try to help as much as we can.

support@JambaAcademy.com

To the fearless domain investors, who see the infinite potential within digital assets, and to the trailblazers who have shaped the domain investing industry, this book is dedicated to your unwavering spirit and entrepreneurial vision.

May it inspire and guide you on your journey to domain investing success.

ACKNOWLEDGMENTS

The completion of this book could not have been possible without the participation and assistance of so many people whose name may not all be enumerated. Their support and contributions are gratefully appreciated.

I would like to thank Sagar, an inspiring entrepreneur and great human-being who motivates me to write this book. I would not be able to get my work done without his continual support and vision. He provides unconditional support for considerable research that was involved in the preparation of this book.

I'd also like to thank the many people who have helped me learn and practice different strategy in the domain name industry throughout the years.

Additionally, my special thanks to Tanwir Khan, for helping me in proof-reading and editing this book. An additional thanks to Komal for designing awesome cover for this book.

If you have a question or there is anything I can help you, please feel free to reach out at support@JambaAcademy.com. Although it is not always possible, I will try to respond to everyone.

Rajender Kumar

A Complete Guide to Domain Investing: Buy, Sell & Profit

Table of Contents

ABOUT THE AUTHOR

Rajender Kumar is a seasoned Business Intelligence and Advanced Analytics professional, specializing in quantitative and qualitative data analysis, automating manual reporting processes, and visualizing complex data to reveal actionable insights that drive strategic business decisions. Certified in key technologies such as AWS, Power BI, Data Analytics, Tableau, and Alteryx, he brings a data-driven mindset to every endeavor.

With in-depth experience in the domain name industry, Rajender has honed his skills through years of hands-on involvement in buying, selling, and monetizing domains. In *A Complete Guide to Domain Investing: Buy, Sell & Profit*, he shares his accumulated knowledge, real-world experiences, and expert strategies gained from navigating the dynamic world of domaining. Readers will uncover hidden secrets of the industry, learn to avoid common beginner pitfalls, and discover proven methods to build profitable portfolios, flip domains for substantial returns, and generate passive income through development and leasing.

Passionate about empowering others, Rajender loves educating and inspiring professionals and entrepreneurs to achieve success and live their dream lives. His interests span writing, finance, investing, technology, marketing, and online income streams, all of which inform his practical, insightful approach to domain investing.

PREFACE

In the ever-evolving digital age, where the internet serves as the backbone of global commerce, communication, and innovation, domain names have emerged as one of the most undervalued yet potent assets available to investors. Think of them not merely as strings of letters and numbers that point to websites, but as prime virtual real estate—locations in the vast cyberspace where businesses build their empires, brands establish their identities, and individuals launch their dreams. Just as physical property in bustling cities like New York or Tokyo commands premium prices due to location and demand, domain names like "Business.com" (sold for $7.5 million in 1999) or "Voice.com" (a staggering $30 million in 2019) demonstrate the enormous financial potential locked within these digital addresses. This preface sets the stage for *A Complete Guide to Domain Investing: Buy, Sell & Profit*, a book crafted to demystify this exciting field and equip you with the tools to navigate it successfully.

Domain investing, often referred to as domaining or domain flipping, involves acquiring domain names at low costs, holding them until their value appreciates, and then selling them for profit. It's a practice that has created millionaires and provided passive income streams for countless entrepreneurs. However, like any investment strategy, it comes with risks—scams, market fluctuations, and poor decision-making can lead to losses. That's precisely why this book exists: to bridge the gap between curiosity and competence, turning novices into knowledgeable investors and helping experienced domainers refine their approaches. Whether you're a tech-savvy professional looking to diversify your portfolio, a side-hustler seeking extra income, or someone intrigued by the intersection of technology and finance, the insights here will empower you to make informed, profitable moves.

The Allure of Domain Names: Why They Matter in 2025 and Beyond

As we stand in August 2025, the domain name market has matured significantly since the early days of the internet. With over 1.8 billion websites online and new top-level domains (TLDs) like .io, .app, and .xyz proliferating, the opportunities for investment have exploded. Domains are no longer just functional; they're branding tools, SEO boosters, and status symbols. For instance, short, memorable domains in popular TLDs like .com remain gold standards because they're easy to remember, type, and market. Emerging trends, such as the rise of Web3 and decentralized domains (though traditional ones still dominate), add layers of complexity and opportunity.

Consider the economic impact: The global domain name industry generates billions annually through registrations, renewals, and secondary market sales. Platforms like GoDaddy Auctions and Sedo report millions in transactions each year, with premium domains fetching prices that rival luxury real estate. But what drives this value? It's a combination of scarcity—there are only so many desirable combinations—brandability, traffic potential, and relevance to trending industries like AI, crypto, e-commerce, and health tech. In this book, we'll explore these factors in depth, helping you identify domains that could appreciate exponentially.

- **Historical Milestones in Domain Sales**:
  - Business.com: Sold for $7.5 million in 1999, setting an early benchmark.
  - Sex.com: Fetched $13 million in 2010, highlighting the premium on provocative or high-traffic keywords.
  - Voice.com: A record $30 million in 2019, underscoring the value in short, versatile names.
  - Cars.com: Went for $872 million in 2014 as part of a larger deal, showing how domains can anchor entire businesses.
  - Recent Trends: In 2024, AI-related domains like AIAssistant.com sold for over $500,000, reflecting tech booms.

These examples aren't anomalies; they're proof that with the right strategy, anyone can participate in this market.

My Personal Journey into Domain Investing

My foray into domain investing wasn't planned—it was born out of necessity and curiosity. Over a decade ago, as a young software developer in a bustling tech hub, I was building personal websites and experimenting with online ventures. One day, I registered a domain for a hobby blog about emerging technologies. It cost me less than $10. Months later, a startup approached me, desperate for that exact name to brand their product. I sold it for $1,500—a 15,000% return on investment. That moment was electrifying; it revealed the hidden economy beneath the surface of the web.

From there, my passion grew. I dove into forums like NamePros and DNForum, absorbing knowledge from veteran domainers. I learned the hard way about pitfalls: Once, I overpaid for a domain based on hype, only to watch its value plummet during a market dip. Another time, I narrowly avoided a scam appraisal service that promised inflated valuations to lure sellers into fraudulent deals. These experiences shaped my approach, emphasizing research, patience, and ethical practices.

As my career advanced, I worked with major registrars, analyzing data on domain trends and sales. I've flipped domains in niches from e-commerce to fintech, monetized others through parking and affiliate programs, and built a portfolio that generates steady passive income. Today, with the domain market evolving amid AI-driven tools and global digital expansion, I'm more excited than ever. This book distills my lessons, blending personal anecdotes with practical advice to help you avoid my mistakes and replicate my successes.

- **Key Lessons from My Early Days:**
    - Start small: Begin with affordable registrations to build experience without high risk.
    - Research relentlessly: Use tools like Estibot for appraisals and ExpiredDomains.net for opportunities.
    - Network: Engage with communities to learn from others' wins and losses.
    - Diversify: Don't put all eggs in one basket—mix TLDs, lengths, and industries.
    - Stay ethical: Avoid cybersquatting; focus on legitimate value creation.

What Sets This Book Apart: A Comprehensive, Actionable Guide

Unlike generic investment books that skim the surface, *A Complete Guide to Domain Investing* is a deep dive tailored for the modern domainer. It's structured progressively, starting from basics and escalating to advanced strategies, ensuring accessibility for all levels. Each chapter includes real-world examples, checklists, and warnings about common errors. We don't just tell you "what" to do; we explain "why" and "how," with step-by-step guides that you can implement immediately.

For beginners, we cover foundational concepts like domain structure (e.g., the difference between SLD and TLD) and selecting registrars based on criteria such as pricing transparency and customer support. Intermediate readers will appreciate sections on research techniques, expired domains, and buying methods, while pros can refine their skills in portfolio management, financial tracking, and domain development.

The book also addresses the psychological aspects of investing—overcoming fear of loss, maintaining discipline during dry spells, and celebrating wins. In a field where information overload is common, we've curated essential resources, from domain history databases to marketplaces, saving you hours of searching.

Unique Features of the Book

- **Practical Tools and Templates**: Checklists for registrar evaluation, negotiation scripts, and portfolio trackers.
- **Case Studies**: Detailed breakdowns of successful flips, including what made them profitable.
- **Risk Management Focus**: In-depth on scams, legal issues (e.g., UDRP disputes), and diversification.
- **Monetization Beyond Selling**: Strategies for parking, leasing, blogging, and affiliate integration.
- **Updated for 2025**: Insights on emerging TLDs, AI in domain valuation, and post-pandemic market shifts.

This holistic approach ensures you're not just reading—you're building a skill set for lifelong success.

The Benefits You'll Reap: Knowledge, Wealth, and Beyond

Investing in domains isn't just about money; it's about empowerment. By mastering this guide, you'll gain profound knowledge that extends beyond domaining into broader digital entrepreneurship. You'll understand how domains fit into the larger ecosystem of online business, SEO, and branding, giving you an edge in any tech-related endeavor.

Financially, the potential is immense. Many domainers start with a small budget—say, $100 for 10 domains—and scale to five- or six-figure portfolios. Through flipping, you could turn a $10 registration into $1,000+ profits repeatedly. Passive income from developed domains (e.g., via ads or affiliates) can provide financial freedom, reducing reliance on traditional jobs.

- **Knowledge Gains**:
    - Deep understanding of domain valuation factors like length, keywords, and extension popularity.
    - Skills in market research, using tools for traffic analysis and historical sales data.
    - Awareness of legal nuances, including trademark avoidance and transfer processes.
    - Expertise in online presence building, from social media to professional email signatures.
- **Monetary Benefits**:
    - Profit from flips: Buy expired domains cheaply and sell at auctions for 10x-100x returns.
    - Cost savings: Learn to spot registrar deals, avoid renewal traps, and minimize appraisal scams.
    - Passive revenue: Earn from parking (up to $50/month per domain) or leasing ($100-$500/month).
    - Portfolio growth: Diversify to hedge against volatility, aiming for annual returns of 20-50%.
    - Career boosts: Turn skills into freelancing, consulting, or full-time domaining roles.
- **Personal and Professional Growth**:
    - Confidence in decision-making through evidence-based strategies.
    - Networking opportunities via communities and marketplaces.
    - Satisfaction from creating value—helping businesses find perfect domains.
    - Long-term security: Build assets that appreciate over time, like digital stocks.

These benefits compound, turning domain investing into a rewarding pursuit.

Overcoming Challenges in Domain Investing

No investment is without hurdles, and domaining is no exception. Market saturation, algorithm changes by search engines, and economic downturns can affect values. Scams are rampant—fake appraisal services promising "guaranteed buyers" or phishing attempts on registrars. This book equips you to tackle these head-on.

For instance, we detail how to identify scams: Look for unsolicited emails, unrealistic valuations, or pressure tactics. We also cover risk mitigation, such as setting budgets, using secure transfers, and diversifying across TLDs and niches.

- **Common Challenges and Solutions**:
    - **Low Liquidity**: Some domains sit unsold; solution: Develop them for income while waiting.
    - **Competition**: High demand for premiums; solution: Focus on niches like local geo-domains or emerging trends.
    - **Legal Risks**: Trademark infringement; solution: Research via USPTO and avoid branded terms.
    - **Technical Barriers**: DNS management; solution: Step-by-step guides on security and transfers.
    - **Emotional Pitfalls**: Greed or fear; solution: Set clear goals and stick to data-driven decisions.

By addressing these, you'll invest with eyes wide open.

Real-World Applications: From Hobby to Empire

Imagine Sarah, a graphic designer who read a similar guide and started small. She bought "EcoFashion.io" for $15 during a promo. After researching trends in sustainable clothing, she parked it with ads, earning $20/month. A year later, amid the green fashion boom, she sold it for $2,500. That's the power of applied knowledge.

Or consider Mike, a corporate worker who built a 50-domain portfolio focused on health tech. Using strategies from books like this, he diversified into .health TLDs, leased some for $200/month each, and flipped others for cumulative profits exceeding $10,000 annually. These stories illustrate how domaining can fit any lifestyle.

In the book, you'll find more such case studies, tailored to different investor profiles—budget-conscious beginners, aggressive flippers, and long-term holders.

Strategies for Different Investor Types

- **Beginners**: Focus on low-cost expired domains; use free tools for research.
- **Intermediate**: Experiment with flipping in specific niches; build online presence for buyer outreach.
- **Advanced**: Manage large portfolios; integrate development for hybrid income.

Throughout the book, we have included valuable resources, tools, and glossaries to enhance your learning experience and facilitate your journey as a domain investor. These resources will aid you in conducting domain research, understanding domain history and sales data, appraising domains, and navigating domain marketplaces.

Whether you are seeking a profitable investment avenue, exploring new career opportunities, or simply intrigued by the world of domain names, "A Complete Guide To Domain Investing: Buy, Sell & Profit" is your definitive companion. We invite you to embark on this exciting journey with us and unlock the potential of domain investing.

Happy reading and successful investing!

WHAT IS REQUIRED TO BE SUCCESSFULL?

A computer system with Internet Access:

You need a decent computer system with internet access on it. It can be your home computer, office computer etc. In the beginning, no need to invest in super expensive hardware.

Capital Investment:

Theoretically, you can register a domain name for as low as $ 6. That realistically not a business. You should start with a budget of at least with $100.

Patience:

It's not a quick rich scheme. It will take time and efforts to find a good domain name and sell it for profit. If you are assuming you can be a millionaire overnight, then this book is not for you. Like any other business, you need to put efforts and time to make profit in domain investing.

More Patience:

Patience is the key in this business. From my personal experience, I can tell that patience is what will help you make profit in domain investing. I learn this in a hard way. In my early career, I sell some domain name for very less profit which later I found that will be much profitable for the buyer.

Take Action for Extended Amount of Time:

To be successful, you need to be proactive and take action based on whatever you learn from this book. You will not be successful, if you are just sitting, reading the book, and hoping something will change automatically. Anything you learn from this book, apply it in real life, only then you can see some result. This is hundred percent mandatory otherwise there is no point in reading this book. I saw people reading books, taking no action and then complaining about the result. It is all about action. You need to take action for an extended amount of time, only then expect something in return and this advice is not only for this book, but you can also apply it in other aspect of your life. Only action leads to success.

WHAT IS NOT REQUIRED?

No Coding Experience Required:

You don't need any programming or coding experience to start domain investing. If you have basic knowledge of computer and browsing internet, that's more than enough.

No Big Investment required:

You can start buying and selling domain name for as low as $100 and initially, it is advisable that you spent more time in learning about the field instead of spending money. With time, your skills of finding the good domain name and finding the potential buyer will be improved and you can invest more and earn more.

No Office Required:

Like most other online business, you can start domain investing from your home computer. No need to invest in office space or rent a building to start this business. With time, when you start making enough profit, you can decide if you need an office to expend your horizon or want to do from your home computer.

No Staff Required:

You don't need a big staff, accountant, programmer, or other employees to start this business. You alone are enough initially to start the business.

No Prior Experience with Domain Investing Required:

You don't need any prior experience in the domain name investing industry. This book is more than enough to guide you and help in taking good decision at time.

1.

BASICS OF DOMAIN NAME

"Success is the natural consequence of consistently applying basic fundamentals."

-E. James Rohn

Before starting the in-depth domain investing business secret, we need to understand the basics of domain name. Here in this chapter, I will explain what domain name is, how it works and some other basic details, a domain investor should know.

1.1 What is Domain Name?

Domain names are a key part of the Internet infrastructure. They provide a human-readable address for any web server available on the Internet. A domain name is a string of text which is used to access website from client browser, and it is mapped to IP address by DNS (Domain Name System).

IP address is the address of any Internet-connected computer. There are two version of IP address, namely, IPv4 address (e.g., 192.168.55.75) or an IPv6 address (e.g., 3037:0bc8:8b22:0000:0bb0:8a2b:0c20:1224). For human, it's very hard to remember these IP addresses and these addresses may change over time based on different circumstances. Domain name provides answer to all such problems as it's easy to remember, human readable and doesn't change over time.

At its core, a domain name is a unique, human-readable label that serves as an address for a website or an online resource. It provides a user-friendly way to access websites, replacing the need to remember complex strings of numerical IP addresses that computers use to identify each other on the internet. Domain names are crucial for creating a recognizable online presence and establishing a brand identity in the vast digital landscape.

1.2 Structure of domain names

A domain name has a simple structure made of several components, separated by dots, and read from right to left. Each component of domain name provides specific information about the domain name. As you can see in below diagram, a domain name consists of top-level domain, second-level domain (which sometime called label), and sub-domain to identify machine type such as www (world wide web). Let's discuss each component in little more details:

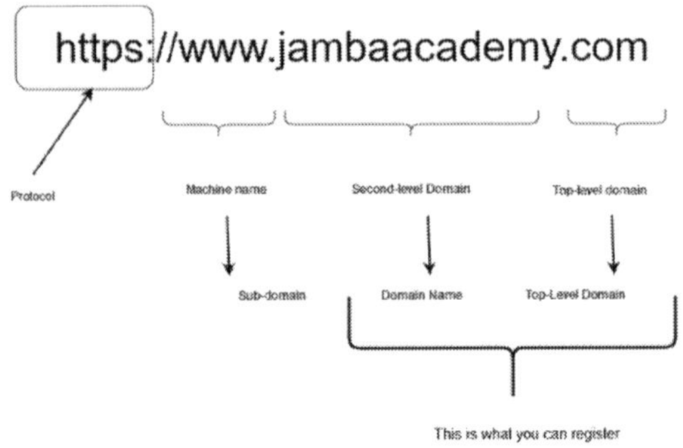

1.3 TLD (Top-Level Domain)

Each domain name must be registered with the Internet Corporation for Assigned Names and Numbers (ICANN). Once registered, it gets a suffix to indicate which top-level domain (TLD) it belongs to. Top level domain is also called "parent domain" or "domain suffixes". TLDs tell users the general purpose of the service behind the domain name. The most generic TLDs (.com, .org, .net) don't require web services to meet any particular criteria, but some TLDs enforce stricter policies so it is clearer what their purpose is. Some common TLDs include:

- .gov for government websites (whitehouse.gov)
- .mil for military websites (af.mil)
- .com for commercial businesses (google.com)
- .edu for educational institutions (harvard.edu)
- .ca for sites in Canada (cbc.ca)
- .org for organizations (wikipedia.org)

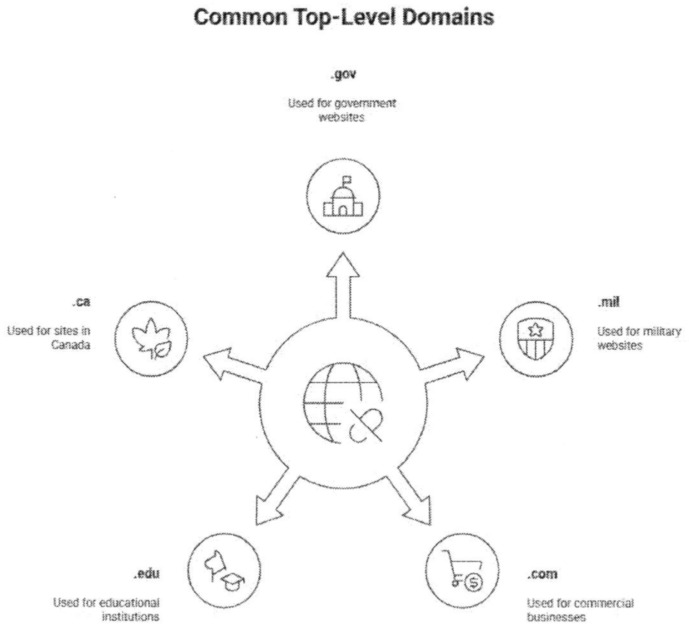

A top-level domain recognizes a certain element regarding the associated website, such as its objective (business, government, education), its owner, or the geographical area from which it originated.

Internet Corporation for Assigned Names and Numbers (ICANN) recognizes the following types of TLDs:

Generic Top-Level Domains (gTLD)

These are the most popular types of TDLs. Some examples include ".edu" for educational sites and ".com" for commercial sites. These types of TLDs are available for registration.

Country-Code Top-Level Domains (ccTLD)

Every ccTLD recognizes a specific country and is generally two letters long. For example, the ccTLD for Australia is ".au". Similarly, ".in" is used for India, ".us" used for USA, ".fr" is used for France and so on. This category of domain name is also called local TLDs and mostly used when you need to target audience of a particular country or language. For example, "Amazon.co.uk" is used for United Kingdom and "Amazon.in" is used for India and "Amazon.com" is used for USA. Each of these website shows product and price in local currency of that country.

Sponsored Top-Level Domains (sTLD)

Sponsored Top-Level Domains are domain extensions that are managed and operated by specific sponsoring organizations or communities. Unlike generic TLDs, such as ".com" or ".org," which are available for registration by anyone, sTLDs are intended for a particular community or purpose. They are designed to bring together like-minded individuals, businesses, or entities under a common domain extension, creating a sense of belonging and reinforcing community values.

One distinguishing characteristic of sTLDs is the involvement of a sponsoring organization that oversees their registration and policies. These organizations, often industry associations, nonprofits, or governing bodies, collaborate to ensure that the sTLD operates in accordance with specific guidelines and serves the interests of the community it represents.

Examples of Sponsored Top-Level Domains include:

1. ".edu" – Sponsored by educational institutions and restricted to accredited degree-granting institutions, such as universities and colleges.

2. ".gov" – Sponsored by governments and reserved exclusively for official government websites.

3. ".museum" – Sponsored by the museum community, serving as a dedicated domain for museums, galleries, and cultural institutions.

4. ".aero" – Sponsored by the aviation industry, intended for aviation-related websites and organizations.

5. ".coop" – Sponsored by cooperative businesses, promoting the cooperative movement and allowing cooperative organizations to showcase their identity online.

Benefits of Sponsored Top-Level Domains (sTLDs):

1. **Community Building**: sTLDs play a crucial role in fostering online communities by creating a shared digital space. They enable businesses, organizations, and individuals within a specific industry or interest group to come together under a common domain extension. This sense of community can lead to increased collaboration, networking opportunities, and a stronger online presence.

2. **Credibility and Trust**: By aligning with a sponsored TLD that represents a specific industry or community, businesses and organizations can enhance their credibility and build trust with their target audience. A sTLD demonstrates a commitment to the values and standards set by the sponsoring organization, lending authenticity and legitimacy to the website or online presence.

3. **Brand Differentiation**: Using a sTLD allows businesses to differentiate themselves from competitors using generic TLDs. It provides a unique and memorable domain extension that aligns with their industry or community, making it easier for customers to identify and connect with their brand.

4. **Niche Targeting**: sTLDs cater to specific industries, interests, or communities, allowing businesses to target their niche audience more effectively. This targeted approach can lead to higher engagement, improved conversion rates, and a better overall user experience.

5. **Enhanced SEO Opportunities**: While the impact of sTLDs on search engine optimization (SEO) is still debated, some studies suggest that search engines may prioritize domain names with relevant extensions. Having a sTLD that aligns with your industry or community may provide a slight advantage in search engine rankings, potentially increasing visibility and organic traffic.

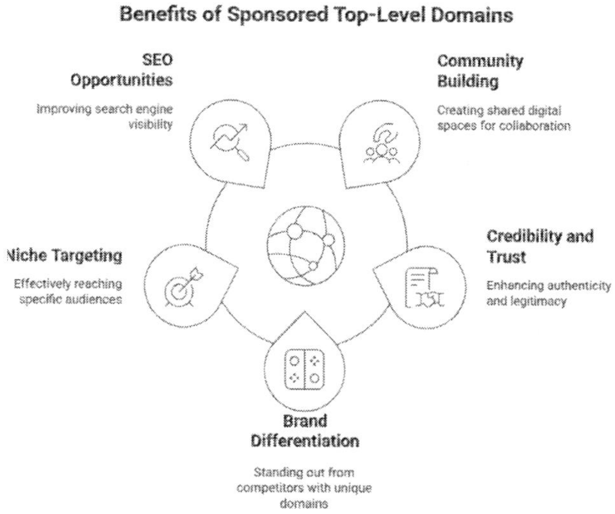

Infrastructure Top-Level Domains

Infrastructure Top-Level Domains (TLDs) are a category of domain extensions that are dedicated to the technical infrastructure and coordination of the internet. Unlike generic TLDs, such as ".com" or ".org," which represent specific industries or purposes, Infrastructure TLDs focus on the underlying systems, protocols, and organizations that enable the smooth functioning of the internet.

These specialized TLDs serve as essential components of the internet's infrastructure, providing a standardized and organized naming system for critical services, networks, and resources. Infrastructure TLDs are managed by organizations responsible for the coordination, stability, and security of these foundational elements.

Examples of Infrastructure Top-Level Domains include:

1. ".arpa" - This TLD stands for Address and Routing Parameter Area and is used for technical infrastructure purposes, such as Reverse DNS (Domain Name System) mapping and other administrative functions.

2. ".root" - This TLD represents the root zone of the Domain Name System (DNS), serving as the starting point for all domain name resolutions. It is essential for the proper functioning of DNS infrastructure.

3. ".int" - This TLD is reserved for international treaty-based organizations, facilitating their online presence and distinguishing them within the digital realm.

4. ".root-servers" - This TLD is used for the authoritative servers that are responsible for the distribution of the internet's root zone file, which contains information about top-level domains and their associated DNS servers.

Significance of Infrastructure Top-Level Domains:

1. **Technical Coordination**: Infrastructure TLDs serve as a means of technical coordination and standardization for various internet infrastructure components. They provide a structured naming system that helps ensure the stability, interoperability, and efficient operation of critical services and protocols.

2. **Security and Stability**: Infrastructure TLDs play a crucial role in maintaining the security and stability of the internet. By managing and overseeing key infrastructure elements, such as root servers and administrative functions, these TLDs contribute to the overall resilience and security of the digital ecosystem.

3. **Organized Naming System**: Infrastructure TLDs establish a well-organized and hierarchical naming system for technical components, making it easier for administrators and users to navigate and identify different elements of the internet's infrastructure. This structured approach enhances efficiency, management, and troubleshooting.

4. **Trust and Reliability**: Infrastructure TLDs instill trust and reliability in the digital infrastructure. These TLDs are managed by reputable organizations and follow strict operational and security guidelines. Their presence reinforces the credibility of the internet's foundational elements, assuring users that they are interacting with reliable and secure services.

5. **Internet Governance**: Infrastructure TLDs contribute to the broader framework of internet governance. They are overseen by organizations and communities involved in the management, standardization, and coordination of the internet's technical infrastructure. These entities work collaboratively to ensure the smooth functioning of critical services and address emerging challenges.

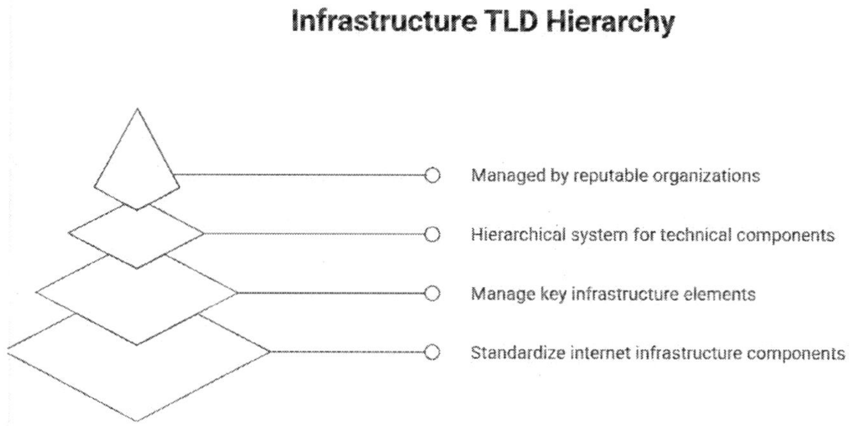

For domain Investing purpose, we will focus only on Generic Top-Level Domains (gTLD) and Country-Code Top-Level Domains (ccTLD).

1.4 Second level Domain Name (SLD or Label or Component)

A Second-Level Domain (SLD) refers to the segment of a domain name that appears to the left of the top-level domain (TLD). It is the customizable portion that enables individuals, businesses, or organizations to create unique web addresses that reflect their brand, purpose, or online presence. For example, in the domain name "example.com," the SLD is "example."

A label (SLD) is a case-insensitive character sequence anywhere from one to sixty-three characters in length, containing only the letters A through Z, digits 0 through 9, and the - (hyphen) character (which may not be the first or last character in the label). amazon, google, yourname, usa, 107-taste, jambaacademy are all examples of valid labels.

Components of a Second-Level Domain (SLD):

1. **Brand Identity**: SLDs play a vital role in building and reinforcing brand identity within a domain name. By incorporating a brand name or a distinctive term in the SLD, organizations can create a web address that aligns with their brand and helps customers easily identify and remember their online presence.

2. **Descriptive Keywords**: SLDs can also include descriptive keywords related to the nature of the website or its content. For instance, a website focusing on technology news might choose an SLD like "technews.com" or "technologyupdates.com." Including relevant keywords in the SLD can improve search engine visibility and attract targeted visitors.

3. **Memorable and User-Friendly**: SLDs contribute to the user-friendliness and memorability of a domain name. When users come across a web address, a distinctive SLD can make a lasting impression and enable easy recall. A memorable SLD can also enhance word-of-mouth referrals and strengthen the overall online presence.

4. **Geographic Significance**: SLDs can incorporate geographic identifiers to target specific regions or audiences. For instance, businesses operating in a particular city or country might include the name of the location in their SLD to indicate their local presence. Examples include "nyrestaurants.com" or "londonhotels.co.uk."

5. **Industry or Niche Specific**: SLDs can be tailored to specific industries, niches, or communities, helping businesses establish a unique online identity within their respective sectors. For example, a photography studio might choose an SLD like "bestphotography.com" or "weddingphotoexpert.com" to differentiate themselves in the photography industry.

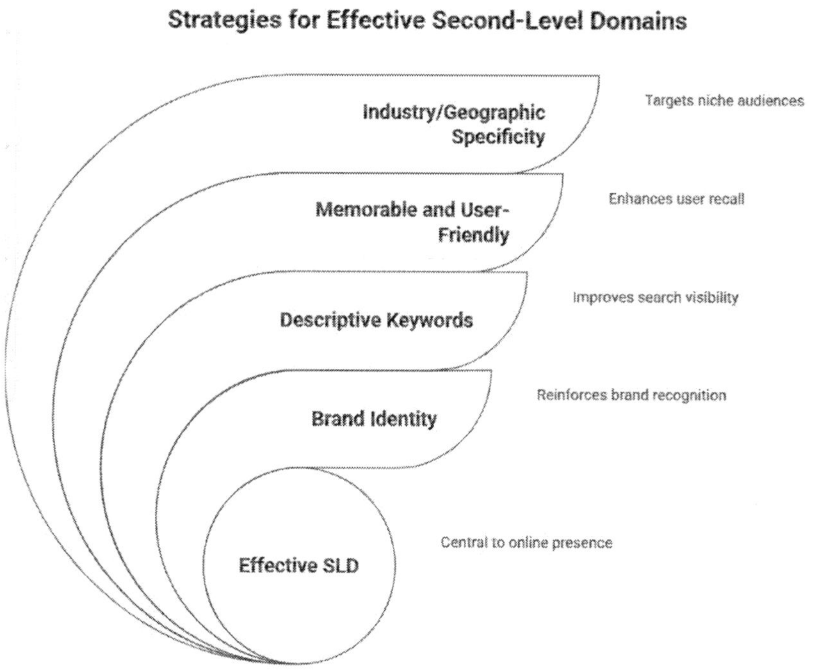

Significance of Second-Level Domain (SLD):

1. **Brand Recognition**: SLDs contribute significantly to brand recognition and recall. A well-chosen SLD that aligns with the brand name or the industry can help establish a strong online presence and enhance brand visibility in the digital space.

2. **Differentiation**: In a competitive online landscape, a unique SLD can set a website apart from competitors and contribute to its distinctiveness. By selecting an SLD that is memorable, relevant, and reflective of the brand or purpose, organizations can stand out and attract target audiences.

3. **Search Engine Optimization (SEO)**: Including relevant keywords in the SLD can improve a website's visibility in search engine results. Search engines consider domain names when ranking web pages, and having descriptive keywords in the SLD can positively impact search engine optimization efforts.

4. **Trust and Credibility**: A well-crafted SLD can enhance the trust and credibility of a website. It portrays professionalism and a clear brand identity, instilling confidence in visitors and potential customers.

5. **Versatility and Adaptability**: SLDs offer flexibility, allowing businesses to adapt their online presence as needed. If a company expands its services or ventures into new markets, having a customizable SLD provides the opportunity to reflect these changes and maintain a consistent brand image.

Second-Level Domain Names (SLDs) are a critical component of a domain name, representing the customizable and distinctive part that precedes the top-level domain (TLD). SLDs enable organizations to establish a unique online identity, enhance brand recognition, and cater to specific industries or communities. Selecting a well-crafted SLD that aligns with the brand or purpose can contribute significantly to establishing a memorable, user-friendly, and differentiated online presence.

1.5 Difference between Domain Name and URL

Domain Name and URL look very similar. But many people may be confused between a Domain vs URL. We already discussed what is domain name. Now, let me introduce what is URL.

Uniform Resource Locator (URL):

Uniform Resource Locator is known as a URL. It is a string that provides the complete address of the web page i.e, this is also known as a web address. In order to access a particular website, you just need to put the URL in the search bar to find the website. For example, the web address of the amazon home page is https://www.amazon.com/. A URL can be divided into different parts.

1. **Protocol**: The protocol specifies the communication rules or protocols used to retrieve the web resource. Common protocols include HTTP (Hypertext Transfer Protocol) and HTTPS (HTTP Secure) for secure connections.

2. **Domain Name**: The domain name identifies the specific website or online resource. It is the address that users type in their web browser's address bar to access a webpage.

3. **Path**: The path indicates the specific location or file within the website or online resource. It provides additional information to navigate to a specific page or directory on the website.

4. **Parameters**: Parameters are additional data appended to the URL, providing instructions or data to the web server or webpage. They are often used for dynamic content generation, form submissions, or tracking purposes.

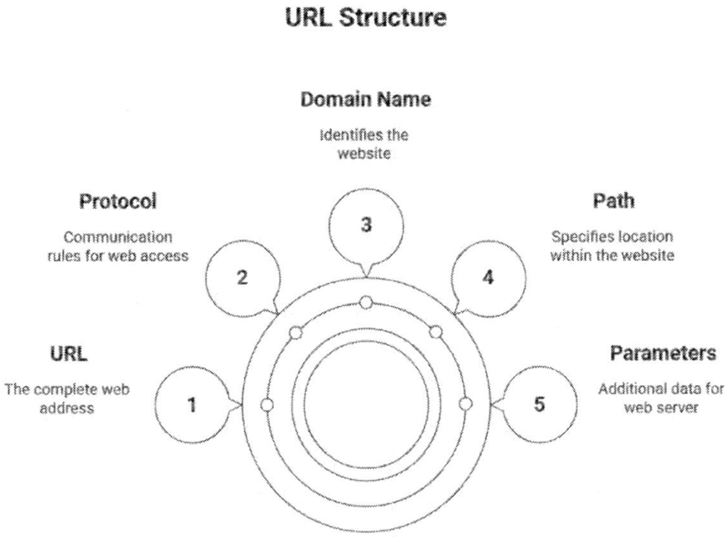

For example, in the below URL, "https" is the method or protocol used to access the resources, "www.jambaacademy.com" is the domain name for the IP address of the server which is hosting the website, and "/file/pdf/2014/03/12/" is the path of the particular file which can be accessed using the URL.

https://www.jambaacademy.com/file/pdf/2014/03/12/

So, in most simple term, domain name is a human-friendly text, and a part of URL and URL is a string that represents the complete web address of any web page. For example, "www.jambaacademy.com" is a domain name and

"https://www.jambaacademy.com/file/pdf/2014/03/12/" is a URL.

Differences between Domain Name and URL:

1. **Scope**: A domain name refers to the overall address used to identify a website or online resource. It consists of the second-level domain (SLD) and the top-level domain (TLD). On the other hand, a URL provides the complete address of a specific web resource, including the protocol, domain name, path, and parameters.

2. **Functionality**: A domain name serves as the human-readable label that represents the address of a website. It acts as a unique identifier for a web presence. In contrast, a URL is a complete address that directs a web browser to a specific webpage or resource within the website. It provides the necessary information for the browser to locate and retrieve the requested content.

3. **Components**: A domain name consists of the SLD and TLD, which help categorize and differentiate websites based on their purpose or industry. A URL comprises multiple components, including the protocol, domain name, path, and parameters, working together to provide a complete address for a specific web resource.

4. **Registration and Management**: Domain names are registered and managed by domain name registrars. Users can purchase and renew domain names to establish their online presence. URLs, on the other hand, are not registered or managed separately. They are formed dynamically based on the specific web resource's location and parameters.

1.6 Who is a domain name registrar?

A domain name registrar is a business that handles the reservation of domain names as well as the assignment of IP addresses for those domain names. In other words, a domain name registrar is any entity which reserves website names for other company or individuals for a payment. Registrar must be accredited by ICANN and certified by registries. It should be noted that registrars don't actually manage and maintain domain names; that part is done by a domain name registry. For some people, registrar and registry look very confusing to each other. These registrars act as intermediaries between domain name registrants (individuals or organizations seeking to register their domain names) and the central registry for domain names.

Responsibilities of Domain Name Registrar:

Here are the main responsibilities of a domain name registrar:

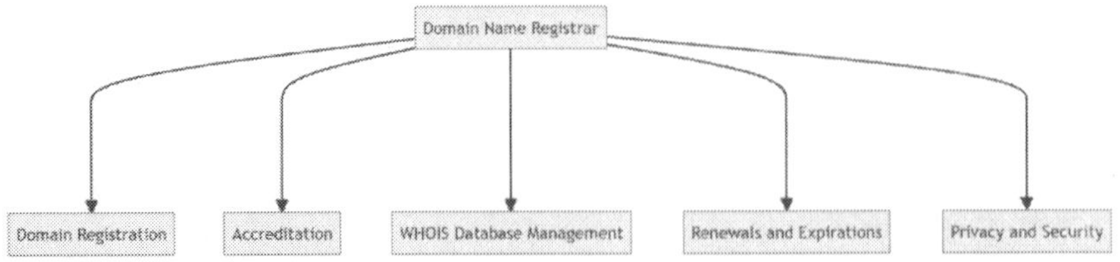

Domain Registration: Domain name registrars exist to facilitate the process of domain name registration for individuals or organizations, providing tools and interfaces necessary for searching availability of desired names for a period specified and then securing those names at their chosen domain registrar. They gather necessary contact data before sending off registration requests directly to central domain registries.

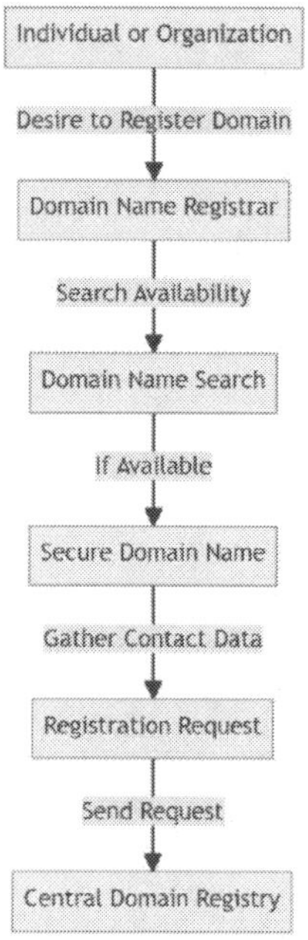

Accreditation: In order for domain name registrars to operate legally as providers of domain registration services, they must first become accredited with either ICANN or their local country-code top level domain registry. Accreditation ensures they adhere to industry standards, policies, and guidelines that foster fair and transparent practices within the domain name ecosystem.

Domain Management: Registrars provide assistance in managing their registered domain names by offering interfaces for DNS (Domain Name System) management that allow registrants to set up DNS name servers, manage DNS records, configure domain settings such as email forwarding or transfers and set domain settings - such as email forwarding or transfers - within an interactive system.

WHOIS Database Management: Registrars maintain the WHOIS database, which holds contact and registration details of domain names registered through them. This publicly accessible information enables individuals to easily identify registered owners; as such, Registrars ensure the WHOIS database remains accurate and up-to-date, reflecting ownership details as well as current contact details of domain name registrants.

Renewals and Expirations: Registrars notify registrants as their domain registrations near expiration, offering options to renew. Registrars also oversee the renewal process to give registrants ample notice before their domains enter redemption period, so as not to miss an opportunity for extension before it goes away completely. Ultimately, domain name restoration occurs should registrant fail to renew before redemption occurs - something domain registrars handle as part of this service as well.

Privacy and Security: Registrars play an essential role in safeguarding domain name registrant privacy and security by offering services like WHOIS Privacy Protection which hides contact details for registrants in public WHOIS databases to reduce spam/unwanted communication risks.

Relationship Between Registrar and Registry Authorities:

Registrars have an integral relationship with central domain registries or registry authorities that involves adhering to policies, paying fees, and adhering to registry guidelines regarding domain name registration and management.

Significance of Domain Name Registrars:

Domain registrars play an essential role in maintaining an efficient domain name ecosystem and providing accessibility of websites and online resources. Their user-friendly process enables individuals and organizations to secure domain names that they need for online presence or brand building; further contributing to stability and security within it.

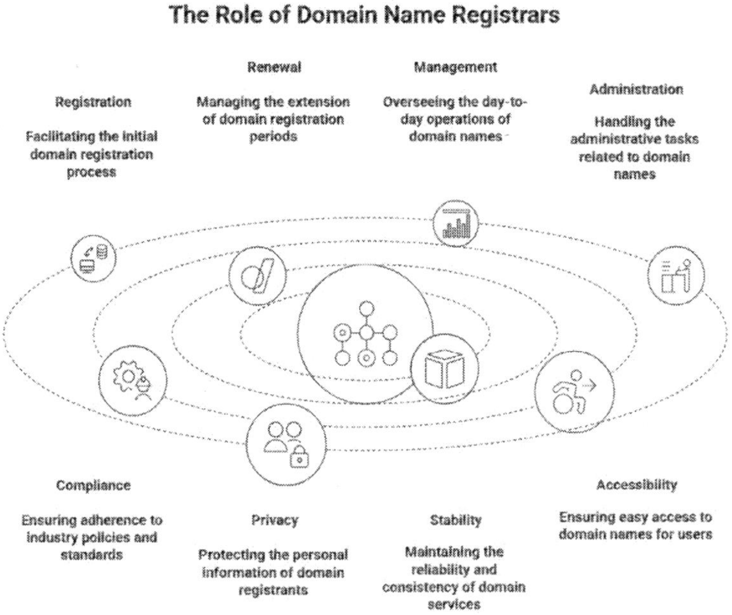

Domain name registrars serve as intermediaries between domain name registrants and the central domain registry, and play an essential role in helping facilitate registration, renewal, management, and administration of domain names. Furthermore, these intermediary services ensure compliance with industry policies while safeguarding registrant privacy while contributing to stability and accessibility of internet digital address space - services essential to individuals, businesses and organizations seeking to establish or sustain online presences.

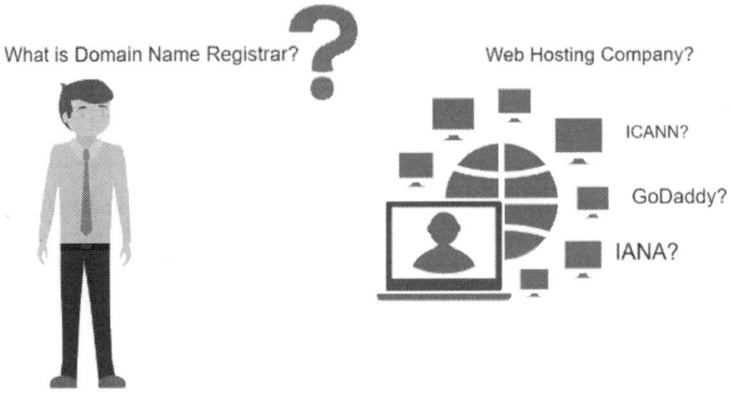

1.7 Difference between a registrar and a registry

As we already explained, domain name registrar is a business or company that needs to have ICANN's accreditation and agreements from registries to sell domain names for registrants. Some of the most popular dealers are NameCheap, GoDaddy, Bluehost, Hostgator, DreamHost, BuyDomains, 1&1, and others.

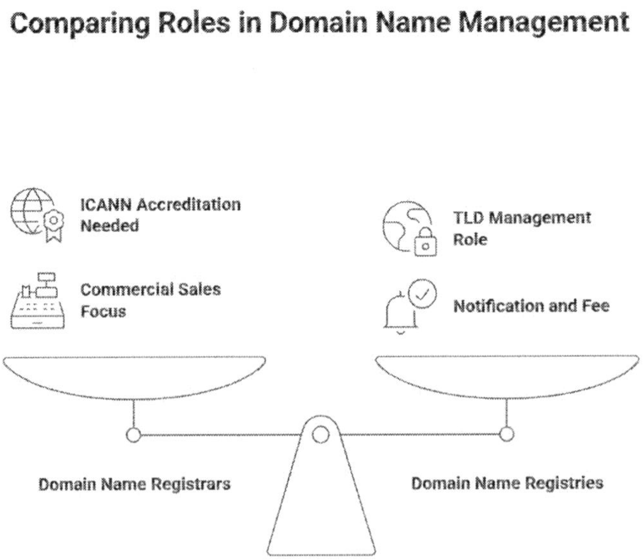

On the other hand, registries are organizations that manage top-level domains (TLDs) '.com' and '.net' – specifically by maintaining the records of which individual domains belong to which people and organizations. These registries are managed by the Internet Assigned Numbers Authority (IANA) – a department of the Internet Corporation for

Assigned Names and Numbers (ICANN), a global organization that coordinates several processes and databases that support the Internet's basic functionality.

Registries delegate the commercial sales of domain name registrations to registrars. For example, when a registrar sells a '.com' domain registration to an end user (or 'registrant'), the registrar must notify VeriSign — the registry for '.com' domains. The registrar must also pay VeriSign a fee, which is factored into the price that the registrar charges the end user.

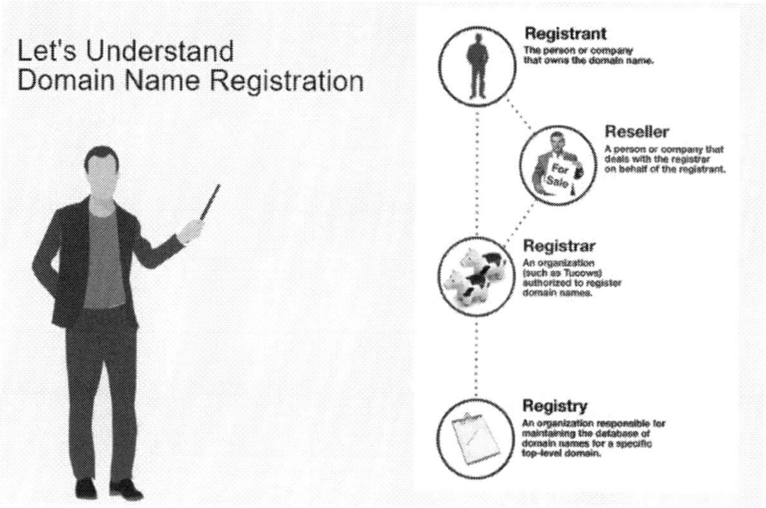

1.8 Difference between a registrar, registry, and registrant

This arrangement works much like a Renting a house in a rental community. A customer who is interested in renting a house visits the property management company office and they assign a realtor (salesman) to the customer. The realtor shows some houses(property) to the customer. If the customer chooses to rent a house, he pays the rent and property management company fee and get the house on rent for a particular period of time. Here, hose doesn't belong to customer or property management company. The owner of the house is some other third-party who get the rent after deducting property management company fee.

A registrar is like a property management company office for domain names, and the registry is like the owner of the property. The registrar facilitates the transactions and provides support services, while the registry is in charge of constructing more domain name. In other word, paying for the domain name is renting it out for as long as you pay for it. Once you stop paying, someone else can take it over!

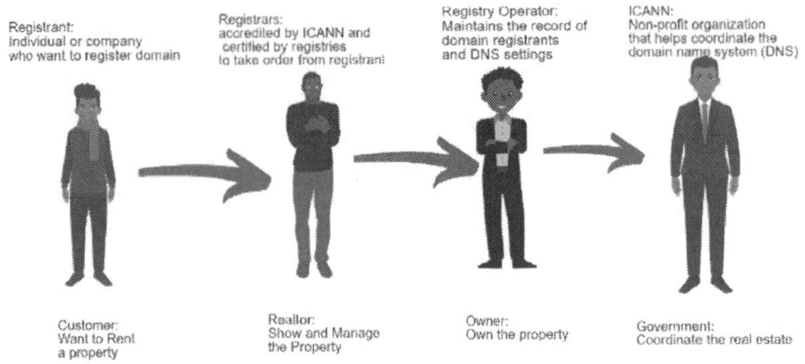

1.9 Can you really 'own' the domain name?

Although people often speak of buying and owning domain names, the truth is that registries own all of their domain names and registrars simply offer customers the opportunity to reserve those domain names for a limited amount of time.

A customer can register a domain name for maximum 10 years in one go. You can continue to use the same domain name for more than 10 years by renewing it again and again. Its domain name registrar responsibility to notify the registrant when their domain name is about to expire.

1.10 Who are Resellers?

Resellers are another type of company that sell domain name registrations. These companies sell domain name on behalf of registrar and charge a small amount of fee for that. For a novice user, it is very hard to find if a company is reseller or actual registrar. The only problem, I saw with reseller is that their customer support is not good. These reseller companies are selling domain name as a side business to make another stream of revenue. They usually don't disclose if they are reseller or actual registrar. Fortunately, there is a list of ICANN accredited and active domain name registrar on the ICANN's website: https://www.icann.org/en/accredited-registrars.

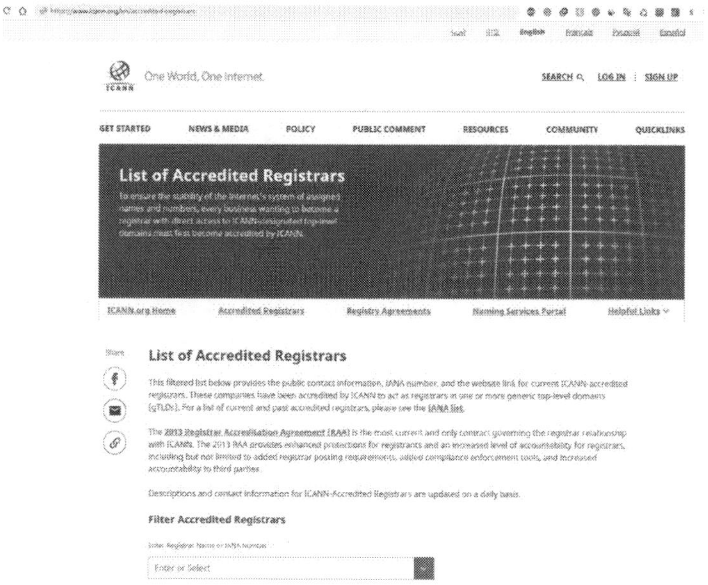

1.11 How registrars provide user privacy?

When you register a new domain name with any registrar, you need to provide your basic contact details. The information which you need to provide usually include your name, phone number, physical address, email address etc.

Most of good domain name registrar provide WhoIs privacy. WhoIs privacy is a way of hiding registrant information and registrar act as a proxy for the registrant. But keep in mind, domain name registrar still have your information in their database. If registrar database is compromised in any way or there is any hack on the registrar database, your information can be compromised. That is another reason to choose a good domain name registrar when you are registering your domain name.

For example, in below screenshot, you can see when I try to register a domain name on namecheap.com (registrar), they provide me an option for domain privacy. Some registrars call it WhoIs privacy. Its usually free, but some registrars charge a small fee for that.

It is always a good idea to get domain privacy as it hides your personal information in the public WhoIs database and avoid spam. Initially, when I start domain investing, I don't know about this, and I receive hundreds of spam email every other day.

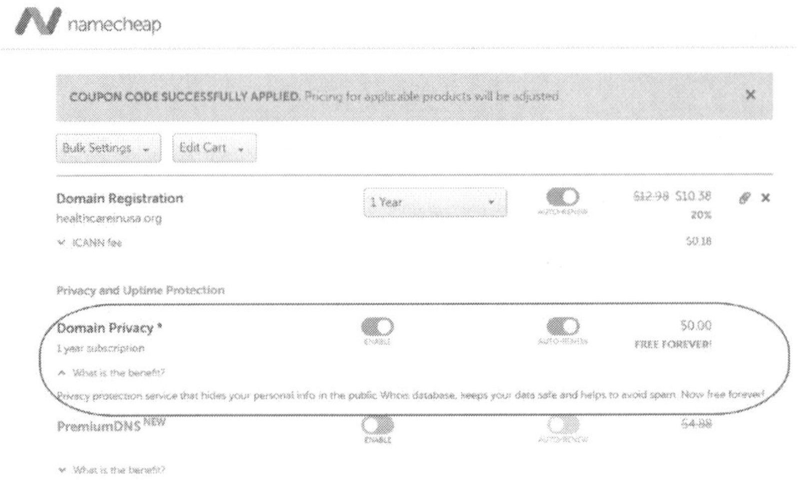

1.12 Domain Name WhoIs Record

WHOIS website provides records about domain name holders. System archive delivers data in a form that every user can understand. When the user wants to check the Whois record, it sends requests to the database holding the records of registrants, IP address blocks, and other information.

Usually, the database provides the following information:

- Name
- Address
- City
- Country
- Phone
- Fax
- E-mail
- Registration Date of domain name
- Expiry date of domain name
- Nameserver information etc.

For example, if we lookup for WhoIs data of facebook, we can find that its registrant name, organization name, their physical address, phone number, when the registration of this domain name is done, its expiry date, nameserver etc. As you can see in the screenshot below, all this information is provided. But its always better to protect your WhoIs information by buying WhoIs privacy from your domain name registrar.

To check yours or some other website's registrar, follow these instructions:

Visit WhoIs Lookup (https://www.whois.com/). Enter the URL of the site you want to inspect.

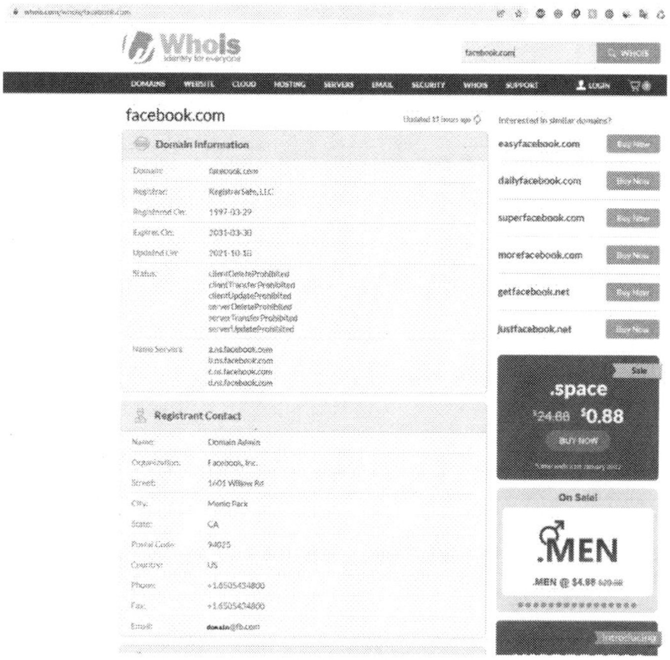

Since anyone can use the WhoIs lookup, companies and individuals might start receiving phishing emails, calls from online fraudsters, or less than reliable offers by marketing firms. Domain name registrars provide Whois privacy services to avoid scams.

1.13 DNS security by registrars

Since domain name registrar hold the personal information of the registrant and other details like nameserver information, IP address of the servers, its registrar responsibility to keep all data and information secure from malicious user, hackers etc.

In the past, some registrars have played a role in domain hijacking attacks, which can either change the registration of a domain name without the original registrants' permission or abuse the privileges of domain hosting and registrar software systems. One example of domain hijacking is an attacker making a particular domain direct to a different website, in order to impersonate the original site or disrupt its business.

ICANN recommends that registrars take a number of steps to prevent domain hijacking, including:

- Better management of AuthInfo Codes — randomly generated codes that play a role in the domain transfer process
- Better implementation of domain locks — settings that keep domains from being transferred
- Improved identity verification for all registration processes
- Improved record keeping for domain changes
- Under the current transfer policy, a losing registrar notifies a registrant upon receiving a pending transfer notice from the registry at its option
- ICANN, the registries, and the registrars should conduct a public awareness campaign to identify the criteria and the procedures registrants must follow to request intervention and obtain immediate restoration of a domain name and DNS configuration

You can find more details about the ICANN recommendation on the ICANN website: https://www.icann.org/groups/ssac/documents/sac-007-en

1.14 How to secure your domain name

When you buy a new domain name and register it with particular registrar, then its registrar responsibility to notify you when your domain name is about to expire. You should be notified in timely manner and should get a chance to renew you domain name. In some cases, registrars will prey on their users' expired domain names by buying those domains the second they expire and then selling them back to the original registrant at an exorbitant price. It's important to choose an honest and trustworthy registrar to avoid these kinds of predatory practices. We will discuss how to identify the best domain name registrar in the next chapter.

Also, another way of securing your domain name is apply **domain transfer lock**. It will help you to secure your domain name from transferring to malicious user.

You can also **apply 2-FA** (two factor authentication) so that nobody can access your account easily.

It's a good idea to not let anyone else (such as an agency) register a domain name for you. Even though it's slightly less hassle that way (since someone else does all the work), it can lead to trouble later on. If someone else registers the domain, you're giving them a hold over you and your website. If you ever want to move away from their services, you can encounter trouble in terms of them not being too eager to transfer the domain over to you and give you full control of it.

There is a possibility of negative experience you can have: They may take too long to transfer your domain name, they may ask some extorsion money to release your domain name, or they simply may decline completely based on some fine print in your initial agreement. Plus, perhaps most importantly, if the agency/person goes bankrupt or loses access to the domain registrar for whatever reason, you could lose your domain name entirely.

Long story short, always register your domains on your own. It's not that difficult anyway.

Till this point, we understand the basics of domain name, domain name registrar, and importance of domain name security. We will discuss how to identify best domain name registrar in the next chapter.

2.

HOW TO SELECT THE BEST DOMAIN REGISTRAR

"Look for your choices, pick the best one, then go with it."

-Pat Riley

In the business of domain investing, it is very important to register your domain name with a good domain name registrar. As we already discussed in the previous chapter, domain name registrars are the companies which provide domain name registration services and manages all domain name on behalf of registry. In this chapter, we will discuss different factor we should consider while registering a new domain name. I will show you how to choose the best domain registrar by comparing their pros and cons. May be some of the domain registrars, I will recommend now (2024), not available in future. Its rapidly changing industry. So, without any further delay, here is the list of factors you should consider while registering your domain name:

2.1 Honest Pricing

I think this is one of the most important factors when we are buying anything and in the field of Investing, you can make money only when you buy low and sell high. Domain name usually cost you anywhere between $2 to $12 a year. Here, I am not talking about the premium domain which can sell for millions of dollars. Also, you are not interacting too often with your domain registrar. You buy once and may be renew it after a year. So, my advice is avoiding all those domain registrars which try to sell you anything higher than $15 a year. If you spent less, then there are good chances of profit when you sell it for a reasonable amount.

Also, for different domain name registrar, price can be very different for the same domain. For example, for "newyorkandtoronto.com" you can see in the below screenshot, pricing from NameCheap, NameSilo, GoDaddy, and domain.com:

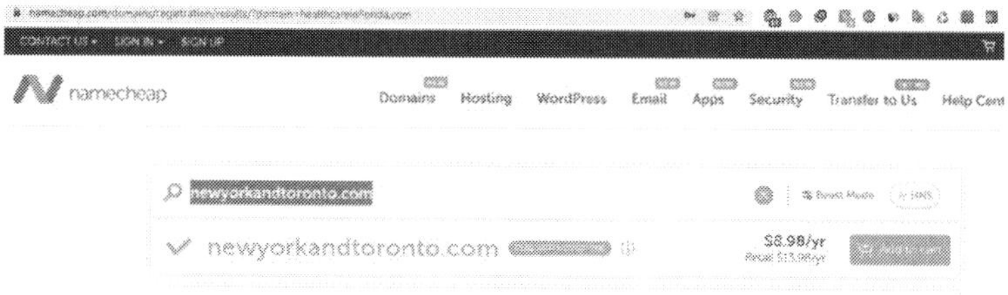

Price on Namecheap for "newyorkandtoronto.com"

Price on NameSilo for "newyorkandtoronto.com"

Price on GoDaddy for "newyorkandtoronto.com"

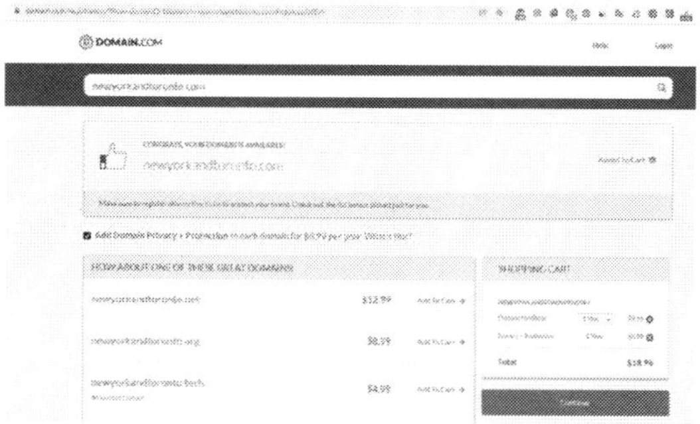

Price on Domain.com for "newyorkandtoronto.com"

Another recommendation is if you are buying domain name in bulk, look for discount, coupons and offers. Sometime, I purchase hundreds of domain name for $0.99 each. It will help you save a lot of money and make you profitable eventually.

2.2 Free WHOIS Protection

As we already discussed in previous chapter, domain name registrar needs to collect your personal information while registering your domain name. This includes you name, address, phone number, email address etc. This information can be accessed by anyone using WhoIs database. But if you don't like to show this information, domain name registrar offers WhoIs protection which sometime called WhoIs privacy or WhoIs guard.

Because of ICANN, some sort of contact information must be connected to your domain name. Therefore, some of the best registrars swap out your personal information with its company's contact information. For example, in the below screenshot, I am trying to get WhoIs information for "JambaAcademy.com" and it is showing NameCheap as the registrar under WHOIS Lookup and the registrant contact is shown as "Privacy service provided by Withheld for Privacy ehf" instead of actual username. A good domain registrar offers free WHOIS Privacy Protection.

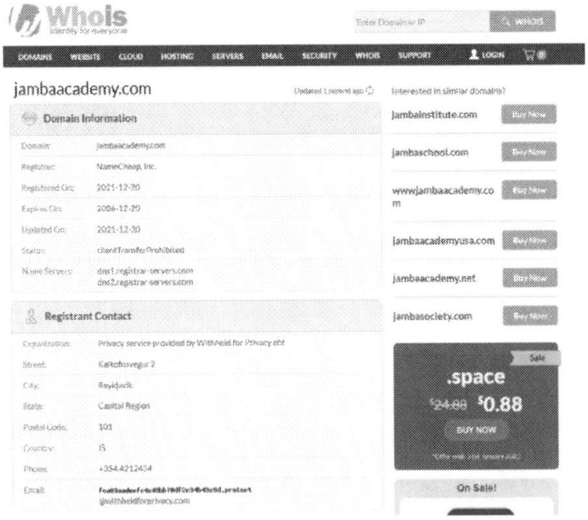

2.3 Options for Registration Timeframes

A good domain name registrar should provide you multiple options for the domain name registration timeframe. You can register a domain name for minimum 1 year and maximum 10 year in one go. You can renew after 10 years again if you want. So, if a registrar requiring you to sign up for more than one year, think again before signing up. In the below screenshot, you can see the different option for timeframe provided by NameCheap:

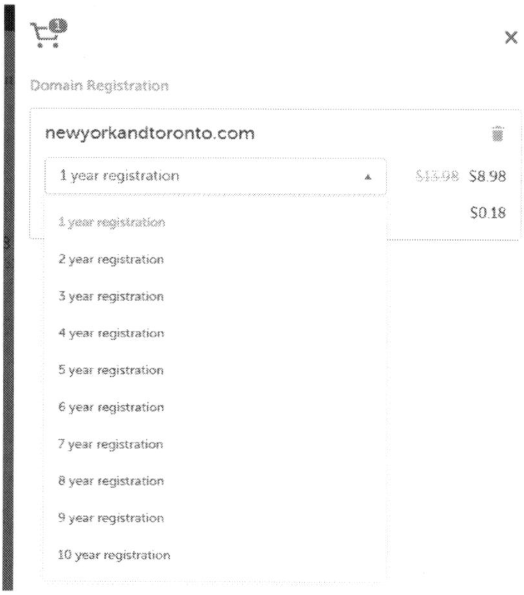

I recommend you register your domain name for only one year, unless there is very heavy discount for multiple year. In domain flipping, you often sell your domain name within one year. For me, almost ninety percent of domain either sell or expire one year. I will discuss in detail which domain name you should renew after one year and which one you leave for expiry. However, if you are registering a domain name for personal use, you should register for a longer period.

2.4 Automated Renewals and Reminders

A good domain registrar should offer the option of auto-renewals so that you don't have to worry when your domain name expires. Also, you should have a valid credit-card on file with domain name registrar so that they can auto-renew your domain name if you want to avail this service. You can see the option of auto-renew provided by in the below screenshot:

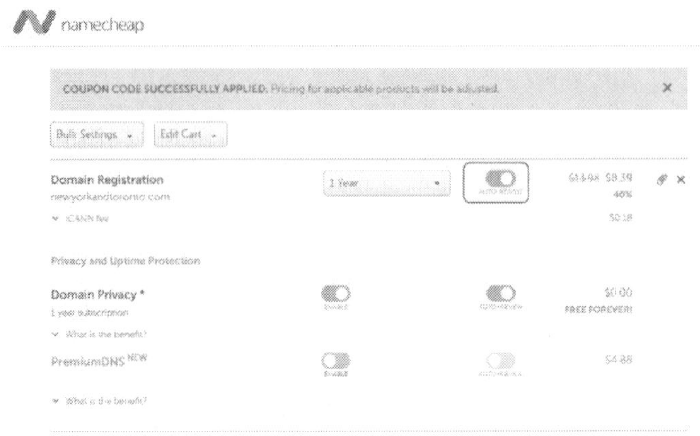

But sometime credit card expires, so a good domain name registrar should also send you reminder email so that you don't lose your domain name. If you don't renew a domain name it eventually gets released to the public for purchase (some registrars have holding times in-between). Someone else can then buy the domain and either keep it or try to sell it back to you for a large sum of money. This is not uncommon, so make sure your credit card is up-to-date and you activate auto-renewals.

2.5 Wide Variety of Top-level Domains (TLDs) Offering

As we already discuss in previous chapter, top-level domains are the highest level in domain hierarchy. It can be anything like .com, .net, .gov, .org, .us, .ca, .dentist, .shop, .mechanic etc. A good domain name registrar should provide a wide variety of top-level domain, so that if you want to register any specific TLD, you can register it. For example, you can see in below screenshot, GoDaddy offers a variety of TLDs:

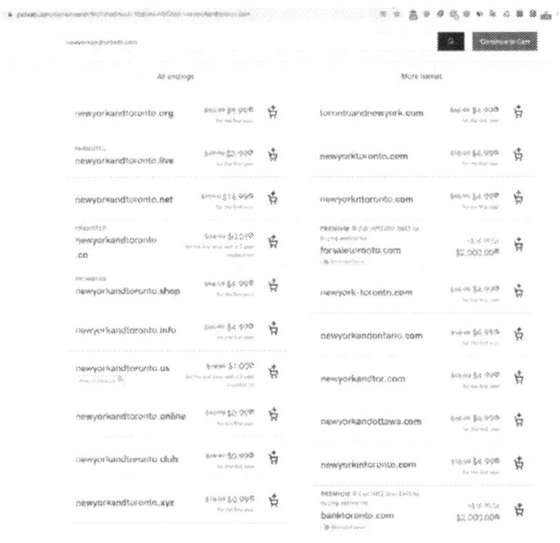

If you are looking for very specific niche TLDs such as countries TLDs, profession TLDs, you can go for niche registrar. If you want to check every possible TLDs available, you can get updated list from IANA (Internet Assigned Numbers Authority).

https://www.iana.org/domains/root/db.

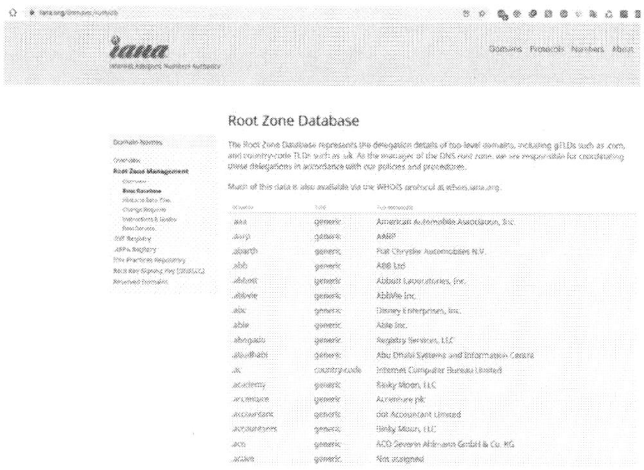

2.6 Domain Transfers

If you are not satisfied with your domain name registrar, you can easily transfer to another registrar. Although most domain registrar offer this service free of cost and make it easy to do for you. But I recommend that you should check transfer policy before selecting your domain name registrar. Some registrars try to make some extra money and intentionally make this process complicated.

The first thing you need to keep in mind is that you cannot transfer a domain name during the first 60 days of the registration. This initial period is decided by ICANN. After that, you are allowed to move it to any other registrar that you want.

2.7 Add-on Services

You may also want to review what other services are offered by your domain registrar. While you may not need these services right now, it is good to know that they have them. Sometime registrars provide free hosting for specific time-period or free SSL certificate when you register your domain name with them.

It all depends on the registrar, but some of the add-ons might include:

- Discounts for bulk domain searches
- Domain privacy
- Website builders
- WordPress hosting service
- Email hosting service
- Tools for online stores
- Site templates
- Regular and managed site hosting
- Dedicated servers
- SSL certificates
- Website security and backups
- SEO services
- Email marketing
- Professional email addresses
- Premium DNS

2.8 Quality Customer Support

Most reputable domain registrars are large companies with lots of employees. This means they should offer everything from chat support to a direct phone line. It's also nice to see an extensive knowledgebase for you to complete your own research. You should check if the registrar is providing good 24/7 customer support. Also, try to find what other people say about the domain registrar. You can read review on many reviews and reputation website about the customer support of registrar.

2.9 Renewal Fee

Sometime domain name registrar offers a good discount on first year of registration, but when you renew after one year, they charge a very high amount as renewal fee. Always check for the renewal fee when registering for a domain name. Also, check the renewal policy at registrar website. This is important if you are registering a domain name for personal use i.e., to develop a website on it. For domain investing or flipping, I think this factor is not very important because I think one year is enough to sell a domain name.

After one year, either I let the domain name expire and don't renew it or it is already sold. That's my strategy for most of the domain name I hold, there are very few domains name which I like to keep for longer period of time. I will explain later how to decide if a domain name is worth renewing or not.

2.10 Ease of Use & Buying Process

A good domain registrar makes the buying process very easy for their customers. They should have a good user interface, and everything should be explained clearly. A quality user interface from a domain registrar involves a simple search tool for finding a domain name, along with a sleek dashboard with clear buttons for parking domains, transferring domains, and editing your domain settings.

I also believe that a great customer experience involves a fluid buying process. If it seems next to impossible to get through the shopping cart without dozens of upsells, think about going with an alternative registrar. For example, if you register a domain on NameCheap or GoDaddy, it is so easy and clear to understand that even a novice user with basic computer knowledge can do it.

These are the most important factor in deciding domain name registrar when you are planning to register a domain name. I know there is lot to consider, I can tell my strategy when I decide a domain name registrar. I first check pricing, other customer review, transfer fee and then customer support.

Anther recommendation is if you are planning to hold a big portfolio (i.e., thousands of domain name), work at least 4-5 domain name registrars. The logic behind this you are not dependent on one company for your entire portfolio. If there is any problem with a particular registrar such as server down, database hack, company shutdown, at least you don't lose all your portfolio. It is similar advice as we say in investing "Don't put all your egg in one basket".

I will provide a list of top domain name registrar below which I am using personally from many years and have a very good experience working with.

2.11 Best Domain Registrars (I have great experience working with)

Here I am providing the list of domain name registrar which I can recommend with confidence and which I am using from long time. I also discuss why I like these and what they offer best in term of pricing, customer support, expiry reminder etc.

2.12 Namecheap (https://www.namecheap.com/)

Founded in 2000, Namecheap is a popular domain name registrar and web host which now manages more than five million domains. Namecheap's excellent website allows searching for individual domains, or in batches of up to 5000. If the domain is taken, you can view the Whois record or offer to buy the domain (via Domain Agents) from the current user.

The best thing I like about Namecheap is its pricing and user interface. It provides domain name in less than $10. During the special time like Black Friday, New year, they offer heavy discounts. I purchased domain name for as low as 99 cents ($0.99) from Namecheap. Their user interface is so easy to use that it takes seconds to search for good domain name and register it. The buying process is very simple, no complexity in the interface or while checkout.

Namecheap offers a wide variety of top-level domains (TLDs). You can easily find a short, easy to remember domain name with specific domain extension (TLDs) such as ".shop", ".online", ".academy", ".in", ".dentist", ".health" etc. Sometime these TLDs works better than ".com" as they are specific to your profession, business, location or niche.

That would be good value all on its own, but Namecheap doesn't stop there: you get WhoisGuard domain privacy for free. Apart from that, you have many other features with Namecheap such as email forwarding, DNS management, 24/7 customer support, SSL certificate. You can use email forwarding to setup a professional email address (such as "info@yourdomainname.com" or "support@yourdomainname.com") and forward all your email to your current email address.

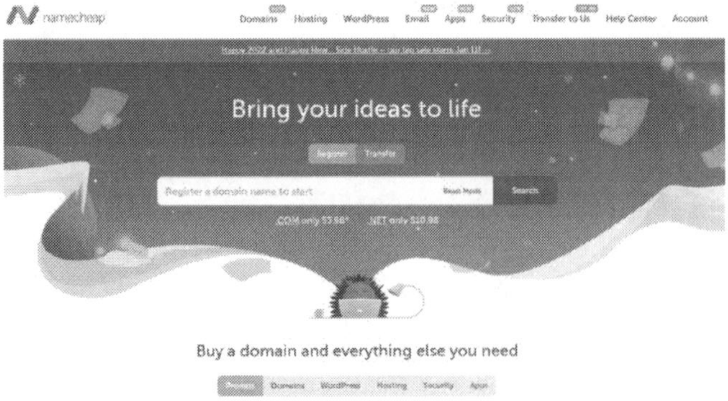

Namecheap also allow you to secure your domain name by transfer locking. You can activate 2-FA (two factor authentication) on your account to make it more secure.

Namecheap's billing is straightforward and honest, with current and renewal prices clearly described in your Namecheap shopping cart, and Auto-Renew turned off. But if there's something you don't understand, helpful FAQ pages and live chat are just a click or two away.

To summarize, Namecheap offers all the feature a good domain name registrar should have:

- Free privacy protection
- Domain name security
- 24/7 live chat support
- Extensive knowledge base
- Full DNS access
- Free PositiveSSL certificate for one year
- 2 FA
- Premium DNS
- Domain Transfer locking
- Honest pricing
- Easy to use Web Interface

2.13 NameSilo

NameSilo is another domain name registrar established in 2009 which makes domain registration quick and easy process. NameSilo offer a good discount if you are registering in bulk quantity. More the number of domain name you register, greater the discount. This is really important for the domain name investor as it help you in reducing your initial investment. You can see in the below screenshot, how is discount increasing with the number of domain name.

	Registrations in Order			Discount Program (active account domains)					
TLD	1 - 49	50 - 100	101 - 500	0+	100+	500+	1,000+	2,500+	5,000+
.com	$9.95	$9.85	$9.75	$9.75	$9.55	$9.35	$9.15	$8.95	$8.75
.net	$11.79	$11.69	$11.59	$11.69	$11.59	$11.49	$11.39	$11.29	$11.19
.org	$10.79	$10.69	$10.59	$10.69	$10.59	$10.40	$10.39	$10.29	$10.19
.club	$3.59	$3.49	$3.39	$3.49	$3.39	$3.29	$3.19	$3.09	$2.99
.biz	$5.75	$5.65	$5.55	$5.65	$5.55	$5.45	$5.35	$5.25	$5.15
.life	$2.99	$2.89	$2.79	$2.89	$2.79	$2.69	$2.59	$2.49	$2.39
.icu	$2.39	$2.29	$2.19	$2.29	$2.19	$2.09	$1.99	$1.89	$1.79
.info	$3.79	$3.69	$3.59	$3.69	$3.59	$3.49	$3.39	$3.29	$3.19
.top	$1.88	$1.78	$1.68	$1.78	$1.68	$1.58	$1.48	$1.38	$1.28
.store	$4.99	$4.89	$4.79	$4.89	$4.79	$4.69	$4.59	$4.49	$4.39
.xyz	$0.99	$0.99	$0.99	$0.99	$0.99	$0.99	$0.99	$0.99	$0.99
.ac	$27.99	$27.89	$27.79	$27.89	$27.79	$27.69	$27.59	$27.49	$27.39
.academy	$12.05	$11.95	$11.85	$11.95	$11.85	$11.75	$11.65	$11.55	$11.45
.accountant	$11.49	$11.39	$11.29	$11.39	$11.29	$11.19	$11.09	$10.99	$10.89
.accountants	$17.80	$17.70	$17.60	$17.70	$17.60	$17.50	$17.40	$17.30	$17.20
.actor	$12.05	$11.95	$11.85	$11.95	$11.85	$11.75	$11.65	$11.55	$11.45
.agency	$3.43	$3.33	$3.23	$3.33	$3.23	$3.13	$3.03	$2.93	$2.83
.airforce	$23.99	$23.89	$23.79	$23.89	$23.79	$23.69	$23.59	$23.49	$23.39
.apartments	$37.99	$37.89	$37.79	$37.89	$37.79	$37.69	$37.59	$37.49	$37.39
.archi	$12.05	$11.95	$11.85	$11.95	$11.85	$11.75	$11.65	$11.55	$11.45
.army	$12.05	$11.95	$11.85	$11.95	$11.85	$11.75	$11.65	$11.55	$11.45
.art	$3.99	$3.89	$3.79	$3.89	$3.79	$3.69	$3.59	$3.49	$3.39
.asia	$4.49	$4.39	$4.29	$4.39	$4.29	$4.19	$4.09	$3.99	$3.89

Besides heavy discount, NameSilo also offers you free WhoIs privacy, free email forwarding, free domain defender protection, free custom WhoIs records, and free DNS management as shown in below screenshot.

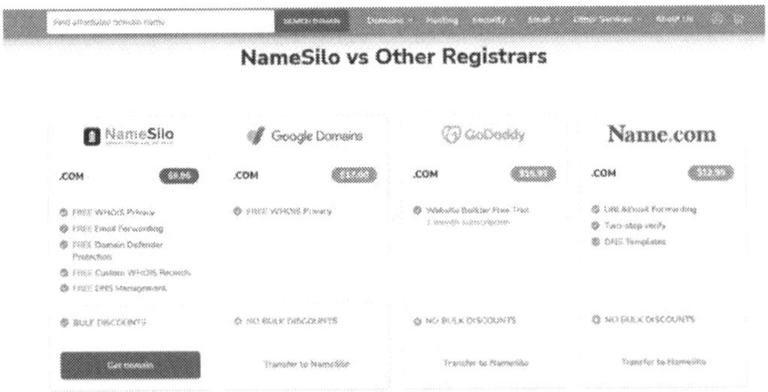

NameSilo also offers many other services, including web hosting, website builders, premium SSL, and DNS. They also have WordPress and email hosting coming soon. I started using NameSilo from last 4 years. Till now, I can say, I have a good experience working with it. Sometimes I need to contact their customer support, they are very responsive in email also. Every time within 24 hours, I received reply for my email. Here is the pros and cons for NameSilo.

Pros:

- Free WhoIs privacy
- Free email forwarding
- Free domain defender protection
- Free custom WhoIs records
- Free DNS management
- Discount for bulk ordering
- Powerful Domain Management Tools
- 2-Factor Authentication
- Clean Easy Process
- Variety of TLDs
- Transparent Pricing

Cons:

- User-Interface looks little outdated
- Bombarding and annoying upsells
- Onboarding process need improvement

2.14 Domain.com

Domain.com offers best array of domains, extensions, and adjacent services. You can find country code specific domain names, generic domain name or some other niche domain name for small and medium businesses. domain.com is a broker for premium domain name.

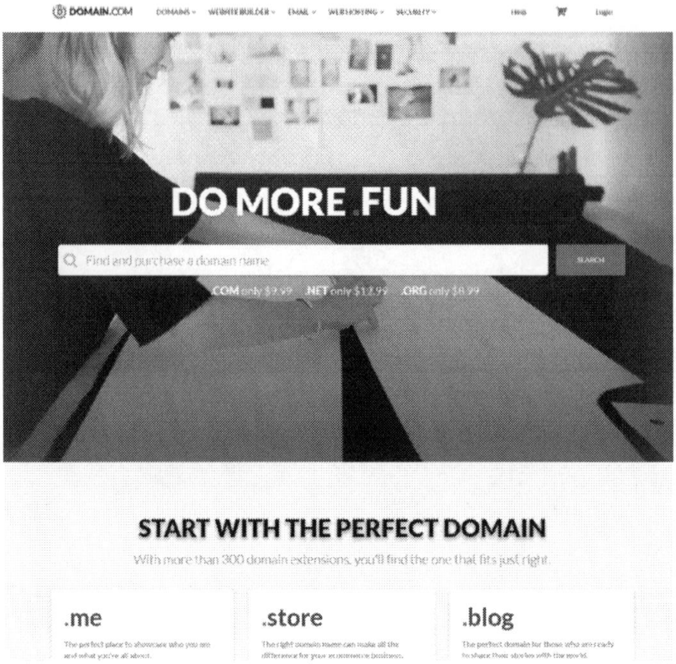

Domain.com is in business of domain registration from more than 20 years and hold a great reputation when it comes to customer support, domain security, and add on services. Domain.com is very transparent in their pricing and renewal fee. The only thing I don't like about their pricing is the renewal fee is quite as compared to other registrar. But as a domain Investor, don't think it is a problem as I assume I can either sell or let expire a domain name within a year.

They are also, very supportive when you are transferring your domain name from other registrar to them. I remember when I transfer all my domain name from 1&1 to domain.com, their customer service is very helpful and friendly in completing the process.

The other problem I saw with domain name is they charge $8.99 for WhoIs guard (whoIs privacy) while their competitors (such as Namecheap) offering that for free.

They also don't support bulk keyword search for the domain, and this is a negative factor if you are searching and registering hundreds of domain name as domain name investor. The lack of bulk keyword search hinder your research process and you end up spending more time in researching. This is annoying sometime.

Domain.com offers a very good and cheap website builder which you can use to develop simple website on your domain name to generate revenue from lead generation or ads. I will discuss these in more details in later chapters. For now, lets discuss, domain.com website builder and their offering.

The Domain.com builder will ask you a couple quick questions and then intelligently set layout and image and content formatting for you, giving you a template to start from in a snap. They offer 550k images to use on the website, so you can go from nothing to a full-fledged homepage in minutes.

Domain.com website builder comes in three options.

The entry-level plan for individuals is just $1.99 per month which offer you to build 6-pages websites in minutes.

The next step up, Business, is $6.99 per month. You're allowed unlimited pages and get site analytics, revision history, and phone support.

Their third plan for those who want to sell product online. It is $12.99/month, and you will get all the essential feature for ecommerce website such as Inventory management and tracking, PayPal integration, Offer coupon codes and promotions

In a nutshell, domain.com is a good, reliable registrar who has almost all the features you need. Here is the pros and cons:

Pros:

- Straightforward & honest pricing
- 24/7 chat, email, and phone support
- Email Forwarding
- Web hosting
- SSL certificates
- Malware protection
- DNS management tools
- Email forwarding
- URL forwarding
- Transfer lock
- Website builder

Cons:

- Lack of bulk keyword search
- WhoIs privacy protection Fee

- High Renewal Fee

2.15 GoDaddy

GoDaddy is one of the oldest and most popular domain registration company. Currently they are managing more than 832 million domain names and serving more than 20 million users with a team of 9000 employees. I am providing this information just to prove that how big it is and how many users trust the company. They provide a wide variety of top level domains ranging from generic domain extensions (such as ".com", ".net") to more specific domain extensions (such as ".co", ".me", ".online"). With GoDaddy, you will get a significant discount for the first year and sometimes they offer discounts for bulk registration. That further helps the domain investor to reduce their initial cost.

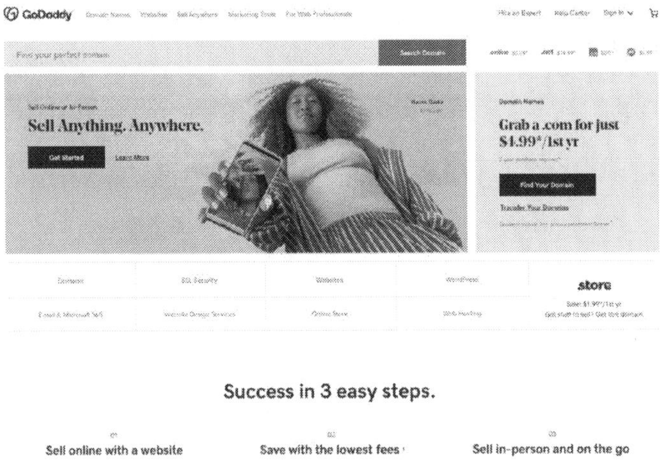

Apart from all these, GoDaddy offers web hosting, website builder, email marketing, SSL certificate etc. GoDaddy also provide free WhoIs privacy and domain lock services. You can bundle the domain name with other services, and it will be cheaper. GoDaddy satisfy all the criteria of a good domain name registrar. I usually browse their website for discounts and cheaper price.

2.16 Google Domains

Google enter in the domain registration market in 2015 and as other services provided by google, google domain is also easy to use, reliable and inexpensive. If you have used other google services such as google chrome, Gmail, google maps, you can easily use google domain. They try to keep it simple and easy to use so that a beginner can also use it. Their pricing start at $7/year and you can get a decent ".com" domain name in $12/year (average). Besides competitive pricing, they also provide other features such as email forwarding, privacy protection, one-click DNSSEC, Google 2-Step Verification, and much more.

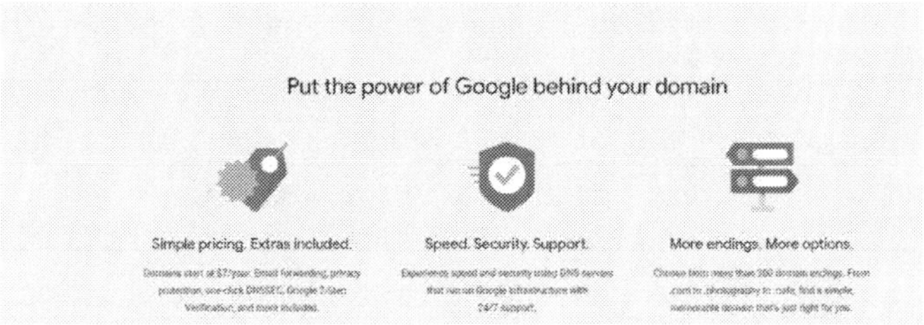

The list of features do not end here, google domain offers domain with more than 300 extensions (TPDs). You can easily pick a domain name according to your need. Few example of extensions are ".com", ".net", ".cafe", ".photography", ".shop" etc.

Google Domains offers a range of trusted website builders that offer both free and paid options. you can easily create a basic information sharing website, or local business website using their free "Google Sites" tool or if you want to write blogs (about travel, your journey, product comparison etc), you can use free Blogger tool. Google also allow you to use with paid tools such as wix, squarespace, bluehost, shopify, weebly to create a more effective website or ecommerce store.

Here is the pros and cons of google domain:

Pros:

- Email forwarding
- Privacy protection
- One-click DNSSEC
- Google 2-Step Verification
- Wide variety of domain extension (more than 300)
- Easy sign-up and buying process

Cons:

- Little expensive as compared to Competition (such as Namecheap, GoDaddy)
- Some extensions are too expensive (For example, .io for $60, .store for $50, .love for $30)
- No bulk pricing options
- No Discount
- No Bulk keyword search

I can recommend google domain if you are developing your own website or for a local business. Personally, I don't use google domain as my registrar, if I have to register hundreds of domain name.

In conclusion, these are my top list of domain registrar which I personally use. There are many other domain registrars who provide very good services. Some of those are Name.com, Enom.com, Dynadot.com, Bluehost.com, DreamHost, HostGator, BuyDomains.com. I used services of these registrar also. Even today, If I find discount on any of these registrars, I go with that. Buying low and selling high is the only way to make profit in domain investing. So, If you find discount or cheaper price on any of those, go with that.

2.17 What is Domain Transfer?

Domain transfer is the process of transferring your domain name registration from one registrar to another. To complete this process, you need EPP Code (Extensible Provisioning Protocol). If you are not happy with your current domain registrar and willing to transfer your domain name to another registrar, you need to get the EPP code from your current registrar and provide this code to the registrar you want to transfer. When the new registrar gets your EPP code, they will initiate the transfer process. During this process, you will receive an approval email to your Registrant Email Address to validate Domain Transfer. The process usually take 5-7 days and you again receive email confirmation when the process complete successfully.

Significance of Domain Transfer:

1. **Registrar Flexibility**: Domain transfer offers the flexibility to switch domain registrars based on individual preferences, needs, or changing circumstances. It allows website owners to choose registrars that provide superior customer

support, enhanced domain management interfaces, improved security features, or competitive pricing.

2. **Consolidation and Management**: Transferring domain names to a single registrar can simplify domain management tasks. Consolidating domain names under one registrar streamlines administrative tasks, reduces complexity, and provides a unified interface for managing all registered domain names.

3. **Domain Renewal**: In some cases, transferring a domain name can provide an opportunity to extend its registration period. If the current registrar's renewal fees are high or if more favorable renewal terms are offered by the new registrar, domain owners can take advantage of the transfer process to secure a longer registration period at a lower cost.

4. **Enhanced Services and Features**: Domain transfers offer the potential to access additional services or features provided by the new registrar. These may include improved DNS management, advanced security options, better domain privacy protection, or value-added services tailored to specific needs or industry sectors.

Important Considerations:

- **Transfer Lock**: Some registrars may have a transfer lock feature enabled by default to prevent unauthorized transfers. Ensure that this lock is disabled before initiating the transfer process.

- **Domain Expiration**: It is crucial to initiate a transfer well before the domain's expiration date to avoid potential complications. Transfers initiated near the expiration date may not be completed in time, resulting in temporary disruption of website and email services.

- **Privacy Protection**: If domain privacy protection (WHOIS privacy) is enabled, ensure that it is transferred along with the domain name to maintain privacy and prevent the exposure of personal contact information.

- **Email Services**: If your domain is associated with email accounts, verify that email services are properly configured and transferred to the new registrar to avoid disruption in email communications.

2.18 Step By Step Guide for Domain Transfer Process

1. To initiate the domain transfer process, you get the EPP code from your current registrar and provide it to the new registrar (you are willing to transfer your domain name).
2. The new registrar will fetch the admin contact details from WhoIs database and send you an approval email on the email id, you used while registering. If the new registrar is unable to get the admin contact information because of current registrar problem or WhoIs privacy, the transfer fails.
3. After getting approval email, you need to approve within 5 days, otherwise, transfer fails.
4. Your domain name must be in active state, transfer lock should be off in current registrar setting, and your domain name must be at least 60 days old, otherwise, transfer fails.
5. If all the above condition fulfill, transfer process goes on and is now considered approved by the registry.
6. Your old domain registrar (loosing registrar) sends you a second approval email to notify to about the transfer process and will usually ask you to cancel the transfer (as they are losing you, customer). If you don't cancel, transfer must be completed within 5-7 days.
7. Your old domain registrar may send you instructions for the transfer approval, you can use them and speedup the process.

3.

WHAT IS DOMAINING/DOMAIN INVESTING/DOMAIN FLIPPING

"Risk comes from not knowing what you are doing."

-Warren Buffett

We already discussed basics of domain name, top-level domain, domain name registrar, and how to identify good domain name registrar. At this point, we already know which domain registrar we are going with for domain registration. Now, let's discuss what is domaining or domain investing or domain flipping.

3.1 What is domaining/ domain investing/ domain flipping?

domaining or domain investing, or domain flipping is the business of buying, selling, developing, and monetizing domain names. Some people also called it "**domain name speculation**".

It is the process of buying a domain name with the intention to sell it for higher price and make profit out of it. As more and more people coming online for selling their products, apps, art, making new contacts, and for other purposes, the demand of more website and eventually more domain name is increasing. With this increase in demand, many individuals find opportunity, by registering (buying) a domain name for low price and finding a person or business who is interested in buying it for high price. These individuals who practice this process of buying and selling domain name are called domainers or domain investors.

WHAT IS DOMAINING?

"Domaining is generally defined as investing in domain names with the intention of making a profit. It is the business of buying, selling, developing, or monetizing domain names."

However, buying and selling is not the only way to make profit in this business. You can use domain parking services to show relevant advertisement to cover the cost of domain name and make some extra earning. The earning using this method is not very high, but, when you have hundreds or thousands of domain name, the cumulative earning become a significant source of income for domainers.

There are other ways to generate revenue from domain name. You can make a lead generation website to provide lead to relevant business and making some commission from that. I personally know some domainers who develop lead generation website in different industries and making good income from it. Some industries like dentist, plastic surgery, hair transplant pays a very high commission for each successful lead.

Another way is to develop affiliate marketing website on the domain name and make profit as affiliate commission when someone buy the product using your affiliate link. This method is more successful in digital products such as WordPress theme, software, plugin, online courses, subscription services, online sign-up for website etc.

3.2 Domaining vs Domain parking vs Domain-warehousing

We used the word domaining, domain parking above. Let's try to understand the difference between these two and a new word Domain-warehousing.

Domaining as we already described is the process of buying a domain name with the intention to sell it for higher price and make profit out of it.

On the other hand, **domain parking** is the process of registering and reserving a domain name without any service or website associated with it. Sometime, when a domain name is registered and not used, domain registrar may use it to show potential advertisements related to keyword of domain name (as they have nameserver and DNS information). Monetized and non-monetized are two classifications for domain parking based on domain name use. Domain monetization is the practice of generating revenue by showing advertisements. In non-monetized classification, an "Under Construction" or a "Coming Soon" message is shown on the domain name. This is normally used when a business is in the process of launching their website.

Domain-warehousing is the practice of registering and holding Internet domain names by the domain name registrar itself (the registration service) or sometime by user (registrant).

Example:

Let's consider a hypothetical scenario to illustrate the differences between domaining, domain parking, and domain warehousing:

John is a seasoned investor in the online domain industry. He purchases multiple domain names with the intention of leveraging them for different purposes.

1. **Domaining**: John is an active domainer. He carefully selects domain names that he believes have high potential value or are in demand within specific industries.

For example, he purchases domain names like "eSportsPro.com," "EcoFriendlyLiving.com," and "PetTrainingTips.net." John's strategy is to hold these domain names and wait for the right opportunity to sell them to interested buyers at a profit. He actively researches market trends, analyzes potential buyer demand, and keeps an eye on industry developments to maximize the value of his domain portfolio.

2. **Domain Parking**: John also engages in domain parking as a way to generate revenue from his unused domain names. He realizes that some domain names in his portfolio are not currently being utilized for specific websites or online businesses. Instead of leaving them dormant, John decides to park these domain names with a domain parking service or platform. When someone visits these parked domains, they are greeted with targeted advertisements. If a visitor clicks on one of these ads, John earns a small commission. For instance, John parks the domain "TravelDestinationsGuide.com" and generates revenue through advertisements related to travel agencies, hotels, and vacation packages.

3. **Domain Warehousing**: John understands the potential value of certain domain names, especially those that are highly generic or sought-after by businesses. He engages in domain warehousing by acquiring domain names that he believes will appreciate in value over time. These domain names are not actively developed into websites or used for any specific purpose. Instead, John holds them as digital assets, banking on the potential demand from businesses or individuals who may want to acquire them in the future. For example, he acquires domain names like "Business.com," "RealEstate.com," and "Insurance.net" with the intention of selling them to the highest bidder or negotiating lucrative deals when the opportunity arises.

In summary, John's involvement in the domain industry showcases the different approaches within the domain space. His domaining activities involve actively buying and selling domain names to capitalize on market demand. He uses domain parking to generate revenue from unused domain names through targeted advertisements. Additionally, he practices domain warehousing by holding valuable domain names as investments, anticipating their appreciation in value over time. Each approach presents unique opportunities and strategies for leveraging domain names in the ever-evolving online landscape.

3.3 Some Examples of Expensive Domain Flipping

To give an idea of how much a domain name can sell for, here I am providing a list of domain name which sold in 2021. By going through the list, you can see how much potential this industry have for profit. Here is the list of top domain sales in **2021**:

Christmas.com – This domain was acquired by Gordon Companies in New York for $3,150,000. The company retails, wholesales, and imports Christmas merchandise such as wreaths, lights, and ornaments.

Angel.com – This domain was sold for $2,000,000 to Angel Studios. Angel dust studios is in the business of TV series and recently raised over a million dollars for their series (called Freelancers).

Exodus.com – Despite the recent pullbacks, investors in crypto are awash in money. These investors have bought a lot of domains, including Exodus.com, for $1,945,000, which is a crypto and bitcoin wallet.

Meme.com – Meme was bought for $1,250,000, and it is currently used for posting memes such as the Grumpy Cat meme.

eBike.com – This domain name was bought by Bosch for $1,008,900. Bosch is in the business of creating eBikes, kitchen appliances and other smart products.

If you need more inspiration, here is another list of expensive domain sale:

RANK	DOMAIN NAME	SALE PRICE	DATE SOLD
1	voice.com	$30,000,000	30-May-19
2	sex.com	$14,000,000	1-Jan-05
3	tesla.com	$11,000,000	6-Dec-18
4	hotels.com	$11,000,000	1-Sep-01
5	fund.com	$9,999,950	11-Mar-08
6	porn.com	$9,500,000	5-Jun-07
7	porno.com	$8,888,888	4-Feb-15
8	fb.com	$8,500,000	1-Sep-10
9	healthinsurance.com	$8,133,000	31-Jul-19
10	we.com	$8,000,000	19-Jun-15
11	diamond.com	$7,500,000	23-May-06
12	beer.com	$7,000,000	1-Jan-04
13	z.com	$6,784,000	3-Dec-14
14	slots.com	$5,500,000	4-Jun-10

15	casino.com	$5,500,000	1-Nov-03
16	toys.com	$5,100,000	1-Mar-09
17	korea.com	$5,000,000	1-Jan-00
18	asseenontv.com	$5,000,000	1-Jan-00
19	clothes.com	$4,900,000	1-May-08
20	ig.com	$4,700,000	18-Sep-13
21	freeporn.com	$4,000,000	1-Feb-08
22	yp.com	$3,850,000	1-Nov-08
23	hg.com	$3,770,000	30-Nov-16
24	mi.com	$3,600,000	30-Apr-14
25	ice.com	$3,500,000	6-Jul-18
26	shop.com	$3,500,000	1-Nov-03
27	wine.com	$3,300,000	1-Sep-03
28	altavista.com	$3,250,000	1-Apr-99
29	software.com	$3,200,000	1-Dec-05
30	whisky.com	$3,100,000	12-Mar-14
31	california.com	$3,000,000	20-Jan-19
32	sex.xxx	$3,000,000	11-Jun-14
33	candy.com	$3,000,000	10-Jun-09
34	vodka.com	$3,000,000	20-Dec-06
35	loans.com	$3,000,000	1-Jan-00
36	wines.com	$2,900,000	1-Jul-04
37	fly.com	$2,890,000	4-Apr-17
38	creditcards.com	$2,750,000	1-Jun-04
39	lotto.com	$2,680,000	31-Dec-17
40	pizza.com	$2,605,000	3-Apr-08
41	social.com	$2,600,000	1-Jul-11
42	gambling.com	$2,500,000	4-May-11
43	tom.com	$2,500,000	1-Dec-99
44	investing.com	$2,450,000	19-Dec-12
45	youxi.com	$2,430,000	12-Mar-14
46	kk.com	$2,400,000	20-Nov-13
47	pharmacy.com	$2,300,000	27-Nov-08
48	coupons.com	$2,200,000	1-Jan-00
49	autos.com	$2,200,000	1-Dec-99
50	delta.com	$2,125,000	31-Jul-00
51	vivo.com	$2,100,000	2-Sep-16
52	114.com	$2,100,000	17-Jul-13

53	computer.com	$2,100,000	5-Dec-07
54	zoom.com	$2,000,000	14-Dec-18
55	eth.com	$2,000,000	22-Oct-17
56	freedom.com	$2,000,000	21-May-17
57	express.com	$2,000,000	1-Mar-00
58	telephone.com	$2,000,000	1-Jan-00
59	england.com	$2,000,000	1-Dec-99
60	37.com	$1,960,800	19-Mar-14
61	savings.com	$1,900,000	1-Feb-03
62	01.com	$1,820,000	29-Jan-17
63	seniors.com	$1,800,000	10-Jul-07
64	mortgage.com	$1,800,000	1-Mar-00
65	20.com	$1,750,000	16-Apr-17
66	dating.com	$1,750,000	16-Jun-10
67	auction.com	$1,700,000	27-Mar-09
68	datarecovery.com	$1,659,000	5-Mar-08
69	branson.com	$1,600,000	1-Jun-06
70	liu.com	$1,556,888	1-Feb-14
71	ticket.com	$1,525,000	16-Oct-09
72	eko.com	$1,500,000	20-Oct-19
73	russia.com	$1,500,000	2-Dec-09
74	tandberg.com	$1,500,000	13-Feb-07
75	cameras.com	$1,500,000	7-Nov-06
76	marketingtoday.com	$1,500,000	1-Sep-05
77	deposit.com	$1,500,000	1-Feb-00
78	vip.com	$1,400,000	1-Dec-03
79	ff.com	$1,400,000	8-Feb-17
80	ebet.com	$1,350,000	23-Oct-13
81	men.com	$1,320,000	1-Feb-00
82	banks.com	$1,300,000	15-Sep-06
83	power.com	$1,261,000	19-Nov-14
84	tm.com	$1,250,000	14-Nov-19
85	jade.com	$1,250,000	29-Feb-16
86	photo.com	$1,250,000	6-May-10
87	vista.com	$1,250,000	14-Nov-07
88	feedback.com	$1,230,000	1-Feb-03
89	super.com	$1,200,000	26-Feb-18
90	myworld.com	$1,200,000	8-Oct-17

91	*la.com*	*$1,200,000*	*8-May-16*
92	*mm.com*	*$1,200,000*	*1-Jul-14*
93	*find.com*	*$1,200,000*	*1-Mar-04*
94	*phone.com*	*$1,200,000*	*1-Feb-03*
95	*scores.com*	*$1,180,000*	*12-Jun-07*
96	*kredit.de*	*$1,169,175*	*2-Dec-08*
97	*dxl.com*	*$1,150,000*	*23-Dec-18*
98	*chinese.com*	*$1,120,008*	*31-Jul-07*
99	*flying.com*	*$1,100,000*	*8-Apr-10*
100	*call.com*	*$1,100,000*	*2-Sep-09*

These are few examples which are available in public sources. Everyday domain sale happens privately as most seller and buyer needs confidentiality. It is believed that almost 75% sales happen privately. Also, this list doesn't include sales happen between established businesses. If you need more example, here I am providing link of Wikipedia and other trusted sources which you can check:

- https://en.wikipedia.org/wiki/List_of_most_expensive_domain_names
- https://www.marketingmind.in/list-of-top-25-most-expensive-domain-names/
- https://fortunly.com/articles/the-most-expensive-domain-names-ever-sold/#gref
- https://alter.com/blog/top-domain-name-sales
- https://www.godaddy.com/garage/the-top-20-most-expensive-domain-names/

3.4 Career Opportunities in Domain Investing

As we already saw the example of expensive domain name, I think that's enough to convince you that domain investing is a real business in today tech-world. But don't assume you buy a domain name for $10 and sell it for million dollars overnight. As with any other business, you need dedication, passion, and time to be successful in this business. Its not a quick rich scheme or a magic stick which you can use to become a millionaire. You need to put a lot of efforts and learn the domain investing skill as any other skill we learn. Its similar to driving a car, if you start driving without any learning, its almost sure that an accident happen. Also, don't assume you make money on every domain you buy. If give my example, almost 80 percent of my domain expire after a year. You need only one big hit to make profit and cover the expenses of all your domain portfolio.

In the example of expensive domain name above, we just saw the tip of iceberg. There are thousands of small transaction (~four figure) happening every day in domain industry. Some people and businesses are willing to pay a lot of money to get their hands on the premium domain names, which makes the business of domain names a very lucrative one. There is very low investment and almost no risk if you do it wisely in domain investing. The return of investment it offers is huge i.e., you are buying something for $10 and selling for $10k. It can definitely be a steady stream of income over time and help you to fulfill your dream.

3.5 What is The Domain Name Life Cycle?

To become a successful domain investor, it is very important to understand the life cycle of domain name as there is lot of potential in expired domain (which we discuss later). Currently thousands of domain name expired and registered every day. There is a standard process of domain registration, renewal, expiration, and deletion. Here, I will explain the complete life cycle of domain name from registration to deletion. Given below are the different stages in the life cycle of domain:

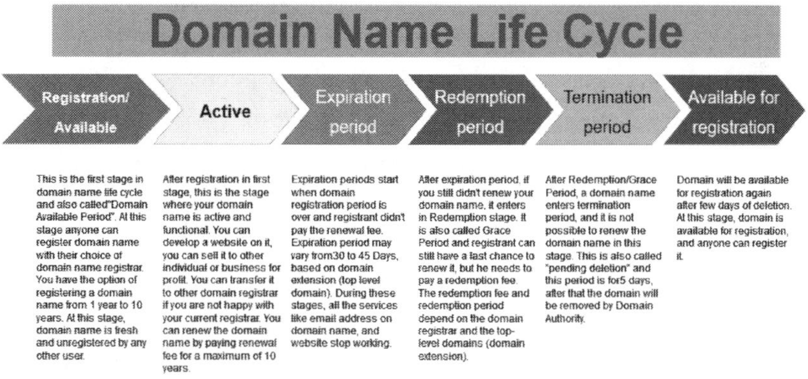

Domain Name Registration/Available:

This is the first stage in domain name life cycle and also called "Domain Available Period". At this stage anyone can register domain name with their choice of domain name registrar. You have the option of registering a domain name from 1 year to 10 years. At this stage, domain name is fresh and unregistered by any other user. You can easily get the domain name at very reasonable price (~$10 -$20 for a year).

Active Domain Name State:

After registration in first stage, this is the stage where your domain name is active and functional. You can develop a website on it, you can sell it to other individual or business for profit. You can transfer it to other domain registrar if you are not happy with your current registrar. You can renew the domain name by paying renewal fee for a maximum of 10 years.

Expired Domain Name State:

Expiration periods start when domain registration period is over and registrant didn't pay the renewal fee. Expiration period may vary from 30 to 45 Days, based on domain extension (top level domain). During these stages, all the services like email address on domain name, and website stop working. Domain registrant can pay the renewal fee during this stage without any penalty and make it active again. If you are using domain for personal business or website, it is recommended that you always extend the domain active period before letting it go to expiration stage.

Redemption/Grace Period:

After expiration period, if you still didn't renew your domain name, it enters in Redemption stage. It is also called Grace Period and registrant can still have a last chance to renew it, but he needs to pay a redemption fee. The redemption fee and redemption period depend on the domain registrar and the top-level domains (domain extension). The redemption fee is usually $80 to $200 and redemption period are usually 30 days. For ".com" domain extension the redemption fee is generally high as compared to other extension.

Termination Period/Pending Deletion:

After Redemption/Grace Period, a domain name enters termination period, and it is not possible to renew the domain name in this stage. This is also called "pending deletion" and this period is for 5 days, after that the domain will be removed by Domain Authority.

Available for Registration:

Domain will be available for registration again after few days of deletion. At this stage, domain is available for registration, and anyone can register it.

This completes the domain name life cycle. As a domain investor, you can take advantage of expired domain name or those domain name which are pending to delete. We will discuss that in deeper detail in later chapter.

3.6 Domain Appraisals

Domain appraisal is defined as the price estimate or valuation of the domain by some individual or a software tool. Domain appraisal is not a random number generated by software, it is in fact based on some factors and statistics. But it may not be accurate as different software tool shows different value for the same domain name. In my opinion, correct price of domain name is what you can actually get someone to pay for it. It is same as saying "beauty is in the eye of the beholder". For one buyer, your domain name may have $100 value whereas for another buyer can offer $100k.

Domain appraisal services can help you in finding a starting price – an amount that you can use as an anchor before doing further research. You can negotiate with the buyer based on domain appraisal price. But I saw domain appraisal price is much different from the actual price of a website. For example, below I am providing the list of recent domain sale (20 Dec 2021 – 02 Jan 2022) with their actual price and price from few domain appraisal tools:

DOMAIN NAME	SOLD FOR	WHERE SOLD	GODADDY APPRAISAL	ESTIBOT APPRAISAL	PC.DOMAINS APPRAISAL
PAYS.COM	$350,000	Sedo	$25,000	$359,000	$4,239
NUTUN.COM	$125,000	Sedo	$2,142	$128,000	$85
ETH.CM	€100,000 = $113,000	DomainHacks.com	$25,000	$2,050,000	$1,934
VIVERSE.COM	$100,000	DomainJunction	$3,642	$103,000	$165
HIRE.BG	€75,600 = $85,428	Sedo	$1,927		$4,117
METAVERSEGROUP.COM	$75,000	Pvt Sale	$1,341		$80
DILDO.COM	$65,000	Sedo	$25,000		$11,386
7BANK.COM	$55,000	Sedo	$5,413		$1,684

MAKSIMOV.COM	$51,000	Sedo	$3,782	$78
HARDFORK.CO	$50,000	Sedo	$1,049	$80
U.FR	€39,990 = $45,189	Sedo	$1,040	$175
DAO.CO	$45,000	Sedo	$11,390	$8,976
HOOKUP.APP	$45,000	Brandforce	$337	$1,200
CLEANPLANET.COM	$40,000	Sedo	$9,637	$600
EXACTTIME.COM	$40,000	Uniregistry Market	$5,870	$345

As you can see, GoDaddy and "pc.domains" price is nowhere near to actual sold price. "Estibot" price is somewhat closer to actual price of the domain name. That may be because Estibot keep track of recent sales and include that information in their algorithm while calculating the estimated price. Estibot is a trusted and widely used free appraisal service and they claim that they provide Unbiased, statistically derived domain name appraisal. Domain registrars, parking companies, and investors trust the Estibot algorithm for fair market value based on historical sales and other criteria. The estimate may be different at a later date or time because age of domain name is also a factor in estimating its price. Again, domain appraisal price is not very important while closing the deal. It is just for the sake of negotiation; you can use it.

Domain appraisal services can be classified as "Free" and "Paid" based on their pricing. I recommend don't waste even a single penny on paid appraisals, they don't have any value. You already saw that different appraisal services provide very different estimate. If a buyer wants you to provide the appraisal value, you can use any of the below free services:

https://www.estibot.com

https://www.DOMAININDEX.com

https://www.Valuate.com

https://www.GoDaddy.com

https://www.sedo.com

https://www.URLAppraisal.net

https://flippa.com/online-business-valuation

https://www.epik.com/appraise/

https://www.freevaluator.com

https://www.pc.domains

https://www.websiteoutlook.com

3.7 Domain Appraisal Factors

Domain appraisal services consider the following factors while evaluating the price or value of a domain name.

Domain Name Extension (TLD):

I think this is the major factor in determining the appraisal value of a domain name. Domain appraisal gives weightage to the domain name if the domain extension match the language of the domain name. It is also important that how popular is the domain extension. For example, ".com" is the most popular and preferred TLD and valuate higher than corresponding ccTLDs or gTLDs.

Domain name Length:

The shorter the domain name, better it is. a one letter domain name has much higher value than a 2 or 3 letter domain name. For example, "z.com" sold for $678000 in 2014 whereas "kk.com" sold for $2400000 in 2013. There is no doubt, other factor is also important and being short is not the only reason behind this sale. But short domain name always has somewhat more value than longer domain name. "fb.com" was sold for $8500000 in 2010 and Facebook is using it only to redirect traffic to facebook.com

Memorability:

Memorability is another factor; these domain appraisal tools take into consideration. If a domain name is easy to remember, it by default gets more direct traffic and more traffic means more money. For example, "pizza.com" sold for $2605000 in 2008 whereas "pizzadfesg.com.com" is available for $4.99 on GoDaddy.

Pronounceability:

Pronounceability is another facto which affect domain appraisal. If a domain name is easy to pronounce, it can get "word of mouth" traffic. It is another form of memorability i.e., if it's easy to pronounce then it's easy to remember and hence more traffic.

Search engine suitability:

If a domain name is suitable for search engine, there is higher chances that it appears more in search result and get more traffic. That's another factor for domain appraisal. Some domain names are optimized for SEO (search engine optimization) and naturally come into search result with little efforts. These domain name have are more valuable than the one which are not search engine friendly. For example, "healthcareinnewyork.com" have better chances to appear in search result (searched from New York) as compared to "healthcareingeneral.com"

Traffic Rank:

Traffic rank is also an important factor in determining the value of domain name. For example, Alexa page rank and search engine PR (page rank) are considered to get the traffic rank. Different appraisal tools give different weightage to traffic rank.

Age of Domain:

How old is the domain name i.e., when was it registered first time? More the age of the domain name, better the appraisal value of it. Although, in recent algorithmic changes, age is not considered a big factor for search result by google search.

Language complexity (Numbers and Hyphens):

How many hyphens or number are present in the domain name? That is also considered by domain appraisal tools as it makes domain name hard to verbalize.

Marketability (Brand value):

Can a domain name be used to make a brand or built business on it? Is it possible to use the domain name as marketing tool for the business?

Typo susceptibility:

How high is the risk of mistyping the domain name? Does the name have any unexpected spellings? If a domain name is more susceptible to typos, there is potential of huge traffic loss which is not good for the business. A typo can be because of a common misspelling, or foreign language spelling, of the intended site, a misspelling based on a typographical error, a plural of a singular domain name.

International usability:

Can the domain name be used on an international scale? Can people from all around the world remember the name? Does the name function locally or globally?

Sales opportunities:

Is there a high sales potential for the domain name in future? For example, if somebody buy a domain name around cryptocurrency in 2008-10, now the same domain name has much higher value.

Historic sales and Market insight:

Some domain appraisal tools track the past sale of domain name and use some artificial intelligence and machine learning algorithm to decide the value of a domain based on this data. For example, Estibot maintain a big database of past domain sales and use it for predicting the value of new domain name. This is the reason Estibot provide closest estimates for all the domain name we present in previous section.

Apart from that, there are some other factors also which domain appraisal tool used in evaluating the domain value. Each domain appraisal tool has different algorithm and different weightage for different factor to get the final value. Some of the additional factor used for domain appraisal are below:

- Monthly search volume for keyword (# of times the keyword is searched on a search engine)
- CPC for keyword (How much advertisers pay per Google AdWords click)
- Comparable sales
- Number of other extensions registered for the keyword
- Current market conditions

3.8 Domain Appraisal Scams

The domain appraisal scam tries to trick domain name owners into paying for an appraisal for their domain name in order to complete a sale. Scammer usually contact the domain name owner with a friendly email and ask if the domain name is available for sale. They send a very good offer to lure the domain name owner and when domain owner ready to sell, scammer ask him to provide a domain appraisal certificate from a website which scammer runs. After domain owner pays for the domain appraisal fee and get the appraisal certificate, scammer never reply. These scammers pretend to be authenticated domain registrar or representative of some big corporation. Even, some scammers pretend to be someone from the team of your domain name registrar company. This is very popular scam in the domain industry and often beginner is an easy target for these scams.

Some registrar changed the process of contacting domain name owner to save their customer from scammer. For example, GoDaddy, the largest domain name registrar, now using contact form instead of providing domain owner contact detail to other people when they inquire about your domain name. A scammer can take advantage of these emails.

Here's what an email sent through the form looks like:

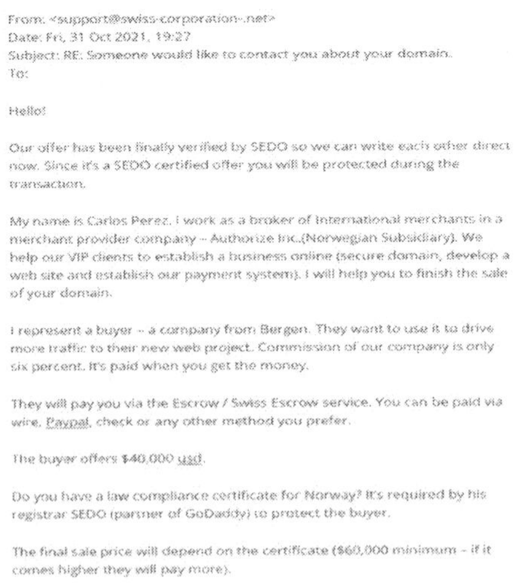
From: <support@swiss-corporation-.net>
Date: Fri, 31 Oct 2021, 19:27
Subject: RE: Someone would like to contact you about your domain.
To:

Hello!

Our offer has been finally verified by SEDO so we can write each other direct now. Since it's a SEDO certified offer you will be protected during the transaction.

My name is Carlos Perez. I work as a broker of International merchants in a merchant provider company – Authorize Inc.(Norwegian Subsidiary). We help our VIP clients to establish a business online (secure domain, develop a web site and establish our payment system). I will help you to finish the sale of your domain.

I represent a buyer – a company from Bergen. They want to use it to drive more traffic to their new web project. Commission of our company is only six percent. It's paid when you get the money.

They will pay you via the Escrow / Swiss Escrow service. You can be paid via wire, Paypal, check or any other method you prefer.

The buyer offers $40,000 usd.

Do you have a law compliance certificate for Norway? It's required by his registrar SEDO (partner of GoDaddy) to protect the buyer.

The final sale price will depend on the certificate ($60,000 minimum – if it comes higher they will pay more).

Never pay any money for such request of appraisal. If someone ask you to provide an appraisal, either ignore the request or ask them to get themselves the domain appraisal.

3.9 Tips to Identify Domain Appraisal Scams:

Safeguarding Your Domain Investments

In the domain industry, domain appraisal services are sought after by domain owners and investors who want to determine the value of their domain names. While there are reputable appraisal services available, it is crucial to be aware of domain appraisal scams that can deceive unsuspecting individuals and exploit their investments. To protect yourself from falling victim to such scams, it is important to be knowledgeable and cautious. In this article, we will provide you with tips to identify domain appraisal scams and safeguard your domain investments.

1. **Research the Appraisal Company:**

   Before engaging with any domain appraisal service, thoroughly research the company or individual offering the service. Look for established and reputable appraisal companies with a track record of providing accurate and unbiased appraisals. Check for online reviews, testimonials, and feedback from other domain owners to assess the credibility and reputation of the appraisal service provider.

2. **Be Wary of Unsolicited Appraisal Offers:**

   If you receive unsolicited emails or messages offering free domain appraisals or claiming that your domain name has high value, proceed with caution. Legitimate appraisal services typically do not reach out randomly to domain owners. Scammers often use unsolicited offers as a tactic to lure victims into their fraudulent schemes.

3. **Evaluate the Appraisal Methodology:**

   Reputable appraisal services employ various factors and methodologies to determine the value of a domain name. They consider factors such as domain length, keyword relevance, market demand, comparable sales data, and industry trends. Be cautious if an appraisal service claims to provide an appraisal solely based on an automated or instant appraisal tool. These tools often lack accuracy and can be manipulated by scammers to deceive domain owners.

4. **Avoid Paying High Fees for Appraisal Certificates:**

   Some scams involve offering domain appraisal certificates at exorbitant prices. These certificates claim to provide an official appraisal value, but in reality, they hold no real value. Legitimate appraisal services do not typically provide physical certificates, as domain valuations can fluctuate over time and are subjective. Be skeptical of any appraisal service that insists on charging a high fee for such certificates.

5. **Cross-Verify Appraisal Results:**

   To ensure the accuracy and legitimacy of an appraisal, consider seeking multiple appraisals from different reputable sources. Compare the results and look for consistency among the appraisals. If one appraisal significantly differs from others, it may indicate an inconsistency or potential scam. Legitimate appraisal services will offer a range of values based on various factors and market conditions.

6. **Trust Your Gut and Exercise Caution:**

   If something feels too good to be true or raises suspicions, trust your instincts. Be cautious of appraisal services that promise extremely high valuations or guarantee quick sales at inflated prices. Remember that domain valuation is subjective and can fluctuate based on market demand and other variables. Avoid rushing into decisions or feeling pressured by high-pressure sales tactics employed by scammers.

7. **Seek Advice from Trusted Professionals:**

   If you are uncertain about the legitimacy of an appraisal service or have doubts about an appraisal offer, seek advice from trusted professionals within the domain industry. Consult with domain brokers, experienced investors, or reputable domain forums and communities to gain insights and recommendations regarding appraisal services.

Identifying domain appraisal scams is crucial for protecting your domain investments and avoiding potential financial losses. By researching appraisal service providers, evaluating methodologies, being wary of unsolicited offers, avoiding high fees for certificates, cross-verifying appraisal results, trusting your instincts, and seeking advice from trusted professionals, you can safeguard yourself against fraudulent domain appraisal schemes. Remain vigilant, stay informed, and exercise caution when engaging with domain appraisal services to ensure the integrity of your domain investments.

4.

RESEARCH FOR HIGH-VALUE DOMAIN INVESTING

"Research is to see what everybody else has seen, and to think what nobody else has thought."

-Albert Szent-Gyorgyi

Before investing a single penny, you should have complete knowledge about the product you are investing in. You must acquire the skill of a good domain investor, if you want to make a profit in this industry. A Pilot start earning after 5000 flights hours, a doctor start earning after spending 5 years in a medical degree. Similarly, if you want to make money in domain investing, you need knowledge, skills and confidence which come with time and efforts. In this chapter, we will discuss what makes a domain name valuable, what are the different strategy you can use to invest in domains. How to do research to identify a valuable domain name.

4.1 What makes a domain name valuable?

"Value of a domain name lies in the eyes of buyer". If a businessmen decided to start a new company with a particular name, he can spend a lot of money to get the related domain name for that business. It depends on the spending power of businessman. For example, If you have a domain name, "instagram.com" or "instagr.am" (here 'am' is top level domain or domain extension) and Mark Zuckerberg (CEO of Facebook) want to buy that domain name for his new application, he can easily offer you millions of dollar for that. For other people, these domain name may have no value. So, it really depends on who is buying the domain name and how much his spending power is.

But there are some factors which can help you identify the valuable domain name. Some domain name for example keyword specific domain name or short domain name are valuable because every business wants a recognizable, brandable, and easy-to-remember domain name for their website. Let's discuss each factor one by one which makes a domain name valuable:

Top-Level Domain Extensions (TLDs):

Top-Level Domain Extensions is the most important factor in deciding the value of domain name. There are more than 700 domain extension available. But I think it is best to keep it old school and focus only on ".com" domain name initially. It is most familiar and one of the oldest extensions on internet. We already saw that in most expensive domain name sale, more than 60 percent are ".com". This proves that ".com" extension domain name have high value as compared to other country code specific or generic extension. It is because ".com" is used from the starting of internet and people are more familiar to ".com" as website extension. It is similar to Bitcoin in cryptocurrency, there are many good cryptocurrencies after Bitcoin (such as Ethereum, Litecoin), but still Bitcoin is most expensive in all of these cryptocurrencies.

If you are not able to find good ".com" domain name, there are plenty of other extension you can focus on. You need to check if extension make sense with the domain keyword. For example, there is a website "remove.bg" to remove the background from images. They choose the domain name wisely which shorten their domain name and make sense also. For resale purpose, there are example of gTLDs which was sold for very high price. For example, "kredit.de" was sold for $1169175 in 2008. Recently, "Hire.bg" was sold for $85428 on sedo, "Kindred.xyz" was sold for $27888 on sedo in January 2022.

The key takeout is trying to find ".com" first, if not able to find valuable ".com" domain, go for gTLDs which make sense.

Keywords:

Keywords are very important factor for search engine and if your domain name have keywords relevant to your content, you will get an edge in search engine ranking. So, if you are planning to develop website on it or even for reselling, keyword domain name sells better. For example, "healthinsurance.com" was sold for $8,133,000 in 2019, "datarecovery.com" was sold for $1,659,000 in 2008.

If you are not able to think keyword, you can brainstorm using google keyword planner. It will provide you average monthly searches, competition for the keyword, and how much advertiser are willing to pay for that keyword (Bid amount). you will also get an idea of similar keyword you can target. My strategy is to choose those (2 or 3 words) keyword where competition is low, searches and bid amount is high.

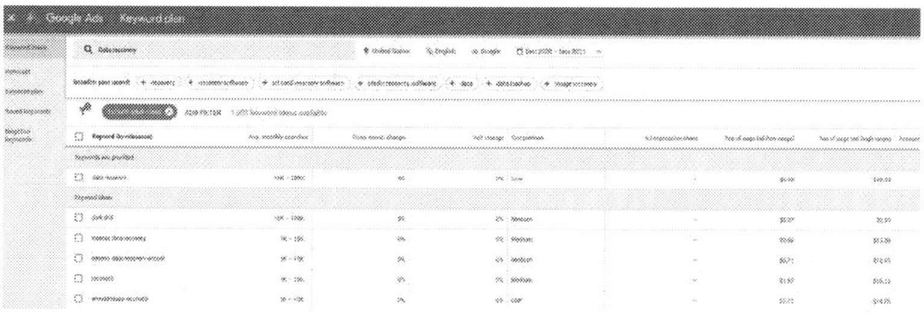

Easy to Pronounce and Spell:

Your domain name should be easy to spell and pronounce. Some people like to have complicated name like Elon Musk baby-name. You may think it's cool and unique, but it is not. There will be time when you have to tell someone your domain name verbally over the phone or in a conference. If it's not easy to pronounce, people will forget it easily or they don't understand it and end up visiting some other website and hence loss of potential traffic. if your domain name is easy to pronounce, people can pass it to their friends or acquaintance, and you will get free "word of mouth" advertising. Your domain name should pass the "radio broadcast" test. What that mean is if someone pronounce your domain name on radio advertisement, people should be able to get it right.

Short Length:

Shorter the domain in length, better the chance of making profit from it. Shorter domain name sells well as it involves less efforts in typing, easy to remember, easy to pronounce and spell and there is very less chances that a visitor types it wrong and end up visiting some other website. That's the reason, any business wants to get the shorter domain name. For example, Facebook spent $ 8.5 million to get "fb.com" from its previous owner

American Farm Bureau Federation. There are plenty other examples such as "ig.com" sell for $ 4.7 million in September 2013, "we.com" sell for $ 8 million in June 2015.

In today competitive market, it is very difficult to get a 3 or 4 letters domain name at good price. But there are still many domains name in 5 or 6 letters category which you can register for less than $12. Shorter domain name has another advantage that you can use big font size when you need to print on billboard or any other print media. It is very helpful to grab attention of potential visitor.

Easy to Remember:

Try to get a domain name which is easy to remember. This will help you in long term as a memorable domain name usually get more traffic. For example, if somebody saw your domain name on billboard while driving, or on print media, they can visit the website later if it is easy to remember. There are some tips you can follow to find a memorable domain name such as find quirky or funny domain name, find unforgettable or unusual name. Use a clever phrase which make people smile and they can easily recall it later when they want to visit the website. For example, "Wintersexpress.com" (Winters Express), "WhorePresents.com" (Who Represents, a sort of database storing the official representatives of famous stars and starlets).

You can try to find domain name which are "call to action" such as "JustDoIt.com", "ThinkDifferent.com", "HaveItYourWay.com", "EscapeToday.com" etc. These are also easy to remember.

Pronoun and Plurals:

If the domain name you are interested in, is not available, try to find some other alternative with pronoun and plural. For example, if "allflavor.com", search for "allflavors.com". Brainstorm the different option you can have and look for availability. You can use pronoun, preposition such as "the, with, in, at" etc.

Age and History of the domain:

Age of domain name is one of the factors for google search algorithm. Try to find older domain name can help you find the great domain name with great search engine reputation. For example, you can try to find expired or deleted domain name which are register a long time ago and which are off market now. http://expireddomains.net/ is one of the best sources to find these hidden gems. I will discuss expired domain in detail in later chapter. But don't spend too much money on a particular domain name, try to keep your investment low only then you can make profit in this business.

Domain Name's Popularity in Google Search Results:

Use Google Keyword Planner to find out the popularity of the domain name. It will help you find out if the domain name is actually valuable or only you are assuming value in it. For example, if you select a domain name to register, try to check how many searches per month are done for the keyword relevant to this domain name. You can also check if other similar domain name with different extension (.net, .org etc.) for search statistics i.e., how much visitor they are receiving each month. There are many free and paid tool for that. I will recommend not to spent money on these tools and use only free tools. For example, you can use "similarweb.com" for stats of a website.

Research Comparable Sales:

Spend some time in researching about the similar sale on different web resources and get an idea of price is suitable for the domain name you are planning to register. There are many good resources to do research about the similar sale of a domain name by keyword or by domain extension. My favorite website for researching of domain sale is namebio.com and dnjournal.com. These two resources provide extensive knowledge about the domain industry. You can spend time on these websites and find out what is selling and valuable enough to register.

Buy What you know (Niche):

Decide a particular Niche and explore the different keywords, terms, and product used in that niche. If you don't know, a niche is the area of expertise or you can define it as a specialization in particular subject, category, or field. It is a subset of bigger market or subject. For example, programming is a subject, but programming in python is a niche. Online earning is a bigger market, affiliate marketing is a niche in that market. So, if you are expert in particular subject, trade, industry, try to explore the domain name related to that industry. You may find some hidden gems which nobody explores yet.

Variation or Alternative:

Try to find the domain name which have very few alternatives available to sale. For example, if you are planning to sell "Dentist.net" for $ 5000 and there is already an alternative "Dentist.com" available to buy for $100, what you think buyer will buy? Check the market for alternative and if there is good alternative available for cheaper price then stay away from buying those domain name. The simple logic is less or no alternative available for your domain name, greater the value of it.

Quality over Quantity:

It is better to register only few qualities domain name instead of registering thousands of unvaluable domain name. In starting of my career, I register so many bad domains name that if I saw those domain name now, I will laugh at my choices. At that time, I am new to this industry and doe's have any knowledge what I should invest and what not. After one year, I didn't make any money from reselling those domain name and dropped almost all. I learn the lesson in hard way, and I don't want you will make the same mistake which I made. You will read this advice again and again from me that spent time in learning and getting knowledge of the industry before spending any money here.

Budget and Pricing:

Decide a budget, you want to spend in domain names and take all your action according to your budget. If you spent too much money initially in buying a particular domain name, then there is very limited scope of making profit from it. For example, if you buy a domain name for $1000, then you need to sell that domain name for at least 2 time (i.e., $ 2000) to make profit and cover all your cost like taxes, initial investment etc. If you buy a domain name in auction, it is very easy to spend high amount for a domain name which doesn't deserve that price. Don't break the rule, follow a budget plan if you don't want to regret later. Many domains flipping portal charge a fee if you want to sell your domain on their portal. Some companies like "Flippa.com" charge a fee of $49 to feature your domain name on their homepage. Don't spend money on such promotion if you are on limited budget.

Initially, when you enter in this business, it is very common to become excited about a domain name, buy it for higher price, and go over-budget. I repeat again, decide your budget, and stick to it. Period.

Use Domain Name Generators to Brainstorm:

After doing all your research, you may find yourself stuck and not able to decide what domain name you should buy. You may come up with a very good keyword and excited to register it and when you check on domain name registrar, it is already taken. This happens to me many times. Fortunately, there are solution for that problem and that is domain name generator. Domain name generator will help you to brainstorm around any keyword and provide you options for available domain name. There are many domains name generator available in the market. Below are few which I personally use for brainstorming around a keyword:

Wordoid (https://wordoid.com/): This domain name generator allows you to put your keyword and provide you many available domains name around that keyword. You can also choose different language, quality, length, and pattern to get the domain name. You can indicate if you want a domain name starting with or ending with a particular keyword.

Lean Domain Search (https://leandomainsearch.com/): This is also another great tool which provide a list of domain name with other relevant keywords. It is simplest and easy to use tool and really useful for brainstorming.

Domain Wheel (https://domainwheel.com/): This tool uses artificial intelligence to generate domain name.

There are many good tools such as GoDaddy, instant domain search (https://instantdomainsearch.com/domain/generator).

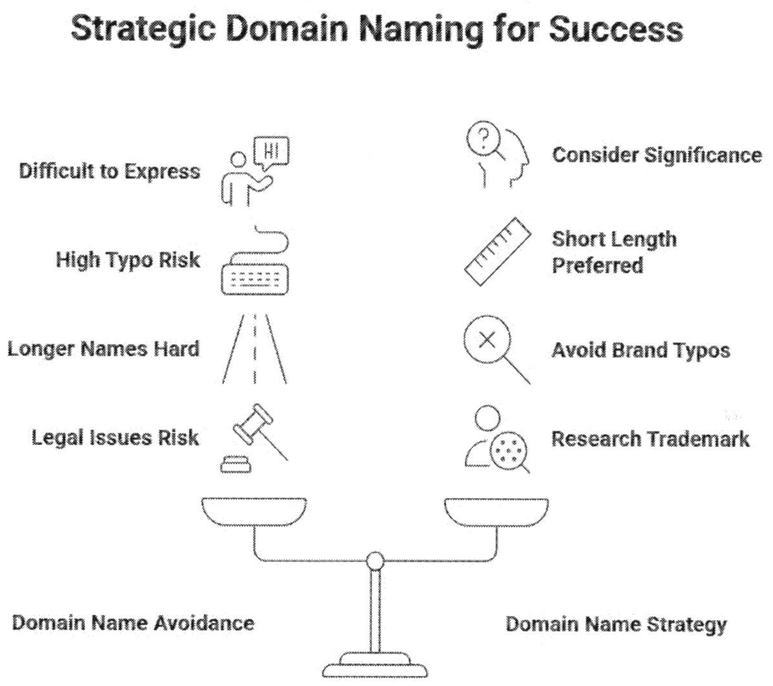

4.2 What You Should Avoid

We already discuss how to find a valuable domain name and what you can look for while researching for domain name. Now let's discuss what you should avoid while researching for domain name:

Avoid Hyphens & Numbers:

Try to avoid hyphens in your domain name as they are difficult to express verbally and make domain difficult to type. It is easy to forget hyphen and your user may end up on someone else's website. That is loss of traffic and revenue for the website.

Same rules apply for number, try to avoid them if your domain name is more than 4 letters. Although there are examples ("37.com" was sold for $1,960,800 in 2014, "01.com" was sold for $1,820,000 in 2017) of number domain name which was sold for very high price, but it's rare to find similar domain in today competitive market. If you are still planning to buy some number domain name, try to find a name which signify something or which is easy to remember. For example, 786 is a holy number for Muslim people, you can try to get "786.com" or 007 is used for James Bond (a Hollywood movie character), you can try to find "007.com". 444 is another number which have spiritual meaning and it signifies the end of one phase of life and beginning of another. There are many another number such as 999 (it is used in bible many times and used as a sign from god that your prayer have been heard and answered), 333 (used as invitation from the universe to move forward), 888, 1212, 1010, 1234, 1and1, 2in1 etc.

The key takeaway is trying to avoid hyphen and number when you are planning to buy a domain name. If you must want to buy a number domain name, try to think the significance of it. Spent some time in researching the value of it and apply other factor such as easy to remember, easy to type (spelling), short length etc.

Avoid using Double Letters:

Double letter in domain name invites the problem of typos and typo squatting. Always avoid using double letter in domain name. It is harder to read, have a high chance of typos and difficult to tell someone about your website. Usually, visitor miss one letter and end up visiting some another website which a potential loss for the business. For example, if you wan a domain name "Internetterminal.com", it is better to think it some other way such as "terminalinternet.com" etc.

Avoid Longer Domain Name:

You are allowed to use a domain name (SLDs) as long as 63 characters, that does not mean you should register that long domain name. Longer domain names are difficult to remember and take few extra efforts to type. So, it is better to avoid domain name which are longer than 10 letters. There is no strict rule which you need to follow for length of domain name. But I usually prefer not to go more than 10 letters unless there is some high value domain name (with great traffic history and high search volume) is available.

Avoid Typos Domain Name of Brand:

Typos are defined as the error in spelling of the domain name. For example, for "yahoo.com", if someone type and visit "yahoo.com" or "yhoo.com", then it come under the category of typos. Although most big business register possible typos domain name and redirect traffic to their original website if someone visit these typos domain name, but still there is some typos domain name available to register.

I recommend not to register these typos as there is law to secure brand and businesses from these typographical errors and you can face serious legal action for hijacking the traffic of other businesses. In the United States, the 1999 Anti-cybersquatting Consumer Protection Act (ACPA) contains a clause (Section 3(a), amending 15 USC 1117 to include sub-section (d)(2)(B)(ii)) aimed at combatting typo squatting. I think it's not worth it to go for these typos domain name.

Avoid Trademark:

Trademark is defined as the word, phrase or name which is legally registered by an individual or a company. You should never register a trademark domain name, otherwise you can face legal issue for trademark infringement. Many big companies have special attorney to find any trademark infringement and taking legal action if there is any. How can you identify if a domain name is registered trademark or not? You can search for free about registered trademarks and any applied-for trademark by using USPTO (U.S. Patent and Trademark Office) service. They offer Trademark Electronic Search System which is very easy to use and provide information about any trademark in seconds. There are many private companies also which you can use to identify other detail (such as social media presence, other domain extensions for same name availability etc.) about the domain name. Knowem (https://knowem.com/) is one such example.

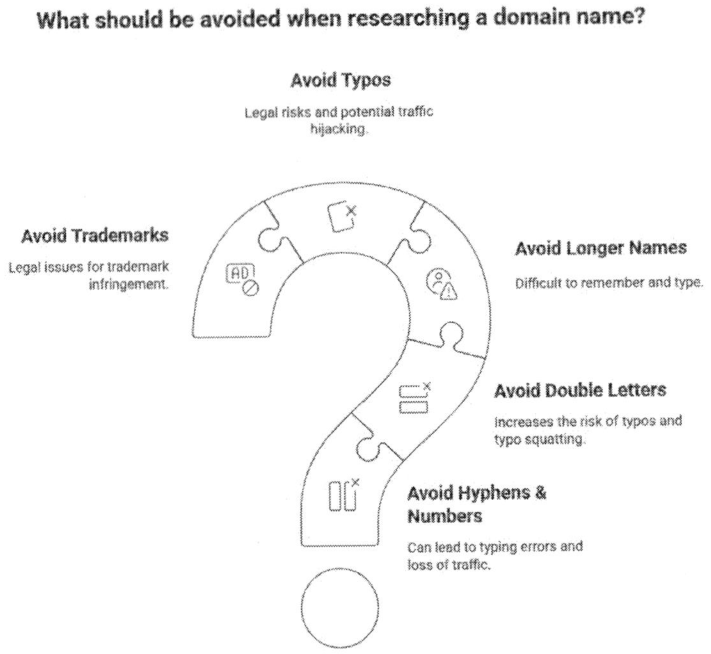

That covers the key points you should consider while researching for domain name. There are many other tips and tricks you should use; I will provide those in upcoming chapters.

5.

HOW TO MAKE A GOOD START (ONLINE PRESENCE)

"Getting smart about having an online presence is one of the strongest sales tactics you could consider."

-Toni Clayton-Hine

Anybody who is looking to buy or sell domain name is doing it online on the internet. That means all your customers (potential buyer) are online. You may say that's obvious, why I am mentioning it here. Sometime obvious things are so obvious that we ignore them. What I am trying to say is if all of your customers are online, you should be online. Your strong online presence is crucial part of your marketing strategy to sell domain online. The potential buyer of domain name can contact you only if it is easy for him to find you online. So, in this chapter, we will discuss why it is important to have a strong online presence and how you can build a strong online portfolio.

5.1 Why it is important to have strong online presence?

You are working hard to find a valuable domain name and then finding a potential buyer. But what if there is a potential buyer for a domain name you are holding, but he didn't have a way to reach out to you, it's a loss for you. So, it is very important to make sure that you are easy to approach online. Here I am providing some more reason why you should have a strong online presence:

1. **Building Credibility and Trust**:

   A strong online presence helps domain investors build credibility and trust within the industry. It provides a platform to showcase expertise, share valuable insights, and demonstrate a deep understanding of the domain market. By curating and sharing relevant content, participating in industry forums, and engaging with potential buyers and sellers, domain investors can establish themselves as knowledgeable and trustworthy professionals.

2. **Expanding Network and Connections**:

   Having a strong online presence enables domain investors to expand their network and build valuable connections within the industry. By actively participating in online communities, forums, and social media platforms, investors can connect with other industry professionals, potential buyers, and sellers. These connections can lead to collaboration opportunities, joint ventures, and access to a broader pool of domain market insights.

3. **Marketing and Branding Opportunities**:

   An effective online presence serves as a powerful marketing and branding tool for domain investors. It allows them to promote their portfolio, showcase their expertise, and highlight their unique selling propositions. Through websites, blogs, and social media channels, investors can create a compelling brand identity, differentiate themselves from competitors, and attract potential buyers and sellers.

4. **Showcasing Domain Portfolio**:

   A strong online presence provides domain investors with a platform to showcase their domain portfolio effectively. By creating a professional website or portfolio website, investors can display their domain names, provide relevant information, and offer an easy way for potential buyers to browse and inquire about specific domains. This increases the visibility of the portfolio and enhances the chances of attracting interested parties.

5. **Maximizing Domain Value**:

   An active online presence helps domain investors maximize the value of their domain investments. By effectively marketing and promoting their domains, investors increase the likelihood of attracting potential buyers who recognize the value and potential of the domains they own. A strong online presence provides the platform to communicate the unique selling points, benefits, and market relevance of each domain, thereby increasing its perceived value and negotiating power during sales transactions.

6. **Staying Updated with Industry Trends**:

An online presence allows domain investors to stay updated with the latest industry trends, news, and market developments. By actively engaging in online communities and following industry influencers, investors can access valuable insights, market analysis, and emerging opportunities. This knowledge enables them to make informed investment decisions, capitalize on emerging trends, and adapt their strategies to stay ahead in the competitive domain market.

7. **Enhancing Visibility and Exposure**:

Having a strong online presence enhances the visibility and exposure of domain investors and their portfolio. Through search engine optimization (SEO) techniques, content marketing, and social media promotion, investors can increase their online visibility, making it easier for potential buyers and sellers to discover them. Increased visibility translates into more inquiries, potential sales, and opportunities to expand their domain network.

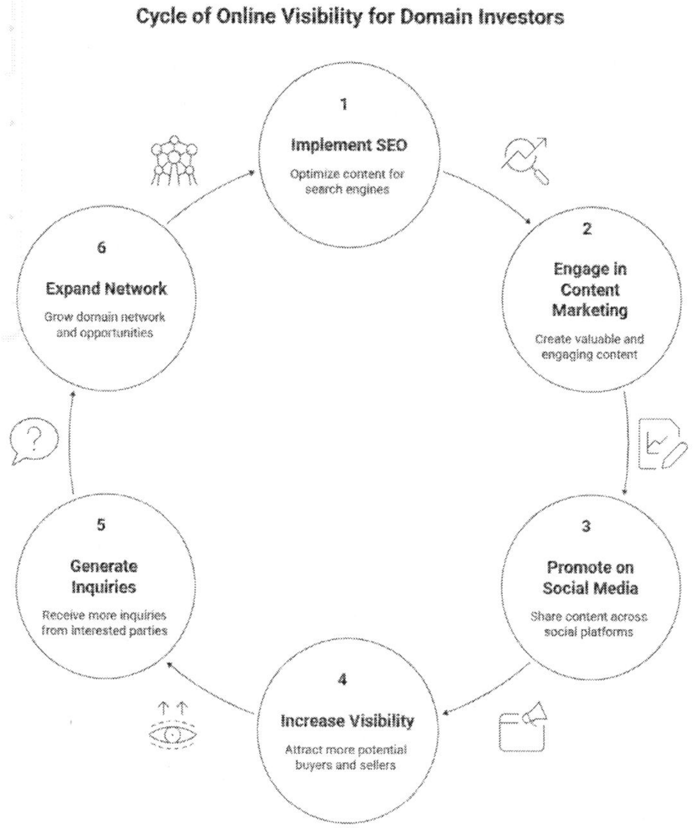

In the domain investment landscape, a strong online presence is not just desirable; it is essential for success. By building credibility, expanding networks, leveraging marketing opportunities, showcasing domain portfolios, maximizing domain value, staying updated with industry trends, and enhancing visibility, domain investors can position themselves as reputable professionals and increase their chances of success in the competitive domain market. Investing time and effort into cultivating a strong online presence is an investment that pays off in terms of increased opportunities, stronger connections, and higher returns on domain investments.

Here is what you can do to build a strong online presence, you should approach this information step-by-step:

5.2 Your website

You should have a website whether it's one page or a full-fledged multipage website. It should have you contact information, a contact form (if you don't like to share your phone number or email id) and some other information about you. You can register a domain name for you name like "FirstNameLastName.com" or "LastNameFirstName.com" if you are stating domain flipping as individual. If a ".com" domain name is not available, you can go for other domain extension such ".net", or your country specific extension such as ".in", ".co.uk" etc. If you want to be little more professional, you can start as a company and register a domain name on your company name. I recommend initially, you should start as individual, later if you are making good money in it, you can register your company.

A simple one-page website is very easy to set up, you can use free html template or even you can use CMS like WordPress. There are thousands of free tutorials available on YouTube to set up a website. Don't spent too much time, effort and money on this, keep it simple.

5.3 Your Social Media Presence

For domain investors, leveraging social media platforms is not only a means of staying connected but also an effective way to enhance their online presence, engage with potential buyers, and expand their network. In this article, we will explore the significance of social media presence for domain investors and provide tips for maximizing its benefits.

Tips for Maximizing Your Social Media Presence as a Domain Investor:

1. **Choose the Right Platforms**:

   Identify the social media platforms that align best with your target audience and industry. LinkedIn is a popular choice for professional networking, while Twitter and Facebook offer broader audience reach. Explore platforms like Instagram and YouTube for visual content and engagement opportunities.

2. **Create a Consistent Brand Image**:

   Develop a strong and consistent brand image across your social media profiles. Use a professional profile picture, a clear and concise bio, and consistent branding elements such as logos or color schemes. This helps in establishing a recognizable and cohesive online presence.

3. **Share Valuable Content**:

   Create and share content that is valuable and relevant to your target audience. Share insights, industry news, domain market trends, tips for domain investors, and updates about your portfolio. Aim to educate, inform, and engage your audience to build credibility and attract potential buyers and sellers.

4. **Engage and Interact**:

   Actively engage with your social media audience by responding to comments, answering inquiries, and participating in discussions. Show genuine interest in the domain community and be helpful and responsive. This fosters a sense of connection and trust, ultimately leading to stronger relationships and potential business opportunities.

5. **Utilize Hashtags**:

   Utilize relevant hashtags in your social media posts to increase visibility and reach a wider audience. Research and include industry-specific hashtags, trending hashtags, and popular keywords to optimize your content for discovery and engagement.

6. **Collaborate with Influencers**:

   Identify influential individuals or brands in the domain industry and explore opportunities for collaboration or guest contributions. Partnering with influencers can expand your reach, attract new followers, and enhance your credibility within the domain community.

7. **Analyze and Adapt**:

   Regularly analyze your social media performance using platform analytics or third-party tools. Identify which types of content resonate best with your audience, track engagement metrics, and adjust your social media strategy accordingly. Continuously adapt and refine your approach to maximize your social media presence's effectiveness.

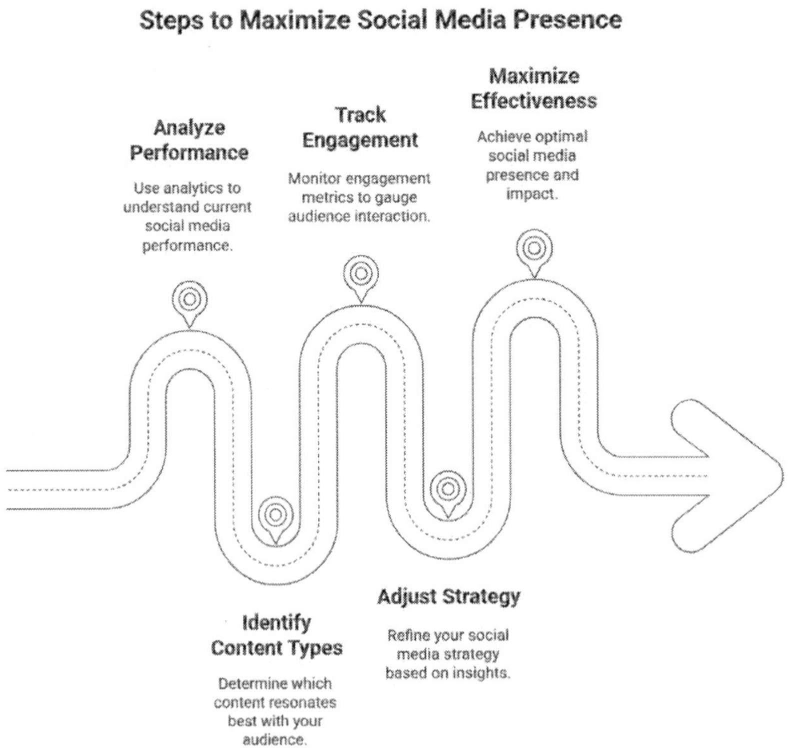

A strong social media presence is a valuable asset for domain investors. It offers opportunities to build brand awareness, engage with the domain community, showcase domain portfolios, gather market insights, and connect with potential buyers and sellers. By leveraging social media platforms strategically, domain investors can enhance their online presence, establish credibility, and unlock a world of networking and business opportunities in the dynamic domain industry.

5.4 Your Email

You should get a professional email id so that when you reach out to someone, they at least open and read your email. Nobody like to spent few seconds of their time if you are sending email from some weird email address like funkyboyforyou@email.com or crazyrahul@email.com. You should have a decent email address including your first name and/or last name and may be some number if FirstNameLastName@email.com not available.

If you want to look like little more professional, you can setup an email like info@YourDomainName.com or support@YourDomainName.com using Google Workspace (GSuite). Google charge $6 per month for one email id for professional email on your domain name and you can use Gmail app in your phone to read and send emails. If you are looking for little cheaper option, you can use Zoho Mail or Namecheap which charge only $ 1 per month.

5.5 Email Signature

Email signature is another way of showing professionalism to your domain name buyer. You can use email signature as a marketing tool and convey your contact information, your website so that its easy for them to contact you. It is great opportunity to connect with other and build trust. A professional email signature should create trust, it should be visually pleasing, and it should provide unique value to your email reader. It should be able to gain your reader attention and provide necessary information to them so that they can contact you easily.

To make a professional email signature, it should have below 5 components:

- Personal and/or Business Details
- Your Contact Information (your Phone number/ Email ID/ Website)
- Personal Picture or Company Logo
- Call-To-Action
- Your Social media Icons with links

Here is an example of professional email signature:

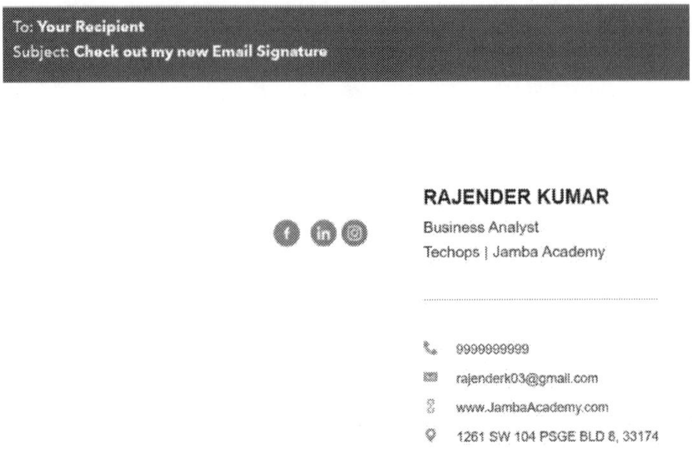

You can create your signature yourself or you can use online tools to create your signature and then copy from there. For example, hubspot (https://www.hubspot.com/email-signature-generator) provide a great tool which you can use to generate very good and visually appealing email signature.

6.

BUYING PROCESS: HOW TO BUY A VALUABLE DOMAIN NAME

"Buy less. Choose well. Make it last. Quality, not quantity. Everybody's buying far too many clothes."

-Vivienne Westwood

We already discussed about how to do research to find a valuable domain name. In this chapter, we will discuss the buying process for a domain name. It may appear obvious that we just need to visit some domain registrar website (e.g., GoDaddy) and register a domain name by paying yearly fee. As I already told, if it looks too obvious, it is the place where you make most mistake. I wasted a lot of money initially because I didn't do proper research and buy some domain name which nobody interested in buying. In this chapter, we will look the domain name research from a different point of view. After that, we will discuss different marketplace where you can buy domain name. At the end, we will discuss the risk associated with domain buying process. Without any further delay, Let's discuss the domain name research process from a different angle.

6.1 Buying Based on Different Category

We can build our portfolio based on different domain name category. Similar to stock market, if you want to make money and reduce risk, you will not put all your investment in one type of stock. You will use the technique of diversification and diversify that in different industry type, different capitalization etc. To build a strong portfolio with high-quality domain names, you should divide your budget in segments and register different domain name from each categories given below.

Generic Names:

Any word found in dictionary can be used as generic name. It is defined as a single word or a set of word which can be used for a service, product, object, subject, place, technology, or events etc. For example, pizza, business, internet, hotels, shoes etc. These all are generic name which is used to represents something and can be found in dictionary. These words look too obvious, but you will be surprised how much these domain names were sold for. Business.com was sold for $ 345 million, Internet.com was sold for $ 18 million, Hotels.com for $ 11 million and Shoes.com for $ 9 million.

A generic domain name is easy to remember, and it is easy to build trust and authority for any business if they use generic domain name. From the name itself, a visitor can identify what website they are going to visit. For example, anyone can know that they are visiting hotels on Hotels.com.

Another advantage of these domain name, they are easy to rank high on search engine like google, Bing etc. Thus, they attract lot of organic traffic, so high revenue for the business.

Geographic Names:

These are the names which include name of city, state or country. These domain name have great potential for local business or services serving locally in a particular place. You can sell these domain name to local businesses or web developers who are looking to build website for a local region.

Top level domain extensions are also available for country which can be used for services offered in that specific region. For example, ".in" for India, ".us" for USA, ".ca" for Canada etc. Now, we can register domain name with extension of some cities also. For example, ".miami", ".doha", ".berlin", ".london" etc. You can combine the generic domain name and geographic extension to get a great domain name. For example, "dentist.miami", "carpenter.london", "massage.thai" etc.

Business (Brandable) Names:

These are the domain name which have a potential to become a great business brand such as "Google", "Facebook", "Microsoft". These are the unique word which or set of word which can be used by someone to build a brand in future. You can go for a single word or a combination of word to get uniqueness. There are different approaches used to find these domain name. For example, a Swedish company combine two word "bit" and "coin" together and register a domain name "bitcoin.com" in 2000. You can imagine how much valuable this name in today market. Another approach is to get some famous last name and register a domain name on that. You can search "Most famous last name in USA (or any other country)" on google and try to get the domain name for that name. Someone in future may build a brand on that name. You can combine last name and some generic word and come up with a great name. "KhanAcademy.com", "SmithLaw.com", "JohnsonControls.com" are some examples.

Future Names:

These are the name which have no value today, but in future they are worth a fortune. It is not easy to predict the future and get domain name today. But you can apply some techniques. For example, if you are working in some industry, you have more knowledge about that industry than someone else. You may guess what word in that industry (or niche) have a potential to become valuable domain name in future. For example, someone doing practice in medical field register the domain name "Ebola.com" much earlier than the disease become wide-spread and managed to sell the domain name to a Russian company for $ 200000.

Two-Word Names:

These are the categories of domain name which is made by combination of two words. You can choose one word as generic word, service, event, place, or profession and another word as last name, first name, or some other generic word. Some examples of past successful sale of this category are "CryptoUniversity.com" (sold for $125,00 in Jan 2022), "MicroFaser.com" (sold for $42,375 on sedo in Jan 2022), "UAEBusiness.com" (sold for $29,380 on sedo in Jan 2022), "CryptoArtGallery.com" (sold for $35,000 on sedo in Jan 2022) etc. There are thousands other examples, you can visit DNJournal.com for latest list of domain name sale.

Number Domain Name:

I know that I advise you in previous section for avoiding number in domain name. But if you approach wisely and od good research in finding a valuable domain name, there are hidden gems in this category. If you find a number with hidden meaning or special significance in specific region, religion, culture, or country, you can try to register that number domain name. For example, number '6' is considered lucky in some part of China because it sounds in their local language 'liu' which is similar to a word meaning 'to flow'. It indicates the smooth progress of life. Similarly, number '3' sounds like 'san' which is similar to word meaning 'Birth'. Number '13' is considered bad or unlucky in wester n countries, but in China it is considered lucky which signifies 'assured growth' or 'definitely vibrant'. There are many other number and combination of number like 168, 520, 777, 888, 1366, 666 which have special significance. You need to be creative to find good domain name in this category.

High Traffic Domain Name:

These are the domain name, which was registered before, but now expired and available to register again. To register domain name in this category, you need to look only one quality that they have history of high search traffic. The domain name in this category may not follow other characteristics of valuable domain name such as memorable, short size, '.com' extension etc. It is completely okay to register a lengthy, unmemorable, and misspelled domain name with high domain authority, great search traffic and good history. These domain names are best suited to develop website on them and generate revenue using ads. Affiliate or lead generation.

Smart Domain Name:

As more and more domain extensions (TLDs) are available for domain name registration, you can use this opportunity wisely and register domain name with some extension which complete the domain name label as a word. It is an intelligent way of incorporating domain name label with the domain extension in a way that it makes sense and relevant to website you built on the domain name. For example, 'remove.bg' is a website which is used to remove the background from the picture, they pick the domain name wisely and it make sense to the purpose of website also. It is memorable, short and easy to spell and pronounce. In the same way, you can think out of the box and register domain name with matching domain extension. For example, '.care' domain extension is good for domain name such as 'day.care', 'life.care', 'medi.care'; '.mo' domain extension is good for 'pro.mo', 'de.mo'; '.fast' domain extension is good for for 'ultra.fast', 'super.fast'. There are thousands of domain name you can think of using this approach. It may not be valuable now, but if you are creative, you can easily make money from them by developing them and may be selling them in future.

To come up with a smart domain name, you can use the list of domain extension provided by IANA (https://data.iana.org/TLD/tlds-alpha-by-domain.txt) and the free dictionary website (https://www.thefreedictionary.com/) for domain name brainstorming. You can search for the word ending with specific extension like 'care', the free dictionary website will provide you hundreds of words.

Specific (Cultural) Domain Name:

If you belong to a specific culture, you have an edge over other domain investor regarding that culture. You know more about the history, food, living style, language, and other important aspect of the culture. You can try to find domain name which have special importance to a set of people. For example, Chinese culture in unique from rest of the world and there is large audience (population of China) which follow that culture. If you know what is important for them, which word connect them, what is most common and easy to remember for them, you can come up with a great domain name.

Expired Names:

Domain names have a registration lifecycle, and you need to pay yearly registration charges every year to renew the domain name. If you do not pay renewal fee on time (or in grace period) at the end of registration period, your domain name will expire and available to register to anyone.

Timely Names:

These are the domain name which are relevant to specific time, year or events. For example, if a big event is happening in near future, you can register a domain name around that and can develop website on that and earn using affiliate marketing or google AdSense. If a domain name fulfilling other criteria (which we discussed in earlier chapter) like memorable, short, ".com", high previous traffic history, good chances of search engine ranking, you can register it.

Honestly, I don't think you should invest in this category until you find a very promising domain name. I am covering it here just for the sake of completeness.

You should not spend all your money on one type of domain name. Think like an investor and choose domain name from each category. Your portfolio should have different type of domain name so that if you are not able to sell one type of domain name, you can others.

6.2 Four Methods of Buying Domain Name

There is different way of acquiring domain name such as auction, direct registration on domain name registrar website, expired domain names etc. Initially you can go for domain registrar for direct registration of your domain name. But, in long term, I recommend you should use a mixed approach i.e., some domain name you registered directly on domain registrar website (which usually cheapest option), some domain name you buy using backorder from http://expireddomains.net/, and some you buy directly form end-user (which I believe most costly approach) Lets discuss each approach one by one.

Direct Registration on Domain Registrar Website:

This is the cheapest option to register a new domain name. But there are more than 400 million domain names already registered and only few good choices are available. You need to think out of the box and be creative while searching for good domain name. You need to brainstorm and put efforts in searching for a valuable domain name, it can be boring and length process. But it's worth it if you are able to find a good domain name as it can save you a lot of money. Someone may think that market is over-saturated as there are thousands of experienced investors competing with you. But there are always opportunities available if you keep your brain open to new idea, niche, and put efforts in research. Using this approach, you can find and register domain name for less than $12 and make a solid portfolio with limited budget. This approach is good for beginner who have enough time and limited budget. Another recommendation is don't assume these domain name sells quickly; it can take years sometime to close a good deal. In that time, you can increase the value of domain by developing it. We will discuss development of domain and other way of making money from it, in later chapter.

Backordering the Expired Domain:

As a domain investor, one of the most effective strategies to acquire valuable domain names is by backordering expired domains. When a domain name expires, it becomes available for registration, and backordering allows you to secure the domain as soon as it becomes available for registration again. Backordering expired domains offers a unique opportunity to acquire sought-after domains with potential resale value or strategic relevance. In this article, we will explore the concept of backordering expired domains and provide insights on how domain investors can use this strategy to make profitable investments.

Understanding the Backordering Process:

1. **Expiration and Grace Period**: When a domain owner fails to renew their domain registration, the domain enters an expiration phase. During this period, the owner typically has a grace period to renew the domain without losing ownership. If the domain is not renewed within the grace period, it becomes available for backordering.

2. **Backorder Services**: Backorder services, offered by various domain registrars and third-party providers, allow domain investors to place a request to acquire an expiring domain. These services monitor the domain's status and attempt to register it as soon as it becomes available.

3. **Competition and Auctions**: It is important to note that multiple investors may backorder the same domain, creating competition. In such cases, the domain may go into an auction where interested parties can bid for the domain. The highest bidder wins the domain.

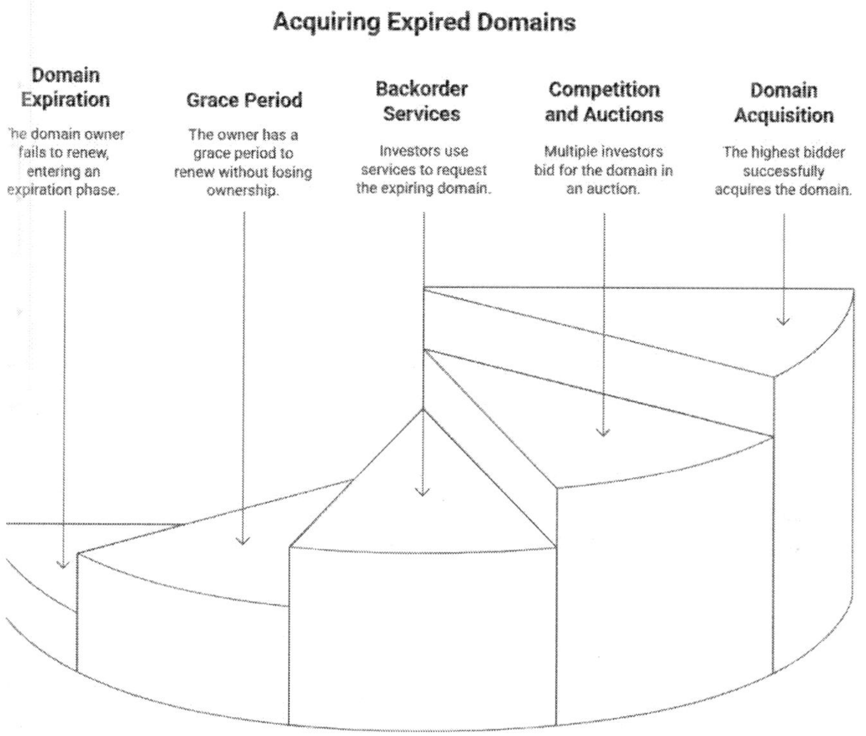

Tips for Successful Backordering:

1. **Research and Identify Valuable Domains**:

   Before backordering, conduct thorough research to identify valuable domains with potential resale value or strategic relevance. Consider factors such as keyword popularity, market demand, industry trends, and historical sales data to assess the domain's investment potential.

2. **Choose Reputable Backorder Services**:

Select reputable backorder services that have a proven track record of successfully securing domains. Look for services that provide advanced monitoring and notification systems, as well as transparent pricing and auction processes.

3. **Set Realistic Budgets**:

Determine your budget for backordering and establish realistic bidding limits if the domain goes into an auction. Be mindful of your investment goals and assess the potential return on investment (ROI) before setting your budget.

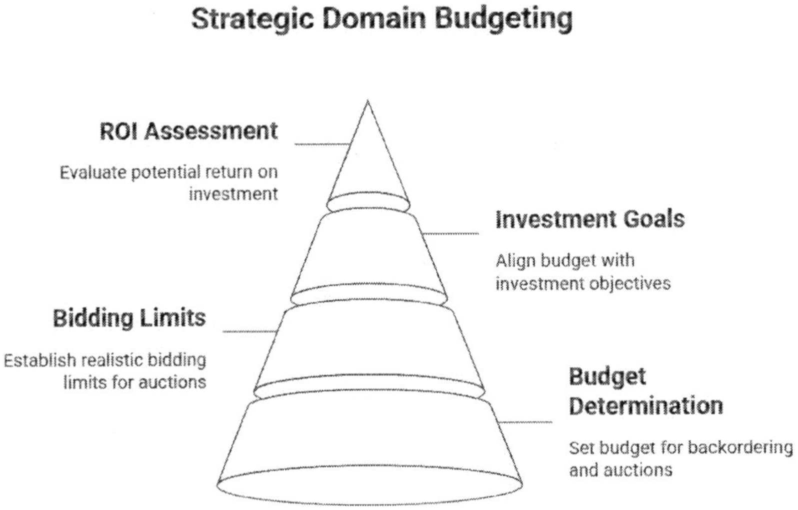

4. **Monitor Expiry Dates and Drop Lists**:

Stay updated on domain expiration dates and regularly monitor domain drop lists. These lists provide information on expiring domains and can help you identify valuable domains that are about to become available for backordering.

5. **Utilize Domain Monitoring Tools**:

Use domain monitoring tools that track the status and availability of specific domains. These tools can notify you when a desired domain becomes available, allowing you to act quickly.

6. **Act Swiftly and Strategically**:

Timing is crucial when backordering expired domains. Place your backorder as soon as possible to maximize your chances of securing the domain. Understand the specific registration rules and processes of the backorder service you are using to ensure you are well-prepared when the domain becomes available.

7. **Assess Legal and Branding Considerations**:

   Before backordering, consider legal and branding implications associated with acquiring expired domains. Ensure that the domain does not infringe on any trademarks or copyrights. Conduct due diligence to assess any potential legal risks or brand conflicts associated with the domain.

8. **Assess Domain Quality and History**:

   Evaluate the domain's quality, including factors such as backlink profile, search engine rankings, and historical usage. Assess the domain's history to ensure it was not associated with spammy or unethical practices that could impact its reputation.

Purchase from End-User or Auction:

As a domain investor, one of the key decisions you'll face is whether to purchase domains directly from end-users or participate in domain auctions. Both strategies offer unique advantages and considerations that can impact your ability to make profitable investments. In this section, we will explore the options of purchasing from end-users or participating in domain auctions, highlighting the factors to consider when choosing the right strategy for your domain investment goals.

Purchasing from End-Users:

Purchasing domains directly from end-users involves negotiating with the current owners who are typically businesses, individuals, or organizations. Here are some key points to consider:

1. **Domain Quality and Relevance**:

   End-user acquisitions can provide opportunities to acquire highly valuable domains that are directly relevant to a specific industry, niche, or business. These domains may have significant market demand and potential resale value due to their specific keyword relevance or brandability.

2. **Customization and Negotiation**:

When dealing with end-users, you have the opportunity to customize the negotiation process. You can tailor your offer, negotiate pricing and terms, and potentially leverage your domain expertise to secure a favorable deal. Building relationships with end-users may lead to future business opportunities or referrals.

3. **Higher Acquisition Costs**:

   Purchasing from end-users often involves higher acquisition costs compared to domain auctions. End-users may have a clearer understanding of the domain's value and its potential for their business, making negotiations more challenging. Be prepared to invest time and effort in the negotiation process, as end-users may hold higher price expectations.

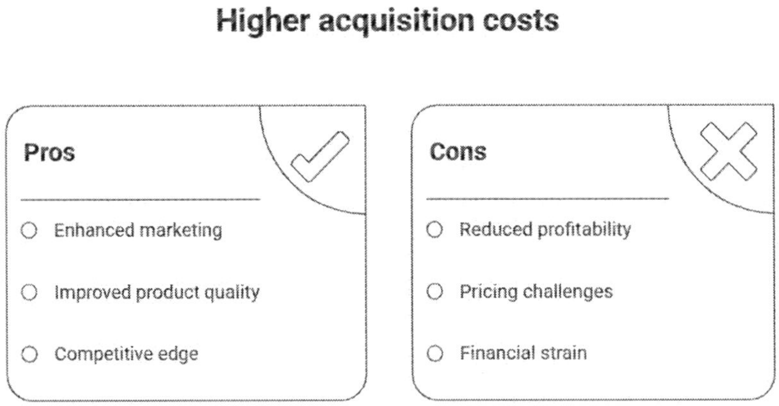

4. **Exclusive Opportunities**:

   Buying from end-users can provide access to exclusive domain opportunities that may not be available in the general marketplace or domain auctions. End-users may have invested significant resources in developing the domain or brand associated with it, making it a unique acquisition opportunity.

Participating in Domain Auctions:

Domain auctions are platforms where multiple buyers compete to acquire domains. Here's what you need to know about participating in domain auctions:

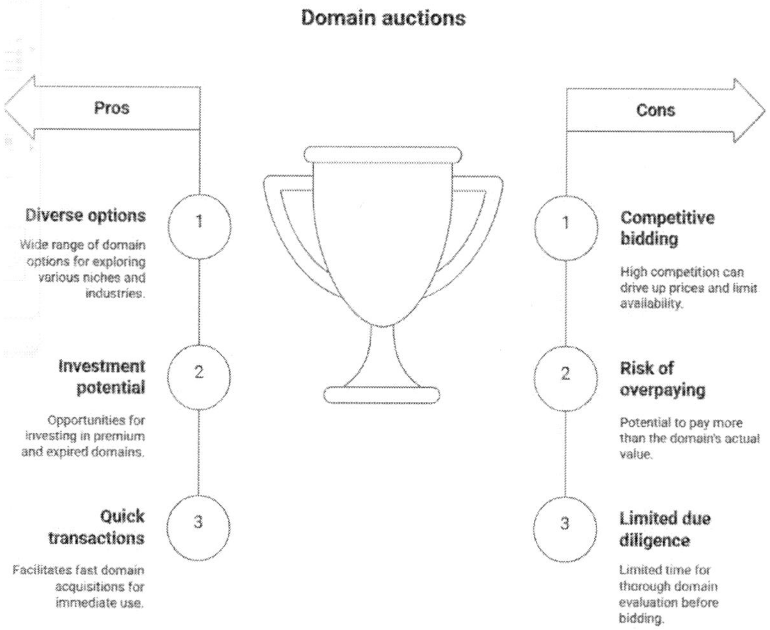

1. **Competitive Pricing**:

   Domain auctions often provide a more competitive pricing environment, with the potential to secure domains at relatively lower costs compared to purchasing from end-users. The bidding process allows for price discovery based on market demand and competition among participants.

2. **Diverse Domain Selection**:

   Auctions offer a wide range of domain options, including expired domains, premium domains, or domains put up for sale by owners seeking quick transactions. This diversity allows you to explore various niches, industries, and investment opportunities.

3. **Time-Sensitive Decisions**:

   Domain auctions operate on a specific timeline, requiring you to make quick decisions. The limited time frame may limit your ability to conduct extensive due diligence on a domain's value or potential. It's crucial to assess the domain's quality, history, and market demand before participating in an auction.

4. **Potential Bargains**:

In certain cases, you may come across undervalued domains or opportunities where bidders overlook a domain's potential value. By carefully analyzing and evaluating the domain's potential, you can identify hidden gems and acquire them at favorable prices.

Factors to Consider in Your Decision:

1. **Investment Budget**:

   Assess your investment budget and determine the maximum amount you are willing to allocate for each domain acquisition. This will help guide your decision-making process and dictate whether you pursue end-user purchases or auction participation.

2. **Investment Strategy**:

   Consider your investment strategy and long-term goals. If you are targeting specific niches or industries, end-user purchases may provide more targeted and relevant opportunities. On the other hand, domain auctions offer a broader selection and allow for diversification in your portfolio.

3. **Time and Effort**:

   Evaluate the time and effort you can dedicate to each acquisition method. Purchasing from end-users typically requires more time, negotiation skills, and relationship building. Auction participation, while time-sensitive, may require less direct interaction and can be more efficient for quick acquisitions.

4. **Market Knowledge**:

   Your understanding of the domain market and industry trends will impact your ability to identify valuable opportunities in both end-user purchases and auctions. Stay updated on market dynamics, keyword trends, and emerging niches to make informed decisions.

Deciding between purchasing from end-users or participating in domain auctions is a critical choice for domain investors. Each strategy offers unique advantages and considerations that should align with your investment budget, strategy, time availability, and market knowledge. Carefully evaluate the domain quality, relevance, pricing dynamics, and potential ROI for each option. Striking a balance between end-user purchases and auction participation can enhance your ability to acquire valuable domains and make profitable investments. Continuously assess your investment goals, adapt your strategies, and diversify your portfolio to maximize success as a domain investor.

6.3 Risk involved in Domaining

Like any investment, there is risk associated with domain investing and if you don't research thoroughly before investing, you can lose all our investment. Risk and return run in parallel in domain investing. It is a very niche investment and require a lot of knowledge, research, efforts, and patience. You don't have to buy and sell every day. In this business, sometimes you spent many weeks without buying or selling any domain name. Without any further delay, lets discuss what are the risk associated with domain investing as below:

Low Liquidity:

Domain investment is not like stocks, bonds, or cryptocurrency which you can liquidate at any time. It is much harder to sell a domain name as compared to other investment. In domain investing, it really depends on luck how soon you can find a buyer. You can list your domain name for sale in different marketplace, but it may take several months or some time years to find the right buyer for your domain name.

No Standardization for Valuation:

In stock market, you can do fundamental analysis, technical analysis and use different ratios to evaluate the value of stock and then wisely decide if its valuable enough to buy the stock or not. But in domain investment, there is no such standardization to evaluate the domain name. It only depends on your research, knowledge, and luck to find a valuable domain name and then a potential buyer for that domain name. There are hundreds of domain appraisal tools to find value of your domain name, but their valuation has no sense. You always get different value for the same domain name on different domain appraisals website.

Legality:

Domain name investor could face legal issue if they registered a trademarked domain name. Businesses usually hire a third party or an attorney firm to secure their trademark and these attorneys are always in search of any trademark infringement. Another problem is someone can sell you a stolen domain name before you get to know that they are not true owner of the domain name. So, it is very important to know what you are investing in, from whom you are buying and always use trusted marketplace (like sedo, flippa etc.) so that you can later prove that you purchased the domain name legally and paid for it.

Appraisals Scam:

We already discussed it what domain appraisal and appraisal scam are. If you find a potential buyer, he is willing to pay the asked price and he ask you to provide an appraisal from a domain appraisal website. It can be a scam as you pay the appraisal fee (usually more or less $100), get the appraisal certificate, and send it to buyer. He will not reply to your message after that, you keep reaching to him, sending messages but all gone. The domain appraisal website from which he asks you to provide the appraisal certificate usually owned and run by him. He managed to get appraisal fee by scamming you and you are not able to do anything now. These scams are very common in domain investing.

Faulty Escrow Payments:

According to Wikipedia, "An escrow is a contractual arrangement in which a third party receives and disburses money or property for the primary transacting parties, with the disbursement dependent on conditions agreed to by the transacting parties." If you didn't understand escrow payment now, don't worry, we will discuss this in detail in later chapter. It is basically a third-party service on which both seller and buyer trust and buyer keep money in escrow account and request the seller for transfer of domain name. At this moment, nobody can withdraw money from the escrow account. After successful transfer of domain name, seller can withdraw money from the escrow account. But sometime, buyer make complex transfer agreement and after transfer of domain name, withdraw money before seller, that is called fault escrow payment.

7.

EXPIRED DOMAIN NAMES

"Your dream doesn't have an expiration date. Take a deep breath and try again."

-K T Witten

An expired domain is a domain that a business, an organization, or a person have registered, they fail to renew it on time, and it is available in market again for registration. If you see a domain that has expired, this means that they can be re-registered. There can be various reason for the expiry of domain name such as owner forget to pay renewal fee on time, auto-renewal is off, or payment method (credit or debit card) expire and no longer active on the date of renewal fee payment, owner intentionally abandon the domain name as the web project they are trying to build on it failed or closed.

7.1 Example of domain expiration and what we can learn from that

The expired domain is a very profitable market. As big companies fail to renew their domain names, discerning domain flippers are quick to buy such domains. If such companies lost out on renewing such domain names, they could lose millions and billions of dollars. These are some of the most popular expired domain names.

1. Yatra

Yatra was the second biggest travel online website that guides Indian tourists. However, it famously failed to renew its domain name. This business of almost $6 billion lost their commercial partnership with India's State bank. They also lost a lot of customers. The company is still struggling to get restore its old business glory days.

2. Region bank

One time, the 22nd biggest bank in the USA, Region Bank failed to renew its domain name registration. This bank boasts of 2400 ATMs and 1700 branches. However, in 2013, they had failed to renew their domain name registration, shutting customers from important banking services for weeks. Anyway, there were forced to publicly apologize for this problem.

3. Dallas Cowboys

One of the biggest failures of domain expiration was with the MLB franchise, the Dallas Cowboys. In 2010, the domain name of this sports franchise expired, and the organization learned a serious lesson. They had to cough out a lot of money to pay whoever registered the domain name before they were able to renew it.

4. Microsoft

Microsoft famously forgot to renew is domain name hotmail.co.uk. At this time, it became difficult for users of the mail service platform to access the website. The company also forgot to renew passport.com, another domain name. This made a lot of embarrassing headlines and gave the company a bad press at the time.

5. Foursquare

Foursquare is the company that has the most embarrassing story about the failure to renew your domain name registration. At that time, foursquare had been able to raise about $10 million for the funding of their business operations. However, they accidentally dropped the ball, when they failed to register their domain name. This led to a massive loss of business for the organization.

What We Can Learn from This

There are a few things that we can learn from this example of domain expiration. First, it is important to renew your domain name before it expires. If you do not renew your domain name, you could lose it to someone else.

Second, if you are considering purchasing an expired domain name, be sure to do your research. There are a number of factors that you should consider, such as the domain's history, its backlink profile, and its age.

Finally, keep in mind that domain expiration is a common occurrence. If you are not careful, you could lose your domain name to someone else.

Tips for Avoiding Domain Expiration

There are a few things that you can do to avoid domain expiration. First, you can set up automatic renewal for your domain name. This will ensure that your domain name is renewed automatically before it expires.

Second, you can check the expiration date for your domain name regularly. This will help you to avoid forgetting to renew your domain name.

Finally, you can use a domain monitoring service. These services will notify you when your domain name is approaching its expiration date.

By following these tips, you can help to ensure that your domain name does not expire. This will help you to protect your online assets and maintain your online presence.

7.2 Why look for expired domains

Domain investing requires diversifying portfolios or finding valuable investments opportunities; exploring expired domains is an effective strategy that offers great returns for domain investors looking to add them or broaden them further. Even though most expired domains expire due to failure by previous owners to renew them on time, expired domains offer tremendous upside if leveraged correctly. In this section we explore why domain investors should explore expired domains as an effective strategy, as well as their advantages for doing so.

Established Domain Authority:

Expired domains often come equipped with established domain authorities that can drastically impact search engine rankings and visibility. Domains boasting quality backlinks and relevant content can allow investors to skip over the initial stages of building authority from scratch; making expired domains ideal investments when looking to launch websites, niche-specific platforms or enhance existing online ventures.

Targeted Traffic Potential:

Certain expired domains still offer significant existing traffic potential. Perhaps previously developed into successful websites attracting visitors and producing organic search traffic. Acquiring such domains gives your new ventures an immediate head start by redirecting that existing traffic directly or monetizing it through advertising/affiliate marketing; you could also redirect it across other websites in your portfolio for maximum web presence and potential revenue generation.

Niche Relevance and Branding:

Expired domains offer niche relevance within specific industries, markets, or geographical regions, making expired domains highly advantageous to domain investors who specialize in niche markets. Acquiring expired domains that align with target audiences' interests can prove highly successful as investors establish brand authority, credibility and recognition within that specific niche space; ultimately increasing chances of attracting the desired clients or customers.

Expired Domains as Investments:

Domains can serve as valuable investments. As digital real estate, domains often appreciate in value over time due to characteristics like brandability, keyword relevance or market demand. Domain investors who identify undervalued expired domains at attractive prices could potentially secure assets that can later be sold off at a profit in future sales transactions.

Development Opportunities:

For domain investors looking for investment opportunities in expired domain names, expired domains provide the perfect canvas on which to build websites, blogs or platforms tailored specifically towards their investment goals. With existing authority ratings, traffic potential and niche relevance all acting as solid building blocks. By producing quality content optimized for search engines as well as offering valuable resources or services that engage visitors while also making profits through various monetization techniques - investors can take full advantage of any developmental opportunity provided by an expired domain and develop websites, blogs or platforms tailored precisely towards achieving their investment goals.

Backlink Opportunities:

Expired domains offer investors access to established backlink profiles that can improve search engine rankings and drive referral traffic, helping boost their SEO. Domain investors can utilize these backlinks strategically in order to maximize the visibility and authority of their online properties while using links from reputable websites as leverage against others in their portfolio, creating an interlinked web of properties.

Competitive Edge:

Acquiring expired domains gives domain investors an edge against their competition in the domain market, giving them the power to take advantage of these valuable domains before others do - often finding valuable domains with high resale potential or which match up perfectly with investment strategies that they implement. By staying vigilant for expiring domains in target markets and keeping an eye on expiring ones as they expire before others, investors can seize value before their competitors and secure potential gems that can help maximize returns and give an investor a distinct edge in domain investing!

Searching for expired domains can be an excellent strategy for domain investors looking to broaden their portfolio, leverage established domain authority, increase targeted traffic flow, or develop niche-specific assets online. By purchasing expired domains, investors can capitalize on existing traffic levels, brand authority, backlink profiles and market relevance to increase returns. Domain investors who conduct proper research, due diligence and keep an eye out for opportunities can unlock the full potential of expired domain names to achieve profitable returns from their investments. Analyzing and understanding of the domain market are critical in making informed decisions and realizing all benefits associated with purchasing these expired domains.

7.3 How to find valuable expired domain name

For domain investors, finding valuable expired domain names is a crucial step in building a profitable domain portfolio. Expired domains can offer established authority, existing traffic, and potential resale value. However, identifying valuable expired domains requires a strategic approach and thorough research. In this article, we will explore effective methods and tools to help domain investors find valuable expired domain names.

1. **Expired Domain Marketplaces and Auctions:**

   One of the primary sources for finding valuable expired domains is through specialized marketplaces and auctions. These platforms connect domain investors with a wide range of expired domains available for purchase. Some popular marketplaces include GoDaddy Auctions, NameJet, and Sedo. These platforms allow investors to filter domains based on metrics such as domain authority, backlink profile, traffic, and niche relevance.

2. **Domain Drop Lists and Catching Services:**

Domain drop lists are curated lists of domains that are about to become available for registration after the expiration period. These lists are often categorized based on various metrics, such as domain length, keyword relevance, and domain authority. Domain catching services, such as DropCatch and SnapNames, specialize in acquiring domains as soon as they become available for registration. These services can help investors secure valuable domains that may have high demand.

3. **Backlink Analysis:**

   Analyzing the backlink profile of expired domains can provide insights into their value. Backlinks from reputable and authoritative websites can indicate the domain's credibility and potential for search engine rankings. Tools like Ahrefs, Moz, and Majestic can assist in examining the quality and quantity of backlinks pointing to an expired domain. Look for domains with relevant and authoritative backlinks that can contribute to your portfolio's overall value.

4. **Domain Metrics and Data Analysis Tools:**

   Several tools provide domain metrics and data analysis, offering valuable information for identifying valuable expired domains. Tools like DomainScope, Domain Hunter Gatherer, and ExpiredDomains.net provide data on metrics such as domain authority, traffic, social signals, and historical domain prices. These metrics help evaluate the potential value and profitability of expired domains before making an investment.

5. **Niche-Specific Forums and Communities:**

   Participating in niche-specific forums and communities can uncover potential leads for valuable expired domains. Engaging with industry experts and domain investors in these communities can provide insights into upcoming expiring domains, emerging trends, and niche-specific opportunities. Forums like NamePros and DigitalPoint offer discussions and marketplace sections where domain investors can connect and share valuable information.

6. **Keyword Research:**

   Conducting thorough keyword research helps domain investors identify valuable expired domains with relevant keywords. Keyword research tools like Google Keyword Planner, SEMrush, and Ahrefs Keyword Explorer assist in identifying popular and trending keywords related to specific niches or industries. By combining keyword research with domain availability checks, investors can uncover potentially valuable expired domains that align with keyword demand.

7. **Historical Auction and Sales Data:**

   Analyzing historical auction and sales data can provide valuable insights into the value of expired domains. Platforms like DNJournal and NameBio track domain sales and auction results, allowing investors to identify trends, assess domain values, and gauge market demand. Analyzing historical data helps investors understand the potential profitability of acquiring expired domains and assists in making informed investment decisions.

8. **Social Media Monitoring:**

   Monitoring social media platforms, especially Twitter, can help identify valuable expired domain names that may be shared by industry professionals, bloggers, or domain experts. Following relevant hashtags and accounts related to domain investing and industry-specific keywords can reveal opportunities and discussions surrounding expiring domains.

Finding valuable expired domain names requires a combination of research, analysis, and utilizing specialized tools and platforms. Domain investors can leverage marketplaces, drop lists, backlink analysis, data analysis tools, niche communities, keyword research, historical data, and social media monitoring to identify potential gems. It is essential to consider metrics such as domain authority, backlinks, traffic, niche relevance, and market demand when evaluating expired domains. By utilizing these strategies and staying up-to-date with industry trends, domain investors can increase their chances of finding valuable expired domains and building a profitable domain portfolio.

7.4 Tools and website to find expired domain name

If you are looking to buy domains, there are several websites and tools that you can use to achieve this.

1. **SEO.domains**: This website has available expired with high authority and traffic. They have an expired domain database that have more than 20,000 domains that come with backlinks and high traffic.

2. **GoDaddy Auctions**: GoDaddy is a good website to flip domains. There are numerous expired domains in the website that can be used. You can find these domains use a tool on the website called GoDaddy auctions.
3. **Domain coasters**: This is another popular website where you can easily buy SEO-optimized expired domains. These domains come with the needed authority, backlinks, and so on. You can find some of the finest domains in the world to easily help your new website rank quickly.
4. **Flippa Auctions**: Flippa is a common place to flip websites. The website is also a good place for you to buy domains that are expired. They have good tools for searching for expired domains. Moreover, you can easily buy an online business or a website if you prefer those over expired domains.
5. **DomCop**: This is an excellent tool that can be used to search for expired domains. Afterwards, if you like the domain, you can then buy it. This tool allows you to look for expired domains based on a wide range of metrics such as Moz Rank, Social Statistics, Traffic Data, SEMRush Rank, Domain Authority, Citation Flows & Majestic Trust, Ahrefs Domain Rating, and so on.
6. **Dynadot:** This is a website that offers an elaborate tool for looking for expired domain sales. With this tool, you can easily seek out expired domains. If you like the results, you can choose to buy one or more. This website also offers a backorder on expired domains.
7. **Namecheap domains**: Namecheap is a very popular platform for flipping domains. It also performs domain registration. Additionally, you can easily get domains that are expired. The good thing is that you can buy them cheaply on this platform.
8. **Namejet**: This platform is famed for its remarket domain offerings. This means that you get an excellent and unique offering of the best expired domains with the highest potential.
9. **Moonsy**: Moonsy is a website whereby you can easily search for and purchased expired domains. The website come with a lot of tools that make domain searching and buying easy. With this site, you can easily purchase domains that are expired. It comes with multiple domains searching tools to find the right domains based on the anchor/site language, traffic and google visibility, metrics, and so on.
10. **SnapNames**: SnapNames have exclusively partnered with the best global domain name registration companies. They have the best tools and technology to help them easily catch the hottest expired domain names in the marketplace before all other platforms. This way, they provide their customers with multiple

tools that use a wide range of intelligent algorithms to capture expired domain names before all other platforms do so.

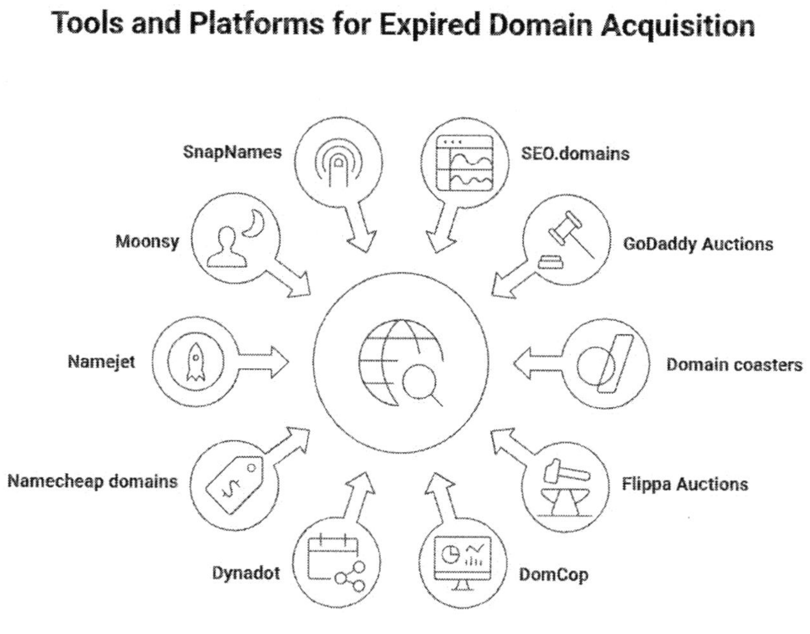

7.5 How To Value Expired Domains

Valuing expired domains is a crucial skill for domain investors looking to make informed investment decisions and build a profitable domain portfolio. Assigning an accurate value to an expired domain involves assessing various factors such as domain metrics, market demand, niche relevance, and potential monetization opportunities. In this article, we will explore the key elements to consider when valuing expired domains.

1. **Domain Metrics:**

   Domain metrics provide quantitative data that assists in assessing the value and potential of an expired domain. Consider the following metrics:

   a. **Domain Authority (DA)**: Domain Authority is a score that predicts how well a domain will rank in search engine results. Tools like Moz's Open Site Explorer and Ahrefs' Domain Rating can help determine the DA of an expired domain. Higher DA indicates a stronger domain with better potential for search engine visibility.

b. **Page Authority (PA)**: Page Authority measures the strength and relevance of a specific page within a domain. Analyzing the PA of specific pages on an expired domain can help determine their potential value.
c. **Backlink Profile**: Analyze the quality, quantity, and relevance of backlinks pointing to the expired domain. Tools like Ahrefs, Moz, and Majestic can provide insights into the backlink profile, helping to assess the domain's authority and potential for organic traffic.
d. **Traffic**: Evaluate the traffic history of the expired domain, if available. Tools like SimilarWeb and SEMrush can provide estimates of the domain's traffic volume and sources. Analyzing the traffic can help gauge the potential value and monetization opportunities.

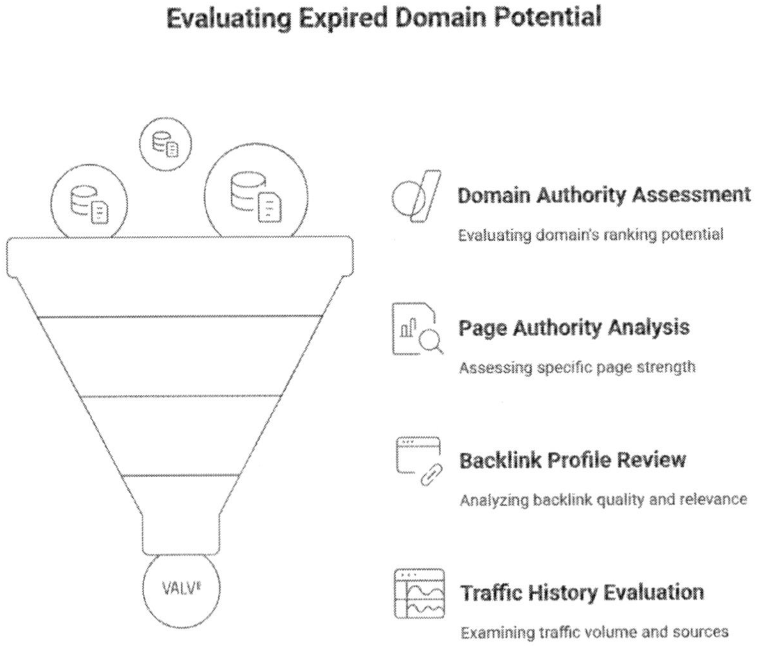

2. **Market Demand and Trends:**

Consider the market demand for the expired domain and assess the current trends within the niche or industry it relates to. Research the demand for similar domains by reviewing sales data, auction results, and industry-specific marketplaces. This research helps understand the potential resale value and the level of interest from potential buyers.

3. **Niche Relevance and Potential:**

Assess the relevance of the expired domain to a specific niche or industry. Determine if the domain name is memorable, brandable, and aligned with the target audience's interests. A domain with niche-specific keywords or a strong brandable name holds greater potential for development or resale value.

4. **Monetization Opportunities:**

   Consider the potential monetization opportunities associated with the expired domain. Evaluate if the domain can generate revenue through advertising, affiliate marketing, e-commerce, lead generation, or other business models. Analyze the niche's commercial viability and the potential for attracting advertisers or generating organic traffic.

5. **Branding Potential:**

   Assess the branding potential of the expired domain. Consider if it has a unique and catchy name that can be easily associated with a brand or business. A strong brandable domain can hold significant value in the marketplace.

6. **Historical Sales Data:**

   Analyze historical sales data to gain insights into similar domain sales and auction results. Platforms like DNJournal and NameBio track domain sales, providing valuable information on comparable domains and their market values. Historical sales data helps determine a fair market value for the expired domain.

7. **Intellectual Property Considerations:**

   Evaluate any potential intellectual property issues associated with the expired domain. Perform due diligence to ensure that the domain does not infringe on trademarks or copyrights. Ignoring intellectual property considerations can lead to legal complications and diminish the value of the domain.

8. **Expert Opinions and Appraisals:**

   Consult domain experts and professionals for their opinions and appraisals. Seek feedback from experienced domain investors or utilize professional domain appraisal services. Their expertise and insights can provide valuable guidance in valuing expired domains accurately.

Valuing expired domains is a complex process that involves considering multiple factors, including domain metrics, market demand, niche relevance, monetization potential, branding, historical sales data, and expert opinions. By conducting thorough research and analysis, domain investors can make informed decisions and assign an accurate value to an expired domain. It is important to continually stay updated on industry trends, monitor market demand, and assess the potential for future growth and profitability. With a solid understanding of these valuation techniques, domain investors can maximize their chances of acquiring valuable expired domains and building a successful domain portfolio.

7.6 What are dropped domains?

In the world of domain investing, understanding the concept of dropped domains is essential. Dropped domains are domains that have not been renewed by their previous owners and are subsequently made available for registration by anyone. These domains go through a specific process known as the "drop cycle," during which they transition from an expired state to becoming available for new registrations. In this article, we will delve into the details of dropped domains, their significance, and the opportunities they present for domain investors.

The Domain Drop Cycle:

When a domain registration expires, it enters a specific period known as the "grace period." During this phase, the previous owner may still renew the domain by paying the renewal fees. If the domain is not renewed within the grace period, it enters the subsequent stages of the drop cycle:

1. **Pending Delete**: After the grace period, the domain enters the "pending delete" phase, during which the registrar prepares to delete the domain from the registry. The duration of the pending delete phase can vary, typically lasting around five days.
2. **Redemption Period**: Some top-level domains (TLDs) have an additional phase called the "redemption period." This period provides a final opportunity for the previous owner to reclaim the domain by paying a redemption fee, which is typically higher than the standard renewal fee. The length of the redemption period can also vary, usually ranging from 30 to 90 days.
3. **Pending Delete Restorable**: Following the redemption period, the domain enters a short period called "pending delete restorable." During this phase, registrars may offer the domain back to the previous owner at a higher cost, providing a last chance to reclaim the domain before it becomes available to the public.

4. **Available for Registration**: Finally, after the completion of the drop cycle, the domain becomes available for new registrations. It is during this stage that domain investors and individuals can attempt to register the dropped domain.

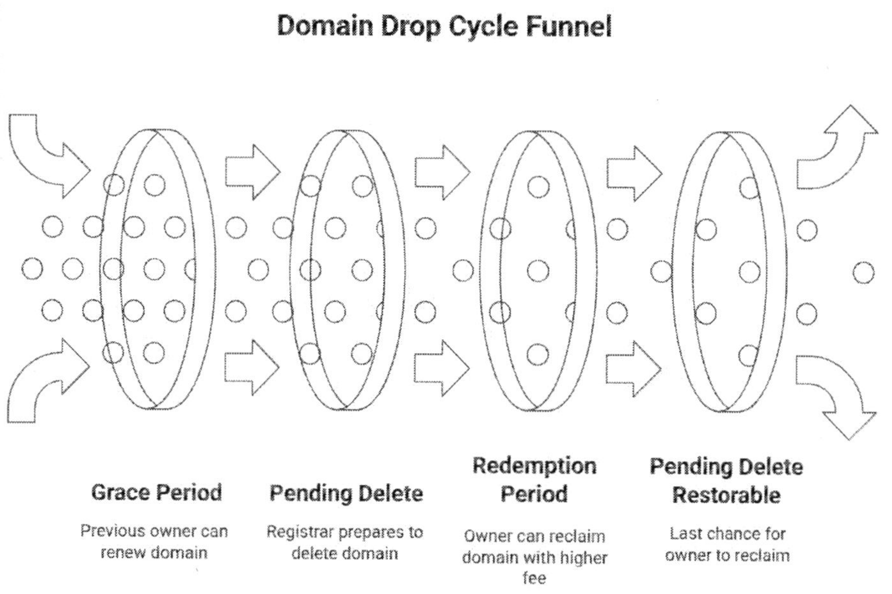

Significance for Domain Investors:

Dropped domains hold significant significance for domain investors due to the opportunities they present. Here's why dropped domains are valuable:

1. **Established Domain History**: Dropped domains often have a history, including backlinks, search engine rankings, and previous development. This established history can provide domain investors with a head start in terms of domain authority and potential traffic.
2. **Valuable Backlinks**: Dropped domains may have accumulated backlinks from reputable websites. These backlinks can contribute to search engine rankings, organic traffic, and overall domain authority. Acquiring a dropped domain with valuable backlinks can be advantageous for SEO purposes.
3. **Brandable and Memorable Names**: Dropped domains often possess brandable and memorable names, making them desirable for businesses and startups. These domains can be developed into successful online ventures or resold at a premium to interested parties seeking a strong brand presence.

4. **Expired Traffic**: Some dropped domains retain existing traffic even after expiration. Acquiring such domains allows domain investors to redirect the traffic to their own websites, monetize it through advertising or affiliate marketing, or resell the domain with the promise of existing traffic.
5. **Investment and Resale Opportunities**: Dropped domains can be valuable investments, particularly if they possess desirable characteristics such as niche relevance, keyword-rich names, or high-demand industry terms. Domain investors can acquire dropped domains at a relatively low cost and later resell them at a profit, capitalizing on market demand and potential buyer interest.

Factors Contributing to the Value of Dropped Domains

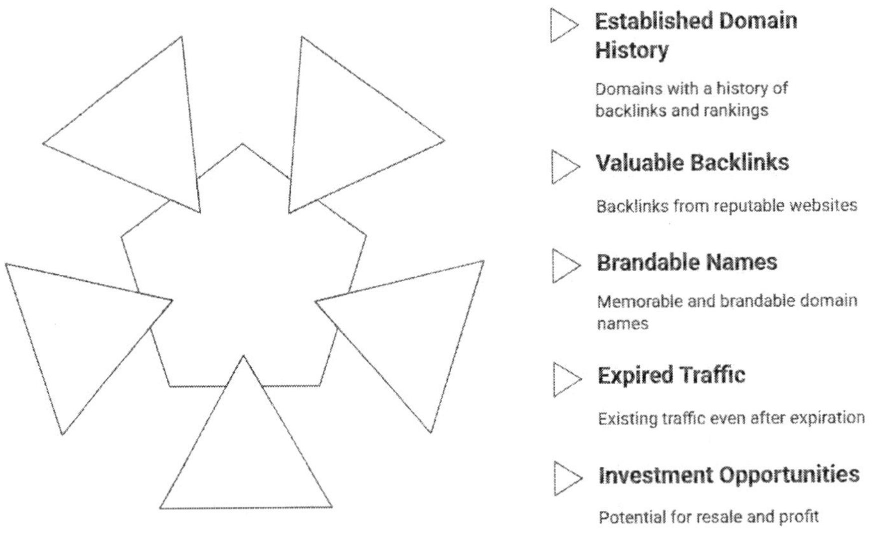

Tools and Resources:

To identify and acquire dropped domains, domain investors often rely on various tools and resources:

1. **Drop-Catching Services**: These services specialize in acquiring dropped domains as soon as they become available. They employ advanced systems to register domains on behalf of investors, increasing their chances of securing valuable dropped domains.

2. **Domain Auctions and Marketplaces**: Many domain auction platforms and marketplaces offer dropped domains for sale. Examples include GoDaddy Auctions, NameJet, and Sedo. These platforms provide a centralized marketplace where investors can bid on and purchase dropped domains.
3. **Domain Monitoring Tools**: Domain monitoring tools allow investors to track and receive alerts about expiring and dropped domains. These tools help identify valuable domains and enable investors to act swiftly to secure them during the drop cycle.

Dropped domains are domains that have not been renewed by their previous owners and are subsequently made available for registration. They offer domain investors significant opportunities in terms of established domain history, valuable backlinks, brandable names, potential traffic, and resale potential. By understanding the drop cycle, utilizing tools and resources, and conducting thorough research, domain investors can identify and acquire valuable dropped domains, leveraging them for their investment strategies and building a profitable domain portfolio.

8.

SELLING: HOW TO SELL DOMAIN NAME

"Selling stuff is easy. All you gotta do is give away stuff that makes people happy ...and then sell stuff that makes 'em even happier."

-Frank Kern

Domain names are some of the most valuable online real estates. They can be used to create websites, establish brand identities, and much more. We already see how we can find good domain name and how we can register them or buy them. Now let's see how we can sell them for a profit. In this chapter, we will walk you through the entire process of selling a domain name. We'll cover everything from finding buyers to negotiating prices and closing the sale. So, whether you're just getting started in domain name sales or you're an experienced pro, this chapter has something for you!

8.1 Criteria For Selling Domain Names

There are a few criteria that you should consider before selling a domain name. Here are a few of the most important:

1. **'.com' domain extension:**

The first criterion for selling a domain name is its domain extension. A domain name with '.com' extension (TLD) is easy to sell as compared to other domain extension. If you are holding a domain name with other extension, you may have to wait a little longer before closing the deal.

2. **Exclusivity:**

The second criterion for selling a domain name is exclusivity. The domain name should be unique and exclusive in a sense that it gives an extra edge to the buyer if in their business if they buy it. For example, if a person is in the business of selling furniture in London and you are holding the domain name 'furniture.com' or 'furniture.london', it is definitely helpful for the buyer to attract more customer online. It is exclusive and unique which exactly represents buyer needs.

3. **Value:**

The third criterion for selling a domain name is value. The domain name should have a high value to justify the time and effort that goes into selling it. If the domain name is not valuable, it will be difficult to find buyers who are willing to pay a high price for it. For example, if you are trying to sell 'best-furniture-in-london-12.com', the domain name doesn't even qualify the basic precheck of a valuable domain name and nobody like to spend money on such name.

4. **Availability:**

The fourth criterion for selling a domain name is availability. The domain name should be available to the public and it should be easy for seller to find your contact details. If they are not able to see the domain name availability or not able to contact you, then there is no way you can sell the domain name for a profit.

5. **Length:**

The fifth criterion for selling a domain name is length. The domain name should not be too long. Lengthy domain name are difficult to type and remember. Buyer usually don't like to spend on length domain name.

6. **Trademark:**

The sixth criterion for selling a domain name is a trademark. The domain name should not contain words which represents a trademark. It often attracts a lawsuit or copyright infringement.

7. **Spam:**

The seventh criterion for selling a domain name is spam. The domain name should not contain any words that are considered to be offensive, illegal, or otherwise prohibited by law. If the domain name contains any of these words, it will be difficult to find buyers who are interested in purchasing it.

8. **Auction lock:**

The eighth criterion for selling a domain name is auction lock. The domain name should not be in a lock period. If that is the case, you need to wait for the time-period till lock removed.

8.2 How to find a buyer for your domain name?

Once you have decided to sell the domain name, you will need to find a buyer who is interested in purchasing it. Here are a few tips for finding a buyer:

Use an online marketplace:

One of the best ways to find a buyer for your domain name is to use an online marketplace. Online marketplaces are websites that allow buyers and sellers to negotiate the price of a domain name. They are a great way to find buyers who are interested in purchasing your domain name. We have a dedicated chapter for domain marketplace, here is brief detail about it:

To get started you will need to follow these steps

Step one: Join an online marketplace

Step two: Create a profile, add your domain name for sale and select the asking price or put for auction.

Step three: wait for buyers to contact you about purchasing your domain name.

Contact potential buyers:

Another way to find a buyer for your domain name is to contact potential buyers directly. This can be done by email or by telephone. It is a great way to find buyers who are interested in purchasing your domain name.

To get started you'll need to follow these steps

Step one: Determine the value of your domain name

Before you can sell your domain name, you need to determine its value. This can be done by researching similar domain names and their sale prices. You can also use domain appraisal tools like Estibot to get a ballpark estimate of your domain name's value.

Step two: Contact buyers

Contacting buyers directly can be an effective way to find a buyer for your domain name. You could email them or contact by telephone. I will discuss

and it's always best when you do this in person, so they know how serious the sale is!

Step three: Negotiate the sale

Once you've found a buyer, it's time to negotiate the sale. This can be done by email or by telephone. It is a great way to find buyers who are interested in purchasing your domain name.

Use a broker:

A third way to find a buyer for your domain name is to use a broker. Brokers are professionals who help buyers and sellers negotiate the price of a domain name. I recommend working with brokerage firm or individual broker only when you are selling a domain name in five figures i.e., more than $10,000 as they charge a high amount of commission for helping you to close the deal.

To get started, you'll need to follow these steps

Step one: Find a broker. A broker can be a an individual, a brokerage firm or a domain marketplace like Sedo, GoDaddy etc.

Step two: Discuss the terms of your deal with your broker. You need to discuss all the terms and conditions (such as their commission, payment method, payment period etc.) with your broker in details.

Step three: Negotiate a price with the buyer. Here, you should have an exact number in your mind below which you will not sell the domain. You should collect information what the buyer will do with the domain name, what is his purchasing power, how much revenue he is expecting to generate in future with the website linked to your domain name. Is the buyer an individual, small business or an international company? This knowledge and your experience will decide how much profit you make from this deal. You should have the courage to say "NO" if you believe you are getting what you think the value of domain name and it depend on all above factor we discussed. For example, in 2008, if you come to me, to sell a domain name "fb.com", I may value it for $10,000 based on my experience and future profit from it. But for the same domain name, Facebook paid 8.5 million dollars.

Step four: Close the deal. When you are satisfied with the price, term and conditions of the sale, you can close the deal, get the money and transfer the domain name to buyer.

Advertise:

Another way to find a buyer for your domain name is to advertise. You can advertise your domain name at places where you believe potential buyer hangout, it can be social media, a webinar, a local meetup, or conference. It is a great way to find buyers when you are sure about the persona of your buyer i.e., what their interest is, where they spent their time, what characteristics they have, their age, location, profession, gender, buying power, income level etc.

To get started, you will need to follow these steps

Step one: You can advertise by creating one page website or using social media ads such as google ads, Facebook ads, Instagram campaign etc.

Step two: You can publish an article or a video about how much profit your potential buyer can make if they buy your domain name for their business. You can do this yourself or hire a freelancer from upwork, fiverr etc.

Step three: When a buyer contacts you, negotiate the price and close the deal.

Network:

A fifth way to find a buyer for your domain name is to network. This can be done by attending industry events or by meeting people online. It is a great way to find buyers with interest in similar niche in which you are holding domain name.

To get started, you'll need to follow these steps

Step one: You should create a list of people you would like to meet in person or online. This can be done using social platform such as LinkedIn (https://www.linkedin.com/) or meetup (https://www.meetup.com/). You can search for people who have business in the same niche, or who post information about the niche in which you have your domain name. It is very easy to search and filter for people in specific category and get their details.

Step two: Next step is to connect them on LinkedIn, find their email ID or phone number and follow them later. It is not easy to find these details from LinkedIn as it is hidden from free user. But you can send a connect request to the user on LinkedIn and later share the domain name you are holding with them offer to sell them. Don't try to sell immediately when you connect them for the first time as n this case, they usually don't accept your connection. It is similar to approaching a girt for friendship. You don't ask "*will you marry me*" when you meet a girl first time. It almost always leads to rejection. You need to first approach your potential client with an intent to connect them. Later you can offer them to sell your domain name. you can send a simple message like below to send an invitation to connect with them:

Dear FIRST NAME,

I was really impressed by the ________. I saw that you are a _________ and interested in _________. I'm also a ____________, and I would like to connect with you as I am also interested in ________.

Looking forward to connecting with you,

YOUR NAME

Step three: Once you are connected, you can send them details about the domain name and how it can help them to get more visitor for their business and to generate more revenue. Your communication and strategy should be to help them, to solve their problem. It should not sound like you are trying to sell them anything.

Social media:

Another way to find a buyer for your domain name is to use social media. This can be done by posting on forums or creating a website. It is a great way to find buyers who are interested in purchasing your domain name.

To get started, you will need to follow these steps

Step one: Create a list of domain names you want to sell

Step two: Research the market value for each domain name

Step three: Create a listing for each domain name

Step four: Promote your listings on social media and other channels

Private sales:

An eighth way to find a buyer for your domain name is to use private sales. This can be done by using an online service such as Craigslist or eBay. It is a great way to find buyers who are interested in purchasing your domain name.

To get started, you will need to follow these steps

Step one: List your domain name for sale

Step two: Find a buyer

Step three: Negotiate the price

Step four: Complete the sale

Domain name brokers:

The ninth way to find a buyer for your domain name is to use a domain name broker. This can be done by using an online service such as DomainNameBroker.com. It is a great way to find buyers who are interested in purchasing your domain name.

To get started, you will need to follow these steps

Step one: Go to DomainNamesBroker.com and register your domain name.

Step two: Once you have registered your domain name, go to the website of each broker that you want to sell a domain name through.

Step three: Search for the option "Add my URL" or "Register my URL". This will let them know that you are interested in selling your domain name.

Step four: Choose a broker that you would like to sell your domain through and click on "Add my URL". This will let them know that you have already registered your domain name with them.

Step five: Once they receive your email, they will send you an offer for the price of the domain name.

Step six: If you are happy with the offer, then you can sell your domain name to them.

Domain name forums:

The tenth way to find a buyer for your domain name is to use a domain name forum. This can be done by using an online service such as NamePros.com. It is a great way to find buyers who are interested in purchasing your domain name.

To get started, you will need to create a free account with NamePros.com. Once you have registered, you can begin posting your domain name for sale in the appropriate forum section.

Networking events:

The eleventh way to find a buyer for your domain name is to use networking events. This can be done by using an online service such as DNForum.com. It is a great way to find buyers who are interested in purchasing your domain name.

To get started, you will need to make an account on DNForum.com and upload your domain names to be sold. You can also add a description of the domain name you want to sell, which is helpful for potential buyers who might want more information about it before purchasing it from you.

You will then need to wait until someone makes an offer on one of your domains. When this happens, you will receive an email notification and you can then decide whether or not to accept the offer.

If you do accept the offer, the buyer will need to pay using a payment service such as PayPal. You will then need to provide the buyer with your contact information so they can arrange for the transfer of ownership of the domain name.

Blogs and podcasts:

The twelfth way to find a buyer for your domain name is to use blogs and podcasts. This can be done by using an online service such as Namepros.com. It is a great way to find buyers who are interested in purchasing your domain name.

To get started, you'll need to follow these steps

Step one: Write the blog post and podcast.

Step two: Create a profile on Namepros.com.

Step three: Once you've created your profile, create an account with Blogspot or WordPress to write articles about how to sell domain names online. Then submit them to Namepros for approval, which usually takes around 24 hours.

Step four: In your profile, include a link to your website or blog.

Step five: Start writing articles and podcasts about how to sell domain names online.

Email:

Another way to find a buyer for your domain name is by sending out an email. This can be done through Google Mail. It is a great way to find buyers who are interested in purchasing your domain name. It is generally recommended to send an email at a time when most of your recipients will be likely to be checking their email. For example, early in the morning or late in the evening.

Subject

The subject line should be very clear and to the point. Do not overcomplicate it with unnecessary words or phrases. You can use a sentence such as "Selling my domain name, [insert domain name]".

Message

Include a brief description of the domain name you want to sell and that it is for sale for $X.XX USD, then include your contact information such as your email address or your website address. You can also offer to negotiate the price of the domain name with the buyer. However, before doing this make sure that you research to see if this is something that the majority of buyers are willing to do.

Email address

Make sure you include your contact information in your email so potential buyers can easily contact you if they would like to purchase your domain name. You should also include an explanation of how interested parties can stop receiving emails from you, especially if they have already shown an interest in purchasing your domain name.

To get started, you'll need to follow these steps:

Step one: Log into Google Mail and create an email with the subject line "I'm looking for an investor/partner.

Step two: Make sure to include your full name and contact information in the email.

Step three: Write a sales pitch about your website and why someone should invest in it.

If you're not sure what to write, then consider writing something like this: Hello, My name is John Doe and I'm looking for an investor/partner that has experience in investing in websites. The website I'm looking to sell is [insert domain name]. You can check it out by visiting its homepage at [insert URL here].

Step four: Make sure to include a link to your website or blog.

Step five: Send the email.

How many emails should I send?

It is generally recommended to send out at least five emails to potential buyers. However, you may want to send more or less depending on the number of potential buyers you have.

Should I include a price in my email?

There is no right or wrong answer when it comes to including a price in your email. However, you should do what you feel most comfortable with. If you're not sure how to price your domain name, then consider using a valuation service such as GoDaddy's Domain Appraisal Tool or Estibot.com.

Should I avoid sending emails during holidays?

There is no right or wrong answer when it comes to this question. However, you may want to consider the fact that many people will be busy with their families and may not have time to check their email.

How to avoid your email ending up in the spam folder?

One way to avoid your email ending up in the spam folder is to make sure that you have a valid email address. You can also use an online service such as Google Mail to send your email. This will help to ensure that your email doesn't end up in the spam folder.

How to track the sent email?

One way to track the sent email is to use an online service such as Google Mail. This will help you to keep track of the email and see if it was delivered to the recipient's inbox or not.

How can you find emails of the company's executives?

You can identify company executives by going to the company's website and trying to find their email addresses. Their email address will usually be under a heading such as "contact" or "management." In Microsoft Office, you can use a resource called Whois that provides contact information on most websites for registered domain owners.

Estibot leads:

Estibot is a leading domain name appraisal and sales platform. It provides a wide range of services related to the buying, selling, and appraising of domain names.

To get started, you'll need to follow these steps

Step one: Create an account

Step two: Get a domain appraisal

To get your domain appraisal, you'll need to enter the following information about your website. You can find this information on the About Us page of your website. You must provide accurate and up-to-date information for Estibot to be able to give you an accurate appraisal.

Step three: Get a quote

Once you have your domain appraisal, you can get a quote for selling it. Estibot will give you an estimate of how much money they think your website is worth.

Step four: Sell your domain name to Estibot

Estibot allows users to sell their domains directly through the platform. This means that you don't need to go through a third party to sell your domain name.

Sedo:

Sedo is a leading domain name marketplace with over 18 million listings and millions of users who buy sell on this platform every month worldwide! It's a great way to find a buyer for your domain name.

To get started, you'll need to follow these steps

Step one: create a Sedo account

Step two: create a listing for your domain name

Domain names can be listed for free, or you can choose to add on premium services like featured listings, which will make your domain name more visible to buyers. When creating your listing, it's important to include as much information as possible so that buyers have all the information, they need to make an informed decision.

Step three: once your domain has been listed and you've received a few offers, it's time to negotiate the sale!

If you're having trouble negotiating a price with buyers, Sedo can help by providing expert advice on how much money should be offered for your domain name. They also assist if there are any issues during the selling process so that you can rest assured that your domain name will be sold quickly and securely.

Afternic:

Afternic is a well-known domain name marketplace with over six million active buyers and sellers. It's a great place to start if you're looking for a buyer for your domain name.

To get you'll need to follow these steps

Step one: create an Afternic account

Step two: list your domain names

Step three: set up Afternic's escrow service to protect yourself and buyers.

8.3 How to close the sale of your domain name?

There are a few things you need to do to close the sale of your domain name.

1. Make sure you have a price in mind and be willing to negotiate

Domain names can be sold for a variety of prices, depending on the TLD (top-level domain name) and how much traffic the name receives. It's important to set a price that you're comfortable with, but also be willing to negotiate if the buyer seems interested.

2. Have all your contact information ready

When you're selling a domain name, you'll need to provide the buyer with your full name, address, phone number, and email address. This is so they can easily get in touch with you to finalize the sale.

3. **Have the domain name ready to transfer**

When you sell a domain name, you'll need to provide the buyer with all of the necessary information so they can take ownership of the domain. This includes your login username and password for your domain name registrar, as well as any contact information listed in the WHOIS record.

4. **Decide how you want to get paid**

The buyer will most likely pay for the domain name via PayPal or another online payment service. Once they have sent you an offer, it's up to you if you want to accept it and transfer ownership of the domain name.

Once you've completed these steps, you're ready to sell your domain name!

8.4 How To Negotiate a Price for Your Domain Name?

Negotiating the price of domain names effectively is essential for domain investors looking to maximize the value of their assets. Successful negotiations can produce positive outcomes that ensure fair compensation while building strong relationships with prospective buyers. In this section we'll share key strategies and techniques for effectively negotiating domain prices.

Research and Prep:

Before initiating negotiations on your domain name, conduct comprehensive research to gain an accurate assessment of its market value. Take into account factors like domain metrics (domain authority/backlinks/CDN rank/competitor domain sales trends/current market conditions. Doing this research will serve as the cornerstone for supporting pricing expectations while upholding domain's worth in negotiations.

Setting Realistic Price Expectations:

Be realistic in setting your price expectations when setting them. Consider all aspects of the domain's unique qualities such as market relevance, brandability, and development potential when setting fair and equitable prices; overpricing can cause buyers to shy away, so find a balance between maximizing profits while drawing serious buyers in.

Put Forward a Professional Image:

Approach negotiations with an appropriate, businesslike demeanor in order to build credibility and establish trust with potential buyers of domain names. Be prompt in replying to inquiries, clear in communication and provide all pertinent domain name data. Demonstrate expertise so buyers feel at ease during transactions with you.

Highlight Unique Selling Points:

In negotiations, when selling your domain name to buyers, be sure to highlight its distinct selling points: brandability, keyword relevance, SEO potential or any other qualities which separate it from similar domains; also be sure to highlight any benefits they'd gain by owning it.

Understand Buyer Needs and Motivation:

Understand your buyer's needs, motivations and intended use for the domain before starting negotiations with them. By showing that your domain meets their goals you increase the odds of reaching a mutually beneficial agreement between you and them.

Be Prepared and Open to Negotiation:

Negotiations involve give and take. Be open and flexible towards reasonable offers or potential compromises as part of a dialogue designed to find an equitable agreement that benefits both sides; avoid rigid positions in favor of exploring creative deal structures such as installment payments, joint ventures or creative ways of paying back debt if it fits within your goals and can benefit buyers.

Patience and Persistence:

Negotiations may take time. Be patient while being persistent in your efforts - avoid rushing the process or pressuring buyers too soon - instead show that you are committed to finding an amicable agreement by investing the necessary time and energy in reaching one.

Seek Professional Assistance:

Should negotiations become complex or challenging, seek professional assistance. Domain brokers or attorneys with experience in domain transactions may provide valuable guidance, navigate legal aspects and facilitate negotiations on your behalf - ultimately making for successful deals!

Document & Agreement:

Once an agreement on price has been made, it's essential that both parties sign an official purchase or agreement that includes essential details about domain name registration price, payment terms, transfer procedure and any additional terms or conditions agreed to between themselves. A legally binding document protects both sides while guaranteeing an uninterrupted process.

Negotiating the price for your domain name requires taking an analytical and professional approach. Thorough research, realistic pricing expectations, effective communication and understanding the buyer's needs are key components to successful negotiations. By employing these strategies and remaining open to flexibility and compromise you can successfully negotiate and increase the odds of finding an equitable price for your domain name. Remember negotiation is a skill which develops over time so continue honing your approach as each negotiation experience presents new lessons to learn from.

8.5 How To Maximize Your Profit?

When selling a domain name, it is important to remember that you want to get as much money as possible. Here are some tips to help you maximize your profits:

- Make a good impression on potential buyers. A simple way to do this is to create a website for the domain name you are selling. This will give people an idea of what they can expect from your site, and it will help them understand that you own the domain name in question.

- Don't just sell names you don't want. It is important to be choosy when selling domain names. Only sell the ones that you know are valuable and will fetch a good price.

- Price your domain name correctly. This can be tricky, but it is important to remember that you want to get as much money as possible for your domain name. Price it too low and people will not be interested in buying it from you. If you price too high, then people may think that the domain name is worth less than what you are asking for.

- Avoid using words like “free” or other similar terms in your domain name listings. This can give off a negative impression to potential buyers and may cause them not to buy from you.

- Be patient when waiting for a sale or response from a buyer. Sometimes it can take up to 24 hours before you hear back from someone interested in buying your domain name. If this happens, do not panic! Just be patient and wait for the right opportunity to come along before selling it again.

- Consider getting help from a professional if necessary. If you are not sure about how to sell domain names, then hiring someone who knows what they're doing may be beneficial for both parties involved in the transaction. These professionals will also know which types of domains are more likely to generate interest among buyers and thus make more money for you in the long run.

- Know when to stop trying and move on. If all else fails, then it may be time to give up on your dream of being a domain name seller and focus your energy elsewhere!

8.6 What If My Domain Name Isn't Getting Sold?

If your domain name isn't getting sold, you may need to consider a few things.

1. Are you ranking for your keyword?

Use webmaster tools to see if there are any errors on your site. If so, fix them and submit your URL again to Google after a few days have gone by. Once you're done with that and all is well, check out the search engine results pages (SERPs) for the keyword you're targeting. If you're not ranking in the top three, it's going to be tough to sell your domain name.

2. Is your offer reasonable?

If you're asking for too much money, people will be turned off. However, if you're offering it for a steal, they may wonder what's wrong with the domain name. Try to find a happy medium when pricing your domain name.

3. Is your domain name easy to remember?

If people can't remember your domain name, they're not going to type it in the address bar. Make sure it's something catchy that will stick in their heads.

4. **Have you made a website?**

If you haven't created a website yet, it's time to do so. You don't need to have all the pages filled in, but make sure it looks professional and that there are no errors on the site. Once you're done with that, submit your URL to Google and other search engines. Then, wait a week or two before checking back on your site's rankings.

5. **Is your domain name relevant?**

Domain names that are relevant to the topic of the website will generally sell for more money. If you're targeting a specific keyword, make sure your domain name includes it. This will help you rank in the search engines and boost your chances of selling your domain name.

9.

DOMAIN MARKETPLACE

"Don't bring your need to the marketplace, bring your skill."

-Jim Rohn

Domain flipping has been recommended as one of the most profitable businesses to make money online in 2023. With the successful selling of many domains over the years, it seems that this business is on a continuous rise to gaining worldwide traction. Domain flipping is one of the best businesses to engage in 2022.

9.1 What is domain flipping?

Domain flipping is the practice of buying cheap domains with high revenue potential and then reselling such for a profit. The main effort in domain flipping comes in being able to identify dormant domains with huge commercial potential.

9.2 Types of domains to flip

When it comes to domain flipping, several types are considered ideal to invest in. These are expired, short, new, and local domains.

Expired domains: By expired domains, you buy domain names with the expired registry. They are usually cheaper than competing domain names. This is because they have not been in the market for some time.

Short domains: For short domains, this could be also profitable for domain flippers. The shorter the domain the better. The short domain name for Cars.com almost brought a total sales price of $1 billion for the seller. This is how important short domain names are.

New domains: You can buy new domains because they are very valuable. You can choose to capitalize on your revenue potential by purchasing new domain extensions.

Local domains: You can buy local domains as they offer you the best opportunity to make money locally. An example is 'Miamihotdogs.com' or 'hotdogs.miami', 'Londonsoccertalents.com' or 'soccertalents.london', and so on.

9.3 Why domain flipping is important

The motivation behind domain flipping is for profit. As valuable assets of internet real estate, domain flipping is a very lucrative business for people who understand the art of the business. Cars.com was one of the most expensive domains that was sold. It was able to fetch $872 million for the seller. If you know how to be at the right location when it matters the most, you will make a lot of money from flipping domains. Flipping a domain could result in massive personal profits for you. People who regularly flip domains make a lot of money that they need to turn the practice into their full-time careers.

9.4 Buying domains for profit

When it comes to buying and selling domain names, there are 5 basic steps involved in the process. These are critical steps that ensure you are on your way to flipping domains for massive profits.

First step: To begin your journey to successfully flipping domains, you need to know how to search for one. Look for a domain with massive revenue potential. You will need to optimize your domain searching strategy to find the right domain that is suitable for you. You will need to know how to look for a domain that comes with a low price and can be sold for a substantial price. Many domains selling websites offer digital tools that help you to look for the right domains to buy.

Second step: As soon as you have seen the right domain that suits your budget, you will have to evaluate this domain. When it comes to evaluating domains, there are several factors that you can use to determine a potentially valuable domain. These factors include:

- Brandability
- Length
- Search friendliness
- Relevance

You will need to check whether you will be able to sell off that domain for a much higher price. You can also check the sales history of similar domains.

Third step: Register the name of your domain as soon as possible. This is after you must have diligently evaluated the domain. You get to register the domain after you must have completed the buying of the domain. This process should be a simple one without taking much of your time.

Fourth step: The next stage in the domain flipping process is to start looking for a buyer for the domain. Finding the right buyer for your domain can be the most difficult stage of this process. Flipping the domain to make a profit is simply to look for a buyer that will pay more money than you did when you first bought the domain. There are various strategies and tools that you can use to purchase the domain to make a lot of profit.

Fifth step: The last step here is to finally sell off your domain. When you are finally able to sell off the domain, whenever the new registry is done, there is usually an ownership transfer. This is an easy process that takes a little time.

9.5 Best Domain Marketplace

If you are looking to flip domains like a professional, you will need to understand price considerations and how it is used in this business. Insecure was sold in 2009 for a whopping $16 million. There are many other websites like vacationrental.com and insurance.com, and so on that have been sold for very profitable prices. Selling at high prices does not mean that you will sell off your domains for very high prices. A good thing to note here is that many popular domains with catchy keywords have been purchased. Pricing considerations for domain selling means that you will need to understand how domain names are sold and how to peg the prices of various domains.

In other to get a proper pricing idea for your domain, you will need to visit websites that trade domains. This way, you will know how much similar domains like yours are listed. You will then be able to set the price the right way.

Namecheap

Namecheap is an internet-based business support website that allows you to buy and sell domain names. Apart from buying and selling domain names, you can also purchase hosting plans, apps, and security features.

How to buy a domain name on Namecheap

You can easily buy any domain name on Namecheap. To do this, simply navigate to the "Domain Marketplace" on the website. After, this checks the "Buy it now" lists. You will then perform the necessary action.

To begin the process of buying the domain name, go to the Namecheap website and sign into your account. Navigate to the "Domains" area of the website and choose "Marketplace." Go to the tab ton" Buy now." Look for the domain name you want and insert it into the shopping cart. As soon as the domain name has been added, the process to checkout and pay for it.

How to sell your domain name on Namecheap

If you are looking to sell off your domain name on Namecheap, this can be done easily. Just sign into your account on Namecheap. Go to the "Domain list" and add the domain you need to sell. Select the "Manage" tab close to the domain.

Scroll downwards towards the area for "Other Domain Settings", and click on the button for "Sell domain." For the next stages of the process, simply input the "Asking Price" and the "List Period." You will be expected to perform other simple functions. When you are done, select the "Sell domain" tab and conclude the process.

Pros

- Have the best pricing in the industry.
- Domain renewal is fast and simple.
- They offer excellent privacy features that are free of charge.
- Modern, clean, and user-friendly system interface.
- Excellent support services.

Cons

- Offer poor quality hosting.
- Some premium domains can be expensive.
- Offer limited email hosting plans.

Flippa

Flippa is the number one global marketplace to buy and sell your domains. This allows you to easily buy and sell any online business. Flippa doesn't don't offer you the opportunity to buy and sell empty domains. You can buy and sell any business for thousands or millions of dollars.

How to sell a domain name on Flippa

To sell your domain name on Flippa is easy and fast. Simply sign up for an account on their website. Then simply list your business for sale. This action will take about 15 minutes. While your domain name is listed, Flippa will match your listings to potential buyers. When you successfully make a sale, you will be expected to pay a minimal fee.

How to buy a domain name on Flippa

With Flippa, you can easily buy a domain name.

To buy a domain name, simply log onto your account on Flippa. You can then perform a search on any domain name that you like. If it is available, you will need to place a bid. If the sales go on well, you will be expected to pay for the domain name.

Pros

- Good for easily buying and selling any type of online business.
- Comes with easily navigable features.
- Availability of great websites for cheap prices.

Cons

- Too many scammers.
- Bad reviews online.
- You will have to search for a long time to get a good deal.

GoDaddy

GoDaddy is an online platform that sells all you need for an online business to succeed. On this website, you can buy domain names, email, websites, online security, and hosting services.

How to sell domain names on GoDaddy

With GoDaddy, you can easily sell off your domain name by using the "List for Sale" feature. To do this, log onto your account. Go to the Simple List View option. Choose the "List for Sale" option. Choose the box "Get started."Input the listing price of your domain name and proceed. After this process, you will need to undergo several processes to confirm your domain listing. Soon after, an interested buyer can spot your domain name and bid for it.

How to buy a domain name on GoDaddy

GoDaddy as one of the number one online portals for buying domains has made the process ridiculously simple. To buy a domain, use the search function to look for the website in the search bar. When you see the website you like, add it to your cart. After this, you will be expected to follow various simple steps. After which you can then pay for the domain name.

Pros

- Excellent domain maintenance.
- Excellent website hosting plans.
- Quality customer support.
- Domain transfer possible.
- Excellent security features.

Cons

- Very expensive domain restoration costs.
- Limited personalized website templates.
- Occasionally slow website hosting plans.

Afternic

Afternic is a premium marketplace for buying and selling domain names. The site has over 5 million excellent domain names for sale. You can easily buy and sell your domain name in this rich marketplace for flipping domains.

How to buy domain names on Afternic

To buy a domain name on Afternic have never been easier. All you need do is to perform a simple search on the database of the website. Negotiate for the right domain deal, complete the transfer process and take ownership of the new domain name.

How to sell domain names on Afternic

To sell your domain name on Afternic, you can begin by creating an account. Add your domain name to the database. Take part in the fast transfer procedure offered by the website. To accelerate your domain sale, you will need to perform several promotional services.

Pros

- Highly convenient for selling domains.
- Good website for making money.

Cons

- Holds funds for six days, which is too long.
- No tracking system used for customer support.
- Bulky web interface for managing domains.
- Review period of domain takes forever.

Sedo

Sedo is a very popular marketplace that makes it possible for startups and companies looking for their ideal website addresses to get this at a cheap price. You can also buy and sell domains on this website. Sedo offers a wide range of professional domain services. They offer broker services, domain appraisals, transfer services, partner programs, and so much more.

How to buy domains on Sedo

With Sedo, you can easily buy any domain that you like in three simple steps. The first stage involves using the domain search tool on the website. There are millions of domains on offer for sale on Sedo's domain database. You can easily compare various domains and buy anyone that suits your preferences. Domain comparison is performed with the use of available detailed information and in-depth statistics. Soon as you see the domain that meets your need, you can then place a bid for it and buy it. The next stage is Sedo's official free domain transfer service which becomes activated as soon as the domain sales have been completed.

How to sell a domain on Sedo

Sedo offers various formats whereby people can sell their domains at good prices. There are several instruments like broker services, auction events, marketplace auctions, and direct auctions. These sales instruments can all be used to sell domains from the platform. To sell your domain, you can get one directly on their marketplace. The "Buy Now" feature of this website allows you to quickly sell off your domains at profitable prices. You can easily make your offer to buyers to allow buyers about the availability of your domain in the marketplace.

Pros

- Sedo is a very popular platform for reselling and buying domains and it is a great place for entry-level domain sellers and buyers.
- Sedo is one of the best domains selling/buying platforms that can be understood easily and quickly. You can easily set up your domain name selling or buying process in easy and fast steps.
- Free domain parking is a premium feature when it comes to domain buying and selling. Many platforms like GoDaddy, will usually make users pay every month for domain parking.
- The website comes with a lot of features that simplify whatever it is that you are looking for. It makes it easy to determine the number of hits that your auction has received. It also shows you the total amount that your parked page has earned you.
- Sedo is a platform where you can easily get premium auctions periodically and they are also free.

Cons

- Sedo is known for charging massive prices as their commission. They usually charge a 10% auction fee with a minimum amount of $50.
- It does not offer a direct domain auction.
- The search interface looks like it was poorly designed.
- There are no visitor site visit stats that are available on the domain. This makes it difficult for customers to track the number of visitors checking their domains.

Namepros

Namepros is among the biggest platforms that support the buying and selling of quality domains with about a million subscribers.

Pros

- A user-friendly and fluid user interface.
- Lots of options to choose from

Cons

- Can take a long time for the user to seal their preferred deals.

Domain.com

Domain.com is the best platform for making it easy for users to easily buy cheap domains in the fastest way possible. The platform also offers free Cloud storage and eco-friendly services.

Pros

- Domain.com offers the best usability as it comes with a simple control panel, purchasing, and domain search features.
- It offers 100% transparency for the prices of the domain on its platform.
- It offers a wide range of TLDs that offer various TLD alternatives which are outside of the usual domain extensions. It currently offers over 411 TLDs.
- Domain.com does not employ obtrusive cross-selling tactics meaning that users can focus on their services without getting distracted.
- An all-in-one offering of complementary products like hosting plans, eCommerce support, website building tools, and so on.

Cons

- Pricing is usually high with domain.com.
- Does not have any onboarding services.

Bido

Bido is another domain selling and buying platform that offers its users the opportunity to sell and buy domains with a clear user interface.

Pros and cons of using Bido

Pros

- Easy domain buying and selling processes.
- The website platform can be cumbersome to use.

Cons

- The website comes with a poor design
- There can be a lot of charges.

Efty website

Efty makes it possible for people to easily sell and buy premium domain names at considerable prices. As a platform for flipping domains, this is the only domain name marketplace that does not get any commission on the completion of domain sales.

Pros

- Does not charge any commission when you sell your domain.
- Easy domain uploading system.
- Easy integration with popular payment providers.
- Have the ability to monitor all domains from different registrars.
- Efty accepts all domains regardless of their registrars.

Cons

- Buyers are unable to pay for domains through Paypal.

eBay Marketplace

eBay is an online auction site that also provides domain selling and buying services for people to easily make money. This is a marketplace for domain resellers and features a wide collection of tools that are meant to help buyers and sellers succeed on the platform.

Pros

- A large collection of domains to choose from.
- Availability of numerous cheap domain options
- Opportunity for various domain extensions.

Cons

- There is no specific domain selling instruments for resellers.
- Largely influenced by its eCommerce features and does not involve specialised domain selling/buying assistance services.

Brandbucket

Brandbucket is beyond a domain selling or buying platform. Rather, it contains a collection of resources for brands and businesses to get domain names for cheap. The website still offers other services like business names, generating business names, creating catchy business names, and so on.

Pros

- Brandbucket allows the user to be able to choose from a wide selection of possible domain names.
- When you make a purchase, you will also automatically receive a logo design apart from the domain design.
- It is s website that promotes user-friendliness.

Cons

- Brandbucket can be quite costly.
- Selection of names is only limited to the domain library of the site.

10.

PORTFOLIO MANAGEMENT

" The essence of investment management is the management of risks, not the management of returns."

-Benjamin Graham

Domain portfolio management is a crucial aspect of success in the domain industry. It involves effectively managing and optimizing a collection of domain names to maximize returns on investment. Whether you are a seasoned domain investor or just starting out, understanding domain portfolio management is essential for achieving long-term profitability and growth. In this chapter, we will explore the key components and strategies involved in domain portfolio management.

10.1 Defining Domain Portfolio Management

Domain portfolio management refers to the practice of overseeing and optimizing an investor's domain names to reach specific goals, which may range from passive income generation, capitalizing on resale opportunities, developing domains into lucrative online ventures, or capitalizing on passive income generation opportunities. Successful domain portfolio management encompasses numerous activities like acquiring valuable domains, conducting market analyses, assessing domain metrics, implementing monetization strategies and tracking performance - each activity which helps optimize your domain portfolio management success and achieve your predetermined goals.

Key Elements of Domain Portfolio Management

Domain Acquisition:

Acquiring domain names strategically is a cornerstone of portfolio management. This involves researching market conditions and industry trends before analyzing possible demand in terms of future demand and its effect on pricing trends. Domain investors may acquire domains using auctions, direct purchases or drop-catching services as means for acquisition.

Organization and Tracking:

For effective domain portfolio management, effective organization is crucial. This involves maintaining a central record of domain names registered and expired as well as monitoring relevant metrics such as registration dates or expirations dates of domains registered under one's name. Domain management tools/ platforms may assist in streamlining these tasks for efficient record keeping.

Domain Valuation:

Deliberate valuation is critical in making informed decisions regarding pricing, acquisition and resale strategies of domain names. Valuing domains includes taking into account factors like domain metrics (domain authority/backlinks/market demand/keyword relevance etc), demand in terms of keywords relevence to potential monetization opportunities - appraisal tools/services can give an estimate of fair market values of domain names.

Monetization Strategies:

Optimizing domain investments requires adopting several monetization strategies. This may involve domain parking, creating functional websites for lease to businesses or actively seeking sales of the domains themselves. Each approach comes with its own benefits and considerations that depend on an investor's goals and market conditions.

Tracking and Optimizing Performance:

Analyzing performance metrics such as traffic, revenue, renewal rates and resale values of domain investments is crucial to their successful portfolio management. By monitoring key performance indicators (KPIs) such as traffic, revenue renewal rates and resale values of domain investments regularly investors can identify underperforming domains; optimize pricing strategies; make informed renewal and drop decisions and allocate resources more effectively than before.

Example of Domain Portfolio Management:

Let's use an example to demonstrate domain portfolio management:

Sarah is an investor specializing in fitness industry domain acquisition. Her goal is to amass an assortment of fitness domain names for passive income through various monetization strategies and build up her diverse domain portfolio accordingly.

Sarah begins by conducting market research to identify emerging fitness trends and niche opportunities. To acquire domains with great keyword relevance, market demand, and future growth potential. For effective portfolio management she uses a central system with tracking renewal dates as part of portfolio administration as well as regularly monitoring their performance by measuring metrics such as traffic or revenue growth.

Sarah employs various strategies to monetize her domains. For some domains she develops informative websites which attract traffic and earn revenue via advertising/affiliate marketing/parking revenue; other domains take advantage of parking revenues through clicks/impressions etc; Sarah even sells certain domains directly, taking advantage of market demand/negotiations skills when selling certain ones off to interested buyers.

Sarah consistently evaluates and revises her strategies based on the performance of her portfolio and any changes within it. She follows trends within the fitness industry and looks out for new monetization opportunities or optimizing pricing according to market conditions based on staying informed, diversifying her investments, and managing them actively - this ensures her investments reach maximum potential and reach desired outcomes.

Domain portfolio management refers to the practice of strategically managing a collection of domain names to maximize their value and returns on investment. It involves activities like domain acquisition, organization, valuation, monetization and performance tracking. Successful portfolio management requires in-depth market knowledge as well as careful evalutation of metrics on domain metrics as well as implementation of appropriate monetization strategies that unlock their full potential within an increasingly dynamic industry. By adopting sound portfolio practices domain investors can unlock all their domain potential while experiencing lasting success within it.

10.2 Setting Portfolio Goals and Targets

Setting clear and achievable goals is an integral element of effective domain portfolio management. In this article, we will delve into the importance and practical considerations involved with setting portfolio targets as well as various kinds of goals as well as offer guidance on setting them.

Why Set Portfolio Goals and Targets?

- **Setting Goals and Focus**: Goal setting can provide domain investors with a sense of direction for their portfolio and can assist with investment decisions, acquisition strategies and overall portfolio management activities.
- **Motivation and Accountability**: Goals act as motivators, driving investors towards success. Additionally, goals create accountability within investors by holding them to stay committed, taking actions steps towards reaching desired outcomes, and taking the necessary actions on a consistent basis.
- **Measure Progress**: Goals provide benchmarks to track progress and assess the performance of domain portfolios, helping investors assess achievements, pinpoint areas for improvement and make more informed decisions regarding investments and strategies for the future.

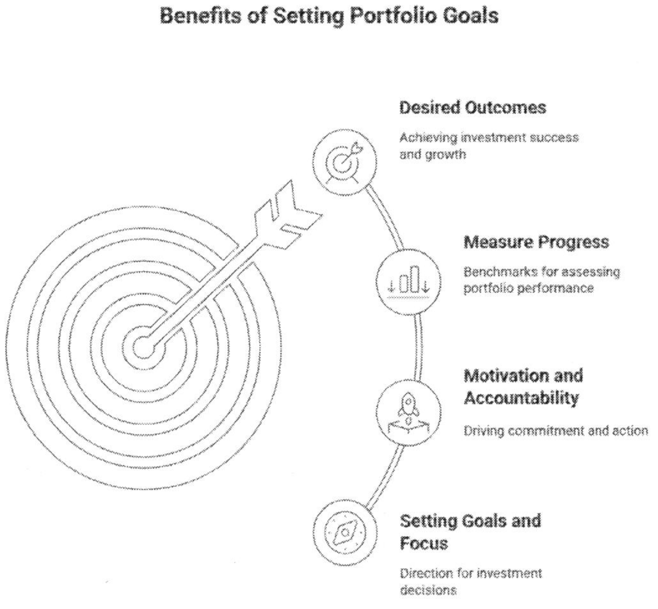

Types of Portfolio Goals:

- **Financial Goals**: When setting portfolio management goals, financial goals focus on the monetary component. Such targets might include targets for annual revenue goals, return on Investment (ROI), profit margin targets or specific monetary milestones set within an allotted timeline.

- **Growth and Expansion Goals**: Growth goals involve expanding one's domain portfolio through purchasing additional domain names, diversifying into different niches or industries or increasing overall portfolio value. Achieve these objectives may require increasing domain numbers by expanding into additional TLDs (Top-Level Domains) or prioritizing domains with high market demand.

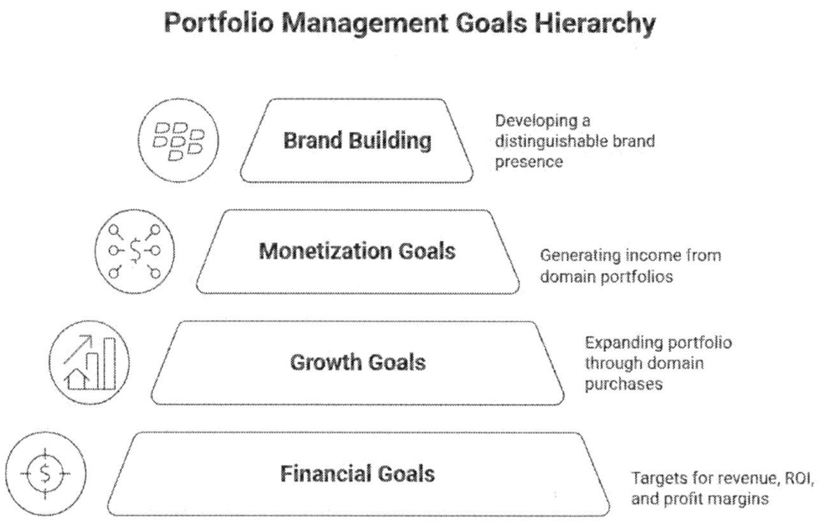

- **Monetization Goals**: Monetization goals aim at making money off domain portfolios through different means, such as passive income from domain parking or revenue from developed websites and e-commerce ventures as well as specific sales targets to be reached through sales/leasing arrangements of domain names.

- **Brand Building Goals**: Brand building goals focus on developing an identifiable, distinguishable brand presence within their respective industry domain. This could involve becoming known for expertise in certain niche areas or forging relationships among professionals within that same field, or through proactive promotion efforts such as networking activities and marketing programs.

Establishing Portfolio Goals and Targets:

- **Starting Out Right**: First step in goal setting should be setting clear and specific goals. Avoid vague or generalized statements and ensure each SMART (specific, measurable, attainable, relevant and timebound) goal is realistic and timely - for instance instead of "I want to make money off my domain portfolio", setting an achievable and timebound SMART goal could mean, "I aim to generate $10,000 annual passive income through domain parking in 12 months' time. "

- **Align Your Goals with Overall Strategy**: Your investment goals should align with and support the overarching investment strategy and reflect desired outcomes. Take into account your investing style, risk tolerance, market trends and available resources when creating goals, making sure they're realistic yet obtainable within your specific context.

- **Break Your Goals Down into Milestones**: When setting larger goals, break them into manageable milestones for easier achievement of success. Each milestone should contribute towards reaching your goal while acting as an indicator of progress towards it.

- **Track Progress and Make Changes**: Take regular stock of how well your goals are coming along and adjust strategies if necessary based on insights gained through tracking progress. Measure and assess portfolio performance through KPIs specific to each goal, then adapt strategies according to what insights are revealed through tracking your goals' progression.

- **Review and Adjust Goals**: As your portfolio develops and market conditions change, periodically revisit and adapt your goals in response to achievements, new opportunities or shifts in investment focus. Doing this ensures they remain aligned with evolving needs and aspirations.

Setting goals and targets is essential to successful domain portfolio management. By setting clear, specific, aligning with overall strategy goals that break them into manageable milestones and regularly tracking progress towards them - you will ensure the smooth running of your portfolio towards its success. Don't forget to review and revise goals according to changing market conditions or personal aspirations changes as necessary! With well-defined goals you will be better equipped for making informed decisions while remaining motivated towards long term profitability in this dynamic industry.

10.3 Diversification and Risk Management

Diversification and risk management are crucial elements of effective domain portfolio management. By diversifying their portfolio and implementing risk management strategies, domain investors can minimize potential losses, protect their investments, and maximize long-term returns. In this article, we will explore the importance of diversification and risk management in domain portfolio management and discuss strategies to achieve them.

The Importance of Diversification:

Diversification involves spreading investments across a variety of domain names, niches, industries, and market segments. It is a fundamental principle in portfolio management that aims to reduce risk by avoiding overexposure to a single domain or market. Here's why diversification is essential:

1. **Risk Reduction**: Diversifying your portfolio helps mitigate the impact of market fluctuations, changes in demand, or specific industry challenges. By spreading investments across multiple domains, you reduce the risk of a single domain adversely affecting your entire portfolio.

2. **Market Opportunities**: Diversification allows you to capitalize on different market opportunities and take advantage of emerging trends. It enables you to participate in various industries and niches, expanding the potential for finding profitable domains and tapping into different customer bases.

3. **Portfolio Stability**: A well-diversified portfolio tends to be more stable and less susceptible to sudden changes in market conditions. By having a mix of domains with varying risk profiles, you can create a balanced portfolio that can withstand market volatility.

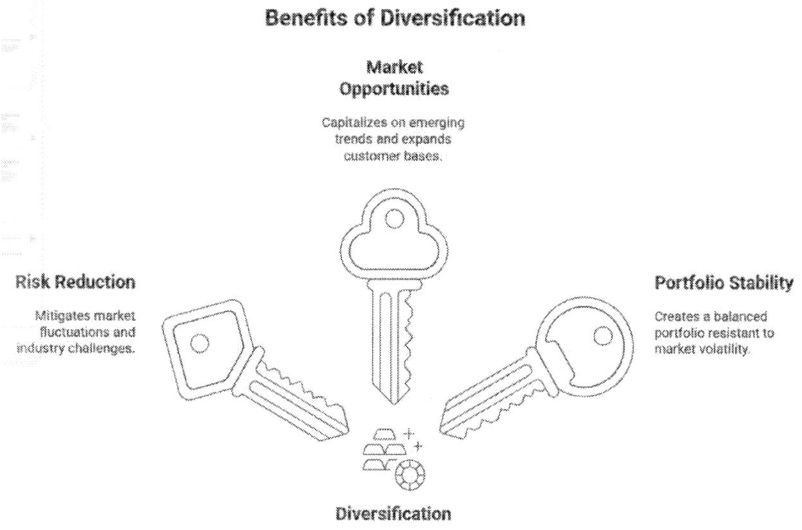

Strategies for Diversification and Risk Management:

1. **Spread Investments Across Different Niches**: Invest in domains across a range of niches or industries. This ensures that your portfolio is not heavily dependent on a single industry's performance or the success of a specific domain.

2. **Consider Different Types of Domains**: Diversify your portfolio by acquiring different types of domains, such as generic, keyword-rich, or brandable domains. Each type of domain carries its own potential risks and rewards, and a mix of these domains can provide a balanced portfolio.

3. **Explore Various TLDs (Top-Level Domains)**: Look beyond traditional TLDs like .com and consider investing in new and emerging TLDs. This allows you to

diversify across different domain extensions and take advantage of unique market opportunities associated with specific TLDs.

4. **Balance Domain Values**: Maintain a balance between high-value domains and lower-value domains in your portfolio. While high-value domains have the potential for significant returns, they may also carry higher risks. Including domains with lower values helps stabilize your portfolio and provides a steady stream of income.
5. **Regularly Review and Assess Performance**: Continually evaluate the performance of domains in your portfolio. Monitor key performance indicators (KPIs) such as traffic, revenue, renewal rates, and resale potential. Identify underperforming domains and consider reallocating resources or divesting from domains that no longer align with your goals.
6. **Stay Informed and Adapt to Market Trends**: Keep a pulse on market trends, emerging technologies, and industry developments. Stay informed about changes in consumer behavior, shifts in demand, and emerging niche markets. This knowledge allows you to adjust your portfolio and make informed investment decisions.
7. **Implement Risk Management Strategies**: Mitigate risk by setting limits on the percentage of your portfolio allocated to a single domain or industry. Implement stop-loss mechanisms to limit potential losses in case a domain's performance declines significantly. Regularly review and update your risk management strategies to ensure they align with your goals and market conditions.

10.4 Tools and Software for Portfolio Organization

Managing a domain portfolio efficiently requires the use of various tools and software that can streamline organization, tracking, analysis, and overall portfolio management tasks. These tools can help domain investors stay organized, monitor performance, and make informed decisions. Here are some essential tools and software for portfolio organization in the domain industry:

1. **Domain Management Platforms**: Domain management platforms provide centralized control and organization of domain portfolios. They allow investors to track domain registration and expiration dates, manage DNS settings, and

monitor portfolio performance. Examples of popular domain management platforms include DomainScope, Domain Portfolio Manager, and DomainBrain.

2. **Spreadsheets and Databases**: Spreadsheets, such as Microsoft Excel or Google Sheets, can be valuable tools for organizing domain portfolios. They provide flexibility for customizing columns, tracking domain information, recording purchase details, and monitoring metrics like traffic and revenue. Databases like Microsoft Access or MySQL can also be used for more extensive and customized portfolio management.

3. **Domain Valuation Tools**: Domain valuation tools assist in determining the value of domain names. They consider various factors such as domain metrics, market demand, keyword relevance, and comparable sales. Some popular domain valuation tools include EstiBot, GoDaddy Domain Appraisal, and Sedo Appraisal.

4. **Analytics and Tracking Tools**: Analytics tools help monitor the performance of domain names by tracking key metrics such as website traffic, revenue, and conversions. Google Analytics is a widely used tool for tracking website traffic, while services like DomainIQ and DomainTools provide insights into domain metrics, WHOIS data, and historical records.

5. **Domain Marketplace Platforms**: Domain marketplace platforms connect domain sellers with potential buyers. They provide a platform for listing and selling domain names. Popular domain marketplace platforms include Sedo, Afternic, Flippa, and Namecheap Marketplace.

6. **Auction Platforms**: Auction platforms offer opportunities for acquiring or selling domains through competitive bidding. They facilitate domain auctions and provide a platform for domain investors to buy or sell domains. Popular auction platforms include GoDaddy Auctions, NameJet, and DropCatch.

7. **WHOIS Lookup Tools**: WHOIS lookup tools allow investors to retrieve information about domain ownership, registration dates, and contact details. These tools help in researching potential acquisitions, monitoring domain ownership changes, and identifying potential buyers. Examples include DomainTools, WHOIS.net, and ICANN WHOIS Lookup.

8. **Monitoring and Alert Services**: Monitoring and alert services notify investors of important domain-related events, such as domain expirations, changes in

ownership, or trademark conflicts. Services like DomainTools' Domain Monitor and DomainIQ's Domain Alerts provide email notifications and alerts for tracking specific domains.

9. **Domain Marketplace Data Tools**: Domain marketplace data tools provide insights into market trends, sales data, and historical domain prices. They help investors analyze market demand, identify valuable domain opportunities, and make informed pricing and acquisition decisions. Examples include NameBio, DNJournal, and DNW's Domain Name Wire.

10. **Domain Drop-Catching Services**: Drop-catching services assist in capturing expired or soon-to-be-released domain names. These services use specialized algorithms and infrastructure to register domains the moment they become available. Popular drop-catching services include DropCatch, NameJet, and SnapNames.

When selecting tools and software for portfolio organization, consider your specific needs, budget, and preferred features. It's advisable to research, test, and explore different options to find the tools that best suit your portfolio management requirements.

11.

FINANCIAL MANAGEMENT

" Financial prosperity is impossible without constant planning and management of money."

- Sunday Adelaja

Financial management plays a critical role in the success and profitability of domain investors in the dynamic and ever-evolving domain industry. Effective financial management involves planning, budgeting, tracking expenses, generating revenue, evaluating performance, managing risks, and setting long-term financial goals. In this chapter, we will explore the importance of financial management in the domain industry and delve into various aspects of managing finances in the context of domain investing.

11.1 Understanding Financial Management

Financial management is an essential aspect of domain investing that involves strategic planning, tracking and optimizing of financial resources related to domain acquisitions, sales, monetization and overall portfolio management. Financial managers employ sound financial principles and practices in order to guarantee profitability while mitigating risks while reaching long-term financial goals.

Financial knowledge in domain investing is indispensable to making informed decisions, optimizing returns on investments, and effectively navigating its complex landscape. Below are key aspects of domain investment financial management:

Budgeting and Expense Management:

Establishing a budget enables domain investors to allocate funds strategically and plan for acquisitions, renewals, marketing efforts and expenses such as hosting fees. Tracking expenses ensure that financial resources are utilized efficiently while costs remain within an acceptable and sustainable framework.

Revenue Generating Strategies:

Financial management requires devising plans to generate revenues from domain investments, whether passive income such as domain parking or active monetization via website development; leasing domains to businesses for lease agreements or engaging in domain sales and auctions are among many of the strategies employed for revenue generating domain investments.

Pricing and Valuation:

Proper domain valuation is key for optimizing profitability, so investors need to become versed in domain valuation methodologies, market trends, buyer behavior as well as how best to price competitively while simultaneously being able to negotiate effectively with prospective buyers.

Tax Considerations and Legal Compliance:

Financial management in domain investing involves understanding tax obligations, reporting requirements and legal compliance specific to domain investments. Navigating intellectual property rights, trademark issues and other legal factors essential in safeguarding investments while upholding legal compliance is imperative in protecting investments while remaining compliant.

Financial Analysis and Performance Evaluation:

Measuring financial performance is integral to measuring domain investments' success, whether or not they produce returns. Evaluating key performance indicators (KPIs), calculating return on investment (ROI), and gauging profitability all provide vital insights into portfolio's health allowing future decisions on investments made with confidence.

Risk Management and Insurance:

Prudent financial practices involve understanding risks. Domain investors need to recognize potential dangers such as market instability, legal disputes or domain theft and then implement risk mitigation plans accordingly. Adding protection with insurance provides additional insurance against unexpected events which might threaten portfolio's financial health

Financial Planning and Long-term Goals:

Financial management requires setting clear financial goals and creating an action plan for reaching them. This involves setting investment objectives, outlining strategies for portfolio growth and planning for long-term sustainability and wealth accumulation.

Engaging Financial Professionals:

Working with financial experts like accountants, financial advisors or lawyers can offer invaluable help with financial management. Such professionals may assist with tax planning strategies, investment portfolio oversight, risk mitigation plans and legal compliance advice.

Domain investors who understand and employ effective financial management practices can increase their financial outcomes while mitigating risks to secure long-term success in the domain industry. Properly planned, monitored, and adjusted domain investments ensure optimal financial returns while taking account of industry realities and goals.

11.2 Budgeting and Expense Management

Budgeting and expense management are crucial components of financial management in domain investing. Creating a budget and effectively managing expenses help domain investors allocate financial resources strategically, control costs, and maximize returns on investment. Here's a detailed overview of budgeting and expense management in the context of domain investing:

Create a Budget:

- Before beginning domain investing, assess your finances to ascertain how much can be allocated towards domain investing. Consider factors like available capital, income generated from existing domains and potential funding sources.
- Setting financial goals for your domain portfolio, such as how many domains to acquire, revenue targets or return on investment (ROI) objectives.
- Segregate your budget into several categories, such as domain acquisitions and renewals, marketing costs, legal and professional fees, portfolio management tools and any other expenses you anticipate incurring.

- Set an effective timeline for your budgeting activities - monthly, quarterly or annually. This will enable you to effectively measure and track financial progress.

Track and Monitor Expenses:

- Keep detailed records of all your domain-related expenses, including domain purchases, renewal fees, auction or brokerage fees, advertising costs, hosting fees, and any other expenses associated with portfolio management.
- Utilize accounting software or spreadsheet tools to track and categorize your expenses accurately. This will enable you to have a clear overview of your spending patterns and identify areas where you can potentially optimize costs.
- Regularly review and update your expense records to ensure accuracy and stay informed about your financial position.

Prioritize Essential Expenses:

- Identify essential expenses that are critical for the functioning and growth of your domain portfolio. This includes domain renewals for valuable domains, essential software or tools for portfolio management, and necessary legal and accounting services.
- Differentiate between essential expenses and discretionary spending. While it's important to invest in your portfolio's growth, be mindful of allocating resources to activities that yield a higher return on investment.

Evaluate and Adjust:

- Continually assess the effectiveness of your budget and expense management strategies. Monitor your financial performance regularly and compare it against your budgeted goals and targets.
- Identify areas where you can potentially reduce costs or reallocate resources. This may involve reviewing domain renewal fees, exploring cost-effective marketing strategies, or reassessing the value and performance of underperforming domains.

- Adjust your budget and expense allocation based on market trends, changes in your portfolio's performance, and shifts in your investment strategy. Flexibility and adaptability are key to optimizing your financial management approach.

Seek Cost-Effective Solutions:

- Look for cost-effective solutions and tools that can help streamline your portfolio management. Explore domain registrar options with competitive pricing, leverage free or affordable portfolio management software, and consider outsourcing certain tasks to reduce overhead costs.

- Take advantage of promotional offers, discounts, or bulk pricing options provided by domain registrars, auction platforms, or other service providers. Be mindful of cost-saving opportunities without compromising quality or essential services.

By effectively budgeting and managing expenses, domain investors can optimize their financial resources, control costs, and improve the overall profitability of their domain portfolio. Consistent monitoring, evaluation, and adjustments to your budget and expense allocation will help ensure financial sustainability and successful long-term domain investing.

11.3 Documenting Domain Acquisitions, Sales, & Expenses

Documenting domain acquisitions, sales, and expenses is a critical aspect of financial management in domain investing. Proper documentation ensures transparency, accuracy, and compliance with tax regulations. It also enables you to track your financial performance, assess the value of your portfolio, and make informed decisions. Here are some important considerations when documenting domain acquisitions, sales, and expenses:

Maintain Detailed Records:

- Keep a comprehensive record of all domain acquisitions, including the purchase date, domain name, purchase price, and any associated costs such as broker fees or escrow fees.

- For domain sales, record the date of sale, domain name, sale price, and any expenses incurred during the sales process, such as commissions or auction fees.
- Document expenses related to domain management, including domain renewals, registration fees, marketing costs, legal and professional fees, and any other relevant expenses.

Organize Documentation:

- Use a centralized system, such as a digital folder or cloud storage, to store all your domain-related documents. Organize them in a logical and structured manner for easy retrieval and reference.
- Consider creating separate folders for acquisitions, sales, expenses, and supporting documents like invoices, receipts, contracts, or correspondence.

Utilize Accounting Software or Spreadsheets:

- Consider using accounting software or spreadsheet tools to track and record your domain transactions and expenses. This helps automate calculations, generate reports, and facilitate analysis.
- Use dedicated columns or fields to input relevant information such as date, domain name, transaction type (acquisition/sale), amounts, and associated expenses.

Capture Supporting Documents:

- Keep copies of invoices, receipts, payment confirmations, or any other supporting documents for each transaction and expense. These documents validate the financial transactions and serve as evidence for auditing or tax purposes.

Stay Compliant with Tax Regulations:

- Familiarize yourself with the tax regulations and reporting requirements specific to domain investing in your jurisdiction. Consult with a tax professional to ensure compliance and maximize tax benefits.

- Maintain accurate and up-to-date records of your domain transactions to facilitate tax reporting, including any capital gains or losses realized from domain sales.

Regularly Review and Reconcile:

- Schedule regular reviews of your documentation to ensure accuracy and completeness. Reconcile your records with financial statements, bank statements, and other relevant financial documents to identify any discrepancies.

- Conduct periodic audits or assessments to assess the financial health of your domain portfolio, identify areas for improvement, and make informed investment decisions.

Properly documenting domain acquisitions, sales, and expenses is not only important for financial management but also for demonstrating the value and history of your domain portfolio. It provides transparency, supports valuation assessments, and helps build credibility when engaging in domain sales or negotiations. By maintaining accurate and organized documentation, you can effectively manage your financial records, meet legal and tax obligations, and make informed decisions to optimize your domain investing endeavors.

12.

DEVELOPING YOUR DOMAIN NAME: TIPS & STRATEGIES

" I use social media as an idea generator, trend mapper and strategic compass for all of our online business ventures."

-Paul Barron

Now you understand how to research for finding valuable domain name, buy and sell domain name and how to build a solid domain portfolio. In domain investing, buying, and selling domains are not the only path for making profit. There are many other alternatives which we discuss in this chapter. If a domain name is not selling or you want to keep it for longer period, you can increase its value and at the same time you can make some profit by developing the domain name. Domain development is one of the most lucrative online businesses today. Besides flipping domain names, there are many ways to make profit in domain name investment. Most of these alternative paths require patience and little effort to generate a steady stream of revenue. We divided all these different approaches into two categories based on the time, efforts and knowledge required to implement them. Here is the two categories which we are going to discuss in this chapter:

Short-term Approach:

This category includes all the methods which require less time, easy to implement and quick in producing results. We need comparably less efforts to implement these methods for generating profit and increasing the value of domains. I will discuss following methods under this category:

- Creating Blog or Website
- Sell Advertising Space
- Domain name parking

- Domain name leasing
- Waiting for best offer

Long-term Approach:

This category includes all the methods which require long time, in-depth knowledge, and a lot of patience to see any considerable results. To implement methods under this category, you need to have in-depth knowledge about specific niche, and you may need to invest additional capital to see any significant results. This category is most suited when you want to keep some domain name for longer period of time and ready to invest your time and efforts in developing them. I will discuss following methods under this category:

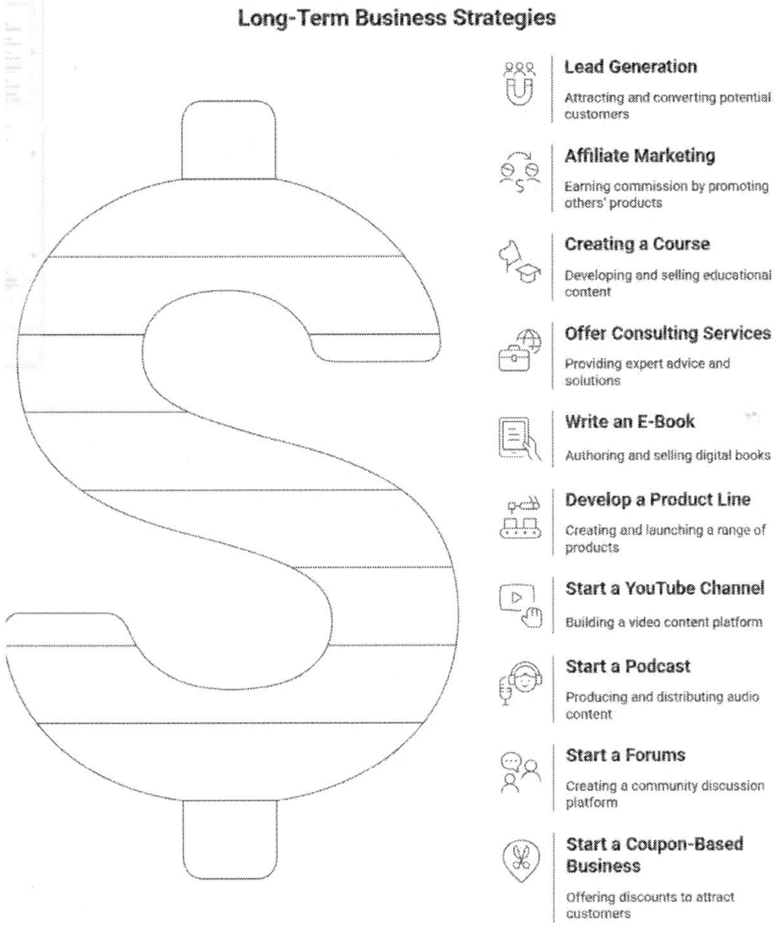

- Lead Generation
- Affiliate marketing
- Creating a Course
- Offer Consulting Services
- Write an E-Book
- Develop a product line
- Start a YouTube Channel
- Start a Podcast
- Start a Forums
- Start a coupon-based business

Don't worry if you have no knowledge about any of these different methods. I will explain them in detail and even if you still don't understand or not ready to invest time in these methods, I will discuss how you can hire freelancers to do it for you. There are thousands of freelancers for doing anything related to your domain name business whether it's developing a website, writing content for your website, creating logo, copywriting, producing video etc. I will discuss about hiring a freelancer in detail. So, without any further delay, let's start with the short-term approach first.

12.1 Create a Blog or Website

Creating a blog or website is a great way to make money from domain development. With artificial intelligence system like wix (https://www.wix.com/), you can easily create, design, and develop website with few clicks. It doesn't require any programming skill, design, or development knowledge. Although wix charge a small amount of fee (starting at $14/month) to provide their system for web-development, it is suitable for those who have no web development knowledge and no time to work manually on their website. If you don't want to pay, there is another solution called CMS (Content Management System) for developing website without any coding. WordPress is the most popular CMS and currently more than 40% of entire internet website built on WordPress i.e., till 2021, more than 455 million websites (out of 1.3 billion website) are using WordPress. Third solution is to use basic HTML (HyperText markup Language) and CSS (Cascading Style Sheet) to develop your website if you have knowledge of these web technology.

There are hundreds of different ways to monetize your website or blog. You can use your website to generate advertising revenue, or you can create mailing list of people interested in specific niche and later promote and sell relevant product to them. We will discuss some of monetization method one by one.

If you're interested in developing a blog or website on your domain name, here are a few steps to help you get started:

Step one: Choose a niche

When you start to develop a blog or website on your domain name, it's important to choose a niche. This will help you focus your efforts on specific direction and target a specific audience. I already defined in previous section that a niche is a segment or small part of a broader market and it usually focus on people with common, specific interest. It's also important to choose a niche that you're interested in and know something about it. Another factor you need to consider is relevancy of your domain name with the niche. For example, if you have registered a domain name "fitnesstracker.com", you should create a website focusing only fitness tracker. Your website should not cover other detail like fitness exercise, or diet plan or fitness equipment. The content of your website should be relevant to keyword of domain if you had registered a keyword specific domain. If you have no keyword in your domain name, you are free to develop website which you think can generate revenue for you. For example, if you have a domain name "golu.com", it (golu) didn't represent any specific product, service, or subject. You are free to develop any brand or niche on this domain name. But always try to develop website in specific niche and target a specific audience. This will help you to monetize your website later.

Step two: Research the market

Before starting a domain development, it's important to do some research on the market. This will help you determine if there is demand for the products and services you plan to offer. It will also help you determine what price points to use for your products and services. There are hundreds of tools to research for the market. For example, you can use the google keyword planner, to check the search volume, competition, and average monthly searches for a keyword. You can find out which keyword have top bid amount and less competition and plan to rank your website for that keyword in search engine. If you are not able to brainstorm new keyword, google keyword planner can also help you to get keyword ideas related to your domain name. You can also spy on competitor website by using google keyword planner tool. Google keyword planner tool can generate keyword suggestions from the URL, and you can use your competitor website URL to get an idea which keyword they are using on their website. You can also use the keyword planner to know what question people are asking and what they are interested in. To get this information, you simply need to filter the result in keyword planner as follow: Filter > Keyword text > contains > enter one of the following: who, what, why, when, where how. If you are developing website for a local region like "plumber.miami", you can use google keyword planner to check keyword volume at city level.

There are many other alternative tools which you can use to research the market for your website. Some of these tools are, Keyword everywhere chrome extension, https://keywordtool.io/, https://keywordplanner.net/, https://ahrefs.com/, https://moz.com/, https://www.spyfu.com/. You can use these tools and research the market and rank your website in google.

Step three: Choose web hosting plan

To develop your blog or website, you need a web server where you can store all your content and host your website. There are thousands of web hosting company available where pricing start as low as $1.99 per month to $ 100 per month based on your requirement. Web hosting server store your content and whenever a visitor visit your website, your hosting provider get the data from server and display to the visitor.

There is different type of web hosting plans based on pricing, type and feature they are offering:

WordPress Hosting plan:

These web servers are specifically designed for WordPress, and they support one-click installation, automated software updates and require minimum efforts to get started. I recommend this hosting plan if you are just starting and don't know much about server installation, server updates etc. These are usually cheapest option to start a website.

Shared Hosting Plan:

In this plan, a large server is shared by many websites and eventually cost is less for all as compared to other plan. This is most suitable for personal website, and small business website which has less than 300,000 page view per month.

VPS (Virtual Private Server) hosting Plan:

In this plan, a physical server is divided virtually into multiple virtual servers. Each partition or virtual server is isolated from the other. It is best suited for medium to high traffic websites.

Dedicated Server:

This plan uses a completely isolated server to host a website. That mean there is no other website hosting on the server and the server completely dedicated to your website. This plan is little expensive as compared to shared hosting and VPS plan.

Cloud Hosting plan:

This plan uses a cluster of multiple servers to minimize downtime of the website. This plan is useful if your website has millions of users, or you are running a big ecommerce website. It offers many features such as automatic load balancing, notification if a server goes down, regional hosting of website in different region or country.

To setup your website, you can consider these different hosting plans and compare several hosting providers. There are many good hosting company which offer very cheap hosting services such as bluehost, GoDaddy, Namecheap, hostinger, google cloud, Amazon web services (AWS), digital ocean etc. Based on your budget and end goal, you can choose different plans from these hosting companies.

Step four: Choose CMS or Technology for website

To develop a website, you need to create content, web pages and other media (such as video, images, infographics etc.) and manage them on the server. You can do it manually yourself if you have knowledge of HTML, CSS, JavaScript or other web development technologies. If you don't want to do it yourself, there are other option called CMS (Content Management System). WordPress is ne of the famous CMS for developing website and it is open source i.e., you don't need to pay for using WordPress on your website. It helps the user to create and update the website without any programming knowledge. It provides an easy-to-use interface which you can use to write content on your website and update the website. WordPress allows updating, customizing, and managing the website from its back-end CMS and components. It provides a login interface for admin using which he can change the setting, appearance, content of the website. Here is some basic information about the WordPress:

WordPress Post:

To create dynamic content such as blog, articles, and other multimedia content, we use WordPress posts. WordPress uses reverse chronological order to display the post on website i.e., newest posts is shown above. This is useful if you continuously updating your website with new articles or blog post. It is very easy to add a new post on the website. You can login into the admin panel and from the dashboard, click on 'Posts' and then 'Add New' to adda new posts on the website. Visitor of the website can comment on the posts and usually post-date, author name is included in the posts. For WordPress post, we usually use social media button so that visitor can share them, and more people can visit the website. Posts are organized using categories and tags.

WordPress Pages:

Pages are used for static content which stay on your website for longer period. For example, home page, privacy policy, disclaimer, contact us page, about us page. These pages are static and not regularly updated. For this static type of content, WordPress pages are used. To add a new page, you need to login into admin panel and from dashboard, you can click on 'Pages' and then 'Add New'. For WordPress pages, social media buttons are not used, and they are static and doesn't make sense to share them. Also, visitor can't comment on the WordPress pages. Pages are organized using a hierarchical structure.

WordPress Theme:

If you want to change the overall appearance, design, structure, layout, navigation, colors, and everything else look-wise, you can use WordPress theme. A WordPress theme is very helpful if you want to make large-scale changes in your website, it helps you drastically changing the overall appearance of the website. There are thousands of free and paid themes available to use on your website. ThemeForest (https://themeforest.net/) is one of the major sources to download WordPress theme. You can find hundreds of customized themes made for specific niche whether its travel, business, online learning, hospitality, restaurant etc. There can be only one theme active at a time on your website. When you install WordPress, there is default theme installed on the website. If you want you can use that, but it is very basic and gives a dull look to your website. I recommend you to use a customizes theme related to niche of your website.

WordPress Plugin:

If you want to add special functionality or a new feature to your website, you can use WordPress plugin. There are thousands of plugins available to download for any functionality you can imagine. Each plugin is built to provide a special feature and functionality for your website. For example, "All in One SEO" plugin is used for improving the on-page SEO of the website. It helps you add SEO title of the page/post, meta description about the content, targeted keywords, generate XML sitemaps, connect your site to Google Search Console, optimize it for social media, and more. If you need any special feature or functionality on your website, you can search for relevant plugin and use it on your website.

Step five: Set-up your website

Now you have domain name, web hosting and CMS for your website, it is time to setup thew website and connect the domain name to your server IP address where website is hosted. Once you install WordPress and install a customized theme, you can visit the homepage of your website. Although there is nothing on your website now, but you can check if its working or not by visiting your URL.

Step five: Create content or blog post

Once your website is set up and ready to go, it's time to start creating content. One of the best ways to do this is by creating blog posts related to your niche. This will help you attract potential customers and establish yourself as an authority in this field. You can use WordPress plugin to optimize on-page SEO so that your page can better rank in search engine.

Step six: Market your business

To make money from domain development, you will need to market your business. There are several ways to do this, including online marketing methods such as SEO and PPC. You can write articles around a specific keyword so that your website rank higher for that keyword. You can also use offline marketing methods such as print advertising and direct mail.

Useful Insight:

It is not easy and feasible to develop all your domain name if you have a portfolio of hundreds of domain name. You need to strike a balance between time spent and revenue generated and develop only those domain names which can perform better in term of search engine ranking. It is worthy to spent time on developing a full website only if you are planning to keep the domain name for longer period. You can always develop small one page website for keyword-oriented domain name which have high chance of getting good traffic from search engine and take less time to develop.

12.2 Sell Advertising Space

Selling advertising space is another way to make money from domain development. You can sell ad space on your blog or website to other companies who want more exposure for their businesses.

This strategy works best when you have built up a good amount of traffic and have a large audience that will see the ads. If you don't have enough traffic yet, then you might consider selling advertising space on web directories instead of your site or blog.

You can also use this strategy if you are just starting with your business and do not have a lot of capital at stake. The main advantage is that it doesn't take much effort to implement this method, but it does require some time before getting any results. The result you received from this method depend on niche you built website on and how much time and efforts you are putting on the website. If you have a ton of useful information to show on the website, you will get more visitor, more clicks on the ads, and eventually more profit.

How to get started?

Generating revenue from advertisement space selling can be a bit daunting, but it's not as difficult as you might think. Here are a few steps to help you get started:

Step one: Choose a Domain Name

You already have the domain name on which you want to develop website for advertisement space. The content of the website and domain name should be relevant to each other. Also, the advertisement you want to show on your website should be relevant to your web content.

Step two: Register a Web Hosting Account

Once you have chosen a domain name, you need to register a web hosting account. This is where you will host your website or blog. There are several different web hosting providers available, so you should do some research before making any decisions.

Step three: Build a website or Blog

Once you have registered your domain name and web hosting account, it's time to start building your website or blog. This can be done through WordPress, Joomla, Drupal, or other content management systems available online today! It will take some time to get your website or blog looking the way you want it, but it's worth the effort.

Step four: Register on ad network

To generate revenue from advertisement, you can't depend on directly selling ads to businesses, you need to register on ad networks. There are two types of advertisement placement on the website. First one is traditional advertising using banner on sidebar or header of article. Second option is to use contextual ads, paid content recommendation, and paid link in between your blog post. There are several ad networks available to help you monetize your website using advertisement. Let's discuss some of the best ad network available today:

Google AdSense (https://www.google.com/adsense/start/): This is Google service which you can register and start using on your website. It is one of popular advertisement service available on internet. It is very easy to register with Google AdSense, you just need to sign up for an AdSense account and you are ready to show ads on your blog or website. Google servers the contextual ads based on your website content and there is an option to allow google to find optimal location for the ads so that more people click on it, and you earn more money. Google ads are optimized for mobile phone and tablets, and you can get even more clicks from mobile phone also. The minimum payout at Google AdSense is $100.

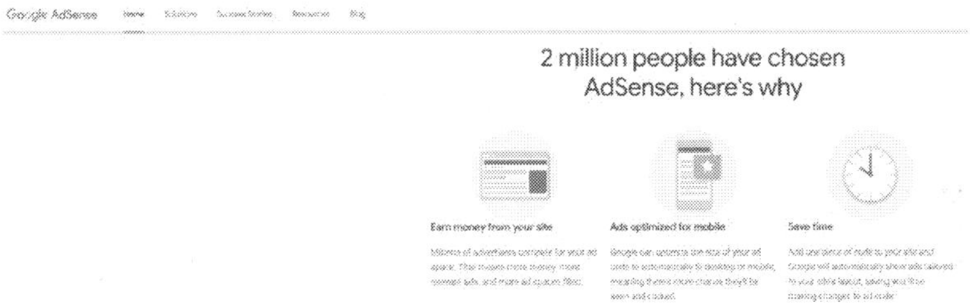

Media.net (https://www.media.net/): It is my second choice if I go for generating revenue using advertisement. Media.net is one of the largest ad networks and have very good reputation in term of payout and ad quality. It provides both text and banner ads, you can test both on your website and choose the one which perform better on your website. It also provides multiple ad formats for one ad tag which further help you to select best ad format for your site and audience. The ads offered by media.net are contextual, relevant, and cookie-free which easily match with the look and feel of your website. The minimum payout at Media.net is $100.

AdThrive (https://adthrive.com/): If you are developing your blog or website in niche like travel, home, hospitality, food, restaurants, parenting, child-care etc., then AdThrive is the best ad network for you. You can also join the network even if you are not in one of these categories, but AdThrive is most suited for above mentioned categories. It offers banner ads of all dimension type which you can easily use on sidebar, header, footer or in between the article. Another advantage of AdThrive is that it offers guaranteed payout even if they don't get paid from the advertiser. Sometime advertiser didn't pay to the ad network and then ad network is not able to pay to creator. This happens with me once in one of my websites. But with AdThrive, they give you 100% guaranty that even if advertiser didn't pay, the will pay to the creator.

To join the AdThrive network, you need to have at least 100,000 page view on your website. Another fact about AdThrive is that it targets mostly US based traffic. So, if you have lot of international traffic, you may not see good result with AdThrive.

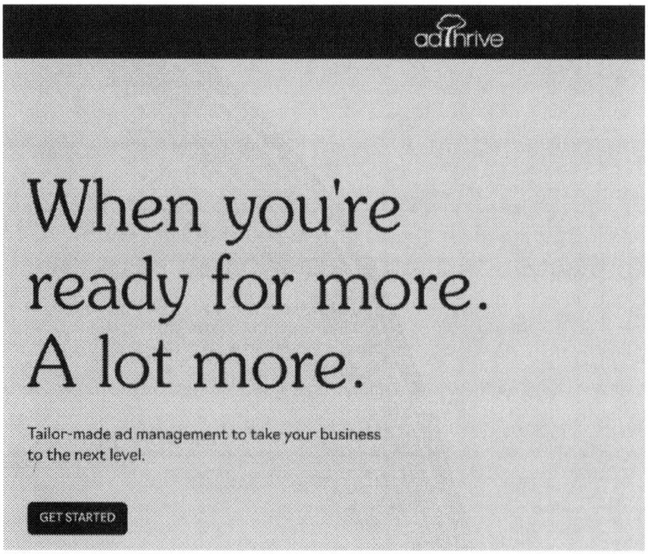

Mediavine (https://www.mediavine.com/): It is the ad network which work on "creator first" approach i.e., they offered guaranteed payout to the creator even if they didn't get paid by advertiser. As compared to AdThrive, minimum traffic requirement for website is 50,000 visit per month to join the Mediavine ad network. It is similar to AdThrive in respect to type of website which should join this network i.e., Mediavine is preferable if your website niche is about lifestyle such as outing, travel, tourism, food, hotels, etc.

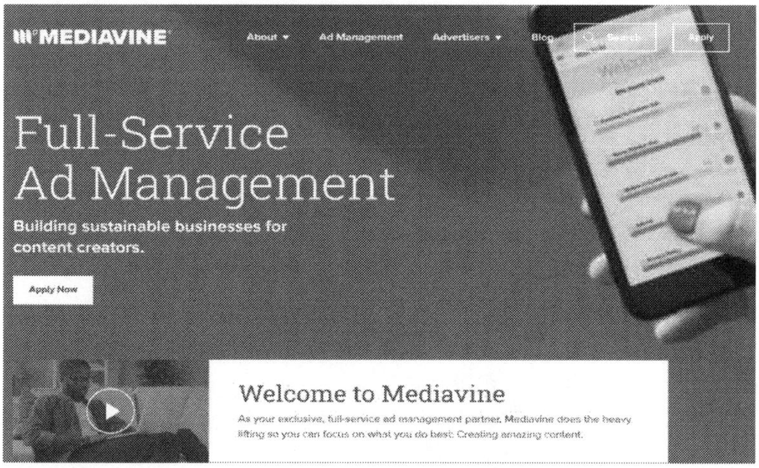

Ezoic (https://www.ezoic.com/): Ezoic uses the machine learning and artificial intelligence technology to find out the best placement of ads, and test different ads on your website to get higher-earning ads setting. It offers flexibility to their customer so that they can run the ads in different setting. For example, if your goal is to sell the domain name in near future, you can run the ads for maximum profit or if you want to keep the domain name for longer period, you can choose to run ads for best user experience. If you are not sure how long you keep the domain name, you can run the ads in a balance mode i.e., maximum profit with great user experience. As compared to other ad network which we discussed above, Ezoic is easy to join with only 10,000 session per month and minimum payout is only $20 i.e., you can withdraw your earning once you reach the minimum threshold of $20.

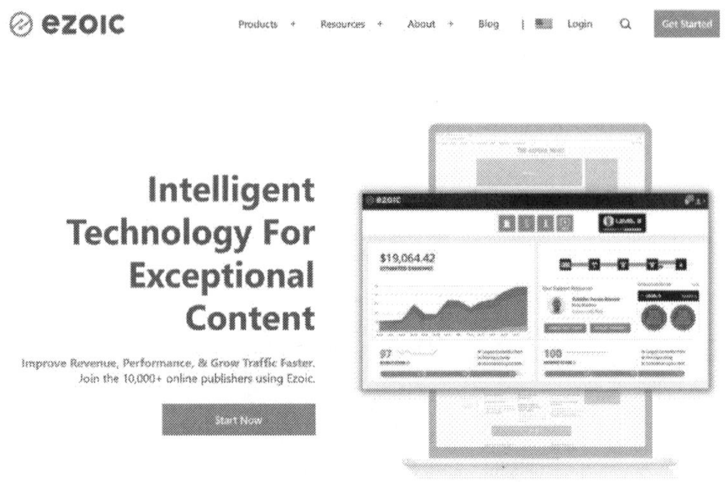

Taboola (https://www.taboola.com/): This ad network is best suited if your website has more than 500,000 visitors per month. Taboola is famous for relevant, interesting, and new ads related to your website content. Currently, there are more than 13000 advertisers registered with Taboola. I think it work best with big publisher and magazines who have more than million visitors each month.

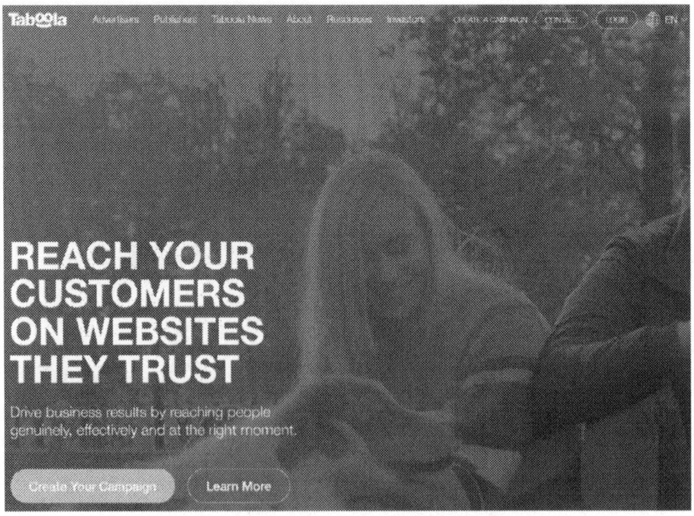

Infolinks (https://www.infolinks.com/): This ad network provides the opportunity to match the ads with keyword on your website. Infolinks provide the links for their ads and when visitor hover over the link, they can see the ads. Apart from that, infolinks also offers ads for notification bar that stick to the bottom of your screen, contextual ads, vertical banner ads for sidebar of your website. Infolinks also claims that they provide high viewability for best performance of ads, and they provide best placement of ads on your website. The minimum payout for infolinks is $50.

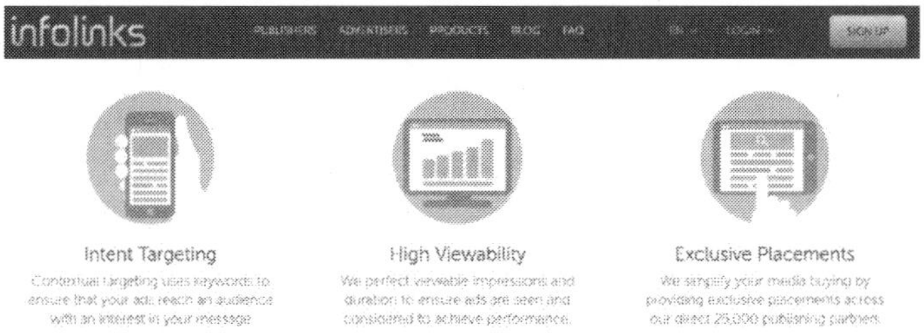

Revcontent (https://www.revcontent.com/): It is content recommendation ad network which focus only on high quality websites. They have a history of rejecting a lot of websites just because they want to work with only quality website. However, if you have a high-quality website, you can apply to revcontent even if you have low traffic as the minimum requirement of revcontent is only 50,000 visitors per month. Also, the minimum payout is only $50.

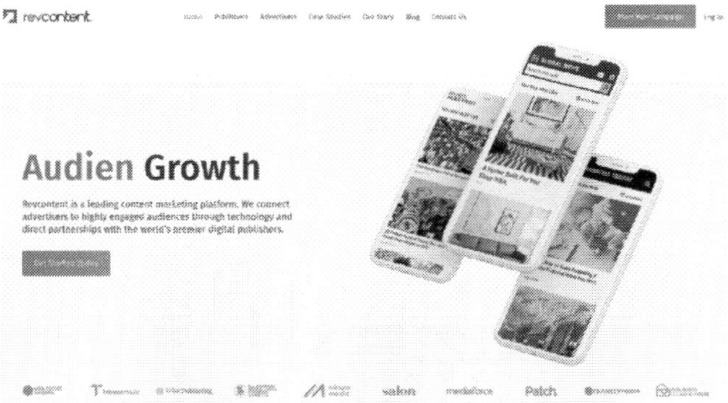

Adversal (https://www.adversal.com/): This ad networks help you to monetize your website by showing video and banner ads on your website. It also provides contextual ads like other ad network and help you by recommending the relevant ads for your website content. It claims to be a "set it and forget it" solution for monetizing your website. You don't need a contract or commitment with this ad network. To join this ad network, you need to have at least 50,000 page views per month.

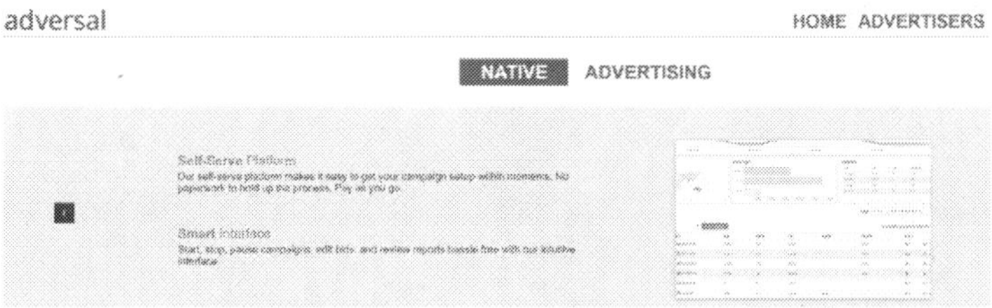

Besides these, there are many other ad networks which you can consider for monetizing your website. Some of these ad networks are BuySellAds (https://www.buysellads.com/), Sovrn (https://www.sovrn.com/), PropellerAds (https://propellerads.com/), and Monumetric (https://www.monumetric.com/) etc.

Step five: Promote your website

Now that you have a website or blog up and running, it's time to start marketing your business. You can do this through online marketing methods such as search engine optimization (SEO), social media marketing, and article marketing. There are also several offline marketing methods that you can use, such as print advertising, direct mail, and telemarketing.

Useful Insight:

Advertising is always a great way of earning some revenue from the domain name. Choose your ad network wisely and don't expect to be a millionaire by this method. It will surely help you to generate some profit, but it will take time to get traffic on your website.

12.3 Domain Name Parking

When you have a great domain name but are not sure what to do with it, domain name parking companies can be a great option. These companies will show advertisement and links on your domain name, meaning that the domain will redirect to one of their websites. In most cases, you will receive a commission on any traffic or sales that the parked website generates.

There are several different domain name parking companies out there, so it is important to do your research before deciding which one to use. Some of the most well-known include Sedo.com, GoDaddy.com, and ParkingCrew.com. All these companies offer a variety of services, so be sure to read the terms and conditions carefully before signing up and paying any money.

how to get started?

To get started, you will need to follow these simple steps:

Step one: research

Before you get started, you must do your research. This means studying different parking companies and their terms and conditions. You should also look over how much each of the companies pays out to their affiliates.

Step two: sign up for an account

Once you have finished your research, you will be ready to sign up for an account. Generally speaking, the sign-up process will be very quick and easy, but you should still read all of the terms and conditions thoroughly before committing to anything.

Step three: place your domain name for sale

After signing up with a parking company, you will need to find a domain name that you would like to use for domain name parking. Offer the domain name to these parking companies to show advertisement. After they accepted your domain name, they start showing relevant ads on it.

Step four: receive payment

You will earn the advertised commission every time one of your visitors visit your domain name and click on any link or ads. Generally, this takes a few days to happen, but it will vary from company to company. More the visitor you get, higher is the income you make from this. There are Different domain parking companies offer different percentage on the commission generated from ads on your domain name. It can be anything from 20 to 80%.

Useful Insight:

Domain name parking is not something which can earn you a huge amount of money. If you are not using any other approach, domain name parking can help you to get some revenue to cover the cost of your yearly domain registration.

12.4 Domain Name Leasing

Domain leasing is a great way to make money from domain development. You can lease a domain name to a company for some time, and then charge them a fee for each time the domain is used. This can be a great way to make some extra money, and it can also help you to build up your domain portfolio.

How to get started?

To get started with domain leasing, you need to follow these steps

Step one: Find a business for leasing your domain

When you have a domain name which look premium and valuable enough that other will be interested to lease it, you need to find a suitable business who can lease it. You can find potential client by doing your research or finding contact information for existing businesses and approaching them. This is often the best option, as you already have an idea about their business, and you know they will need a new website at some point.

If you don't want to do that hard work, there are several companies which can help you to lease out your domain name. you just need to list your domain name on these companies/marketplaces, set a price and allow them to find a renter. Let's discuss few major companies active in the field of domain leasing and their offerings:

Epik (https://www.epik.com/buy/lease-domains/): This is one of the best marketplaces for leasing out your domain name. Epik offers a domain name leasing and renting option as well as domain management option. Here, a domain lessor (who own the domain name) lists the domain name and term and conditions for leasing domain. Domain lessor can also set a selling price if he is interested in selling it. Domain lessee (who is interested in leasing out your domain name) can search and find the appropriate domain name, lease it out and save a payment method for monthly billing.

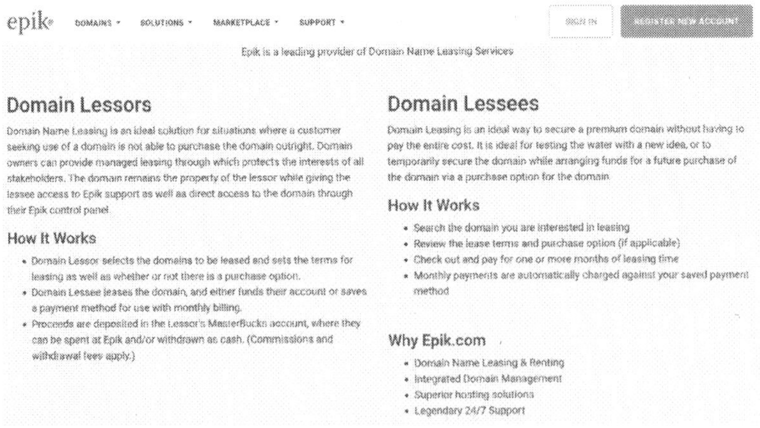

Venture (https://venture.com/): Venture is best marketplaces if you are looking to lease out the premium domain name. It features the best domain name on their website home page with monthly rent. You can find the great domain name with few clicks. You can also select the domain name based on different categories such as acronym, arts, travel, science etc.

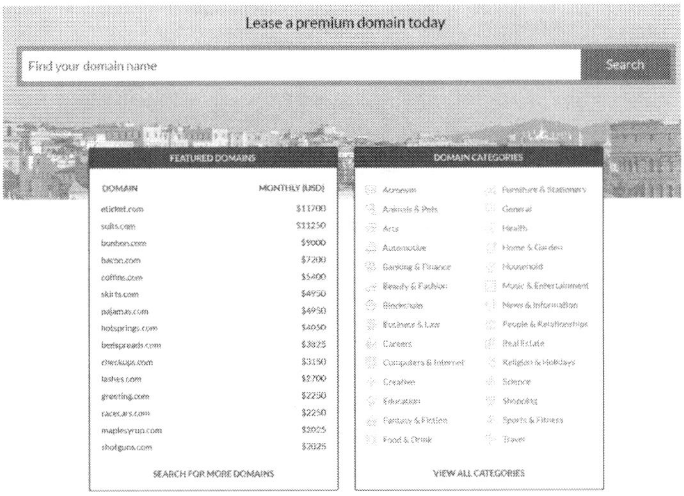

One World Hosting (https://oneworldhosting.com/lease.html): It offers leasing program to protect your ownership of the domain name. The leasing term can be anywhere between 1 to 3 years. One world hosting is in the domain business from 16 years and have a very good reputation in domain leasing.

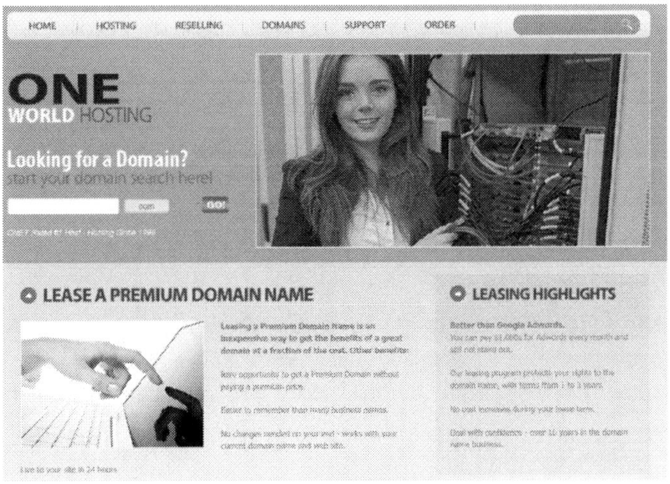

Step two: Sign a leasing agreement

Once you have found someone who wants to lease your domain, sign an agreement. You should outline the duration of the lease, and what they will need to do if they want to renew it. Then, create a schedule for how much each time the domain is used will cost them. This way, you will be able to charge them a fixed amount for entire duration or a monthly rental fee.

Step three: Collect payment

Once you have signed an agreement with a leasing client, you should collect payment at the beginning of every month. You can do this using PayPal or another online payment system, and it is best if you include everything in the monthly fee so that your client isn't in control of the cost.

Step four: Update the leasing agreement

You should update your leasing agreement every year to make sure that it is still suitable for both you and your client. This will make the process of leasing very secure, and it will allow you to continue accepting money from them.

Useful Insight:

Domain leasing is only useful if you are holding some premium domain name. You can use domain appraisal tools to determine the value of your domain name and with experience, you can tell if a domain name is worthy enough to offer for leasing.

12.5 Waiting for best offer

If you are a full time professional or doing other business and take domain investing as side hustle, you may not have time to develop your domain name. In that case, you can hold and wait for best offer for your domain name. This strategy is good only if you have other source of income, you can afford yearly cost of domain name and you are holding premium domain name. I don't recommend holding hundreds of random domain name which has no value as you end up wasting your money in that case. It is always better to develop something on your domain name and generate some revenue so that a domain name covers at least its yearly cost. If you don't want to do yourself, you can always hire freelancer to develop your domain name.

12.6 Lead generation

To start with lead generation, first you need to understand what a lead is. A lead can be any individual who is interested in buying a service or products, but he is not ready yet. You have experience it before in your everyday life. For example, if you like a laptop, you read about its configuration, size, price etc. You browse different website to explore the same laptop, but you are not ready yet, reason can be anything such as you may want to explore other similar laptop, you are waiting for a deal (e.g., black Friday, new year etc.), you have not enough savings to spent on the laptop. In this case, you are a lead for the business.

Lead generation is the process of collecting information and contact details (email id, phone number etc.) of such people who are interested in a product or service but not ready yet. You can collect the information by attracting your target audience usually either by writing engaging content or by offering something for free.

How to get started?

So, how do you get started in this business? Here are a few steps:

Step one: Identify your target audience

To be successful in lead generation, you need to identify your target audience. You need to create a buyer persona for your target audience which can have different details about your potential lead. For example, you need to identify what is the age, location, job title, purchasing power, age, gender, interests of your ideal customer. You need to define exactly who should be your ideal customer and what are problem they are facing which your product can solve.

Step two: Produce engaging and informative content

Once you have your buyer persona, you can start producing attracting and engaging content. The content should be engaging for your potential customer not for you i.e., think about the interest and problem of your buyer before writing any article or producing any video or multimedia.

Step three: Attract the visitor who are looking for solution

Promote your content at all places where you think your potential client is visiting. You can use on-page SEO, engaging content to get the organic traffic or you can use paid traffic using Facebook ads, Instagram ads and google ads. Before using any paid method, always think of return on investment (ROI) i.e., the money you are spending on ads should be maximum 10% of the revenue you generate from lead.

Step four: Collect their contact detail and other information

Collect the visitor information when they visit your web page or social media page so that you can contact them later. To get the contact information, you need to offer something for free, it can be an eBook, trial version of software, anything that can help the visitors and add value in their life.

Step five: Qualify your lead and get paid

At the last step, you need to convert the lead into a prospect and then ultimately a paying customer. To do that, you can send weekly newsletter, special promotions or additional content to your potential lead and attract them to buy the product. If you are generating lead for third party, then direct them to their sale page and get paid when they buy the service or product.

12.7 Affiliate marketing

If you can promote and market another person product on your website and earn a commission for each sale, it is called affiliate marketing. Affiliate marketing is good for those domain name which are relevant to some product, belong to some niche or have specific keyword which can help to rank your website in search engine ranking. For example, if you are holding domain name such as "top10gadgets.com", you can easily earn commission by recommending 10 phones, 10 watches, 10 laptops, 10 keyboards etc. on your website. You can write an article for each gadget type and compare their features, make it engaging and informative and in between you can put your affiliate link for promoting the products. Every time someone read your article and make a purchase using the affiliate link from the article, you will earn a commission. There is no extra cost to buyer as he will get the product in same price if he purchases it without using your link.

It is one of the easiest methods to generate passive revenue from your domain name. There are thousands of online marketplace and website where you can sign up for affiliate marketing and become their affiliate and earn extra cash promoting their products. It can be a physical product such as household items, electronics, clothes etc. or it can be a digital product such as eBooks, software, data, plugin, WordPress theme etc. From my personal experience, I can tell digital products always pay higher commission per sale as compared to physical products. The commission you get can be anywhere between 3% to 60% of the product price.

How to get started?

So, how do you get started in this business? Here are a few steps:

Step one: Choose a niche

To become a successful affiliate marketer, you need to choose a niche or product category which you are interested in marketing. It should be relevant to your domain name, and you should have some knowledge or experience in using the product. I don't recommend promoting products which you don't know anything about. If you have some domain name and you have no knowledge about the relevant products, you can always order some relevant product, try it and if you like the product, you can promote it. Another way of gaining knowledge is to read about the product, watch video on YouTube, check the review of customer who already bought it.

Step two: Register on different affiliate platform

Now you know your niche and it's time to register on different affiliate marketplace to start promoting product. To choose a best affiliate marketing program is crucial part of getting success in affiliate marketing. If you don't choose wisely, you may have to wait for months to get your first payout. On the other hand, a wise choice can get your first earning within a week. It is "make or break" situation and you should spend time wisely to research different affiliate program. Here I am providing list of affiliate program which works for me, and I have great experience in working with. Here is my recommendation:

Amazon Associates Affiliate Program (https://affiliate-program.amazon.com/): Amazon offers one of the best affiliate programs and it is very reputable, trusted, and oldest affiliate program in the market. You can promote almost anything available on amazon ranging from household items to electronics. Link creation in amazon is very easy, with few click you can get affiliate link of any product. There are more than 400 million products available on amazon which you can choose for your affiliate program. The minimum payout threshold for amazon is only $10.

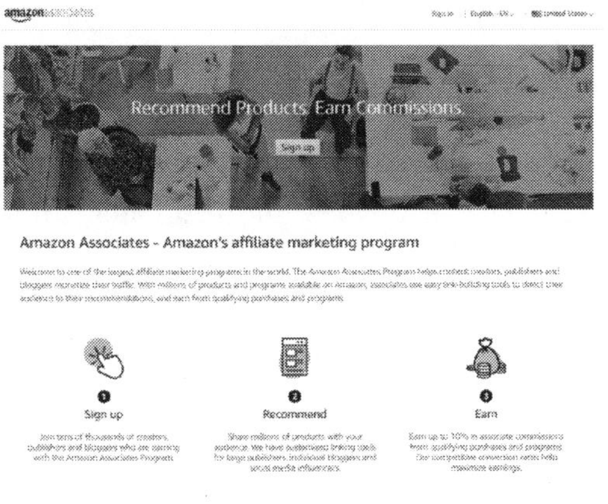

CJ (Commission Junction) Affiliate Program (https://www.cj.com/): CJ or commission junction affiliate program represent more than 2000 big brands such as Walgreen, Disney shops, Staples, Samsung, trip advisor etc. Although CJ provide a great support to their affiliate marketer, you need some affiliate experience to be successful on commission junction. They provide a n intuitive interface and dashboard where you can use different metrics to check performance of different products. The minimum payout threshold for CJ is $50.

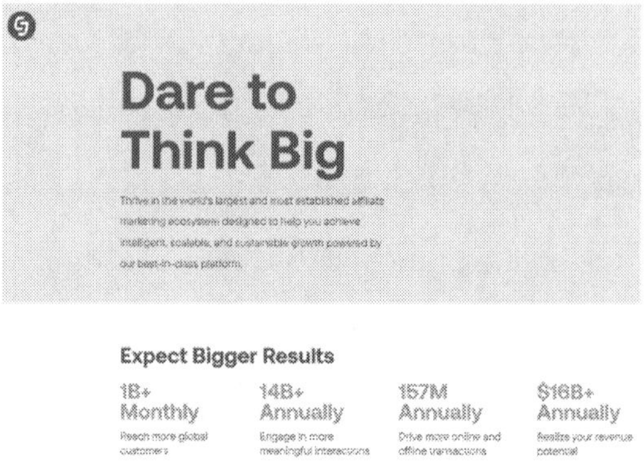

ShareASale Affiliate Program (https://www.shareasale.com/info/): ShareASale is one of most prominent affiliate markets which have more than 5000 affiliate programs. You should choose ShareASale if you are looking for new brands and tangential products. They offer simplest and easy to use dashboard to measure performance of your affiliate links. The minimum payout for ShareASale is $50.

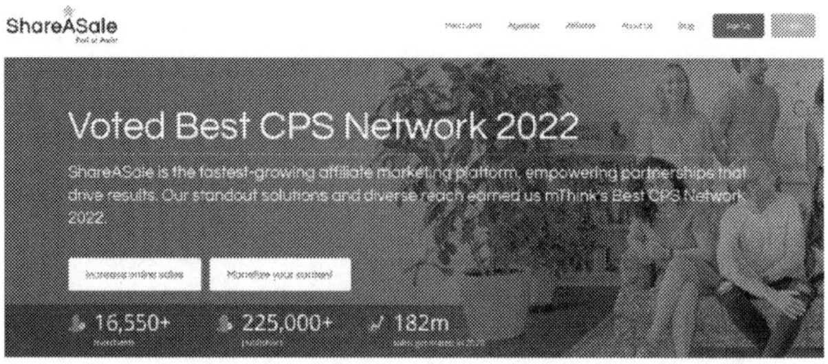

ClickBank Affiliate Program (https://www.clickbank.com/): If you are looking to promote digital products, ClickBank is the solution for you. ClickBank is started in 1998 and one of the oldest affiliate networks. It provides a super easy solution for digital products in almost all categories. You can signup easily even if you have no website ready yet. The minimum payout threshold is $50.

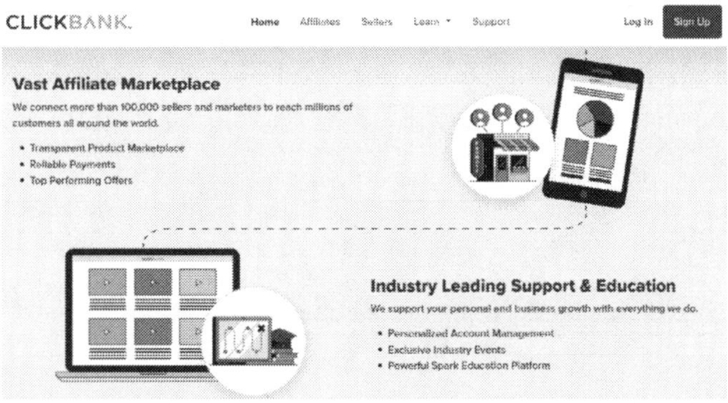

Besides these, there are many other affiliate networks which you can consider when you start working and have good experience in affiliate marketing. Here is some of my other recommendation:

Rakuten Advertising Affiliate Program

Impact Affiliate Program

Awin Affiliate Program

Etsy Affiliate Program

eBay Partner Network Affiliate Program

Fiverr Affiliate Program

PepperJam Network

FlexOffers Affiliate Program

Avangate Affiliate Program

MaxBounty Affiliate Program

LinkConnector Affiliate Program

Step three: Select the product to affiliate

After registering on the affiliate program on different affiliate market or network, you need to select the product which you can promote using your website or blog. Always remember, don't promote a product just because you will get high commission on each sale. Promote only if you really trust a brand and you think it will be useful and best at that price in the market. If you care about your visitors, customers only then you can stay longer in this business. If you promote product of low quality, people start losing trust in you and your website.

Step four: Get link of product

Now you have a list of products which you intend to promote on your blog. Next step is to get the affiliate link of product from the affiliate market you already signed up. For most of the affiliate market, it is straightforward and super easy to do. You just need to login and find the product using the search button and then click on 'get link', most of the market provide multiple forms of the link i.e., you can choose to have a text link to share, short link, text and image or image only with embedded link. The steps of getting link can be little different from market to markets, but it is super easy to figure out.

Step five: Promote on your website

One you have your affiliate links, you just need to embed those in your content, blog post, or article. You need to write engaging articles for your website. You can promote your website and article by on-page SEO, meta0description and getting backlink from other website. Higher the rank of your website in search engine, more people will visit your web page and higher the chances of generating great commission from your affiliate link.

Useful Insight:

Affiliate marketing is all about trust. You need to build trust with your audience and keep providing them high quality and valuable products. Don't put your interest first, f you want to be a successful affiliate marketer. Here are some key point and useful insight which you consider while doing affiliate marketing:

- I am repeating it again you should recommend only quality product which you have used before or have trust that they are valuable enough for the price your audience is paying for that.
- Don't rely on only one affiliate market or network. Promote products from different affiliate market. In this way, if someday one affiliate market is out of business, you have other option to work with.
- Check different metrics and optimize your conversion rate. Update your contents and affiliate link frequently.

- Get analytics detail about your traffic source. You can use the google analytics to find details such as bounce rate, geo location, what device your audience mostly using (mobile, tablet or computer), what time of day you are getting most visitors, what is the age, gender of your visitors etc.

12.8 Develop a digital product line

Developing a digital product line is another way to make money from domain development. This strategy involves creating and selling products that are digital in nature i.e., you can create product such as software, online tools (e.g., pdf to word converter,), image processing tools (e.g., image background remover online, edit picture online), and SEO tools etc.

You can either create these products yourself or partner with other companies that offer these types of services. By doing this, you will be able to offer your customers a solution for which either you can charge once or on monthly basis.

This approach has the advantage of being low risk because you don't have to invest in any inventory, and you don't have to worry about shipping products. It also has the potential to generate a lot of revenue if done correctly.

How to get started?

So, how do you get started in this business? Here are a few steps:

Step one: Choose a niche

One of the keys to success in this business is to choose a niche. This will help you to focus your efforts and make it easier to attract customers. Don't try to solve all problem of the world with your website. Identify a single and specific problem, built a solution around it and focus only on audience which need this solution.

Step two: Offer a high-quality product

When it comes to domain development, quality is key. Make sure that you offer a high-quality product that meets the needs of your customers. If you search online, there are hundreds of digital solutions for every single problem. How you distinguish yourself and why people should visit your website? If you can answer this question and offer a high-quality product or solution, you get success in the business.

Step three: Focus on customer service

Customer service is essential in this business. Make sure that you focus on providing excellent customer service and you will be able to attract and retain customers. Try to get feedback from customer on their experience about your product and always try to improve your product based on their feedback. Besides this, offer money back guaranty for a limited time if they don't like the product. This will help in long term to earn the trust of people and you can sell more.

Step four: Promote your business

Promotion is key in this business. You need to make sure that you are doing everything you can to get the word out about your products and services. Promote on all places where you think your potential customer exist. For example, if you are selling some WordPress plugin which is useful for restaurant business website, try to promote your product where restaurant owner or web developer are present. It can be social media group, YouTube channel, webinar or a local conference.

Useful Insight:

Before starting to develop any digital product, ready to put a lot of efforts and time in it. It is not easy and not short-term method. It requires a lot of dedication, knowledge and maybe some investment if you are thinking to hire a freelancer. Like any other approach, only quality products which solve a specific problem of the user will give good results.

12.9 Start a Forum or Blog

Starting a forum or blog is another way to make money from domain development. You can use this website as an outlet for your thoughts and opinions on the topic of domains, which will help to attract visitors who are interested in what you have to say. This strategy works best when you have built up some expertise in this area so that people want to listen.

How to get started?

Step one:

Gather information about topics related to your topic (or niche) and create an outline of what you want your blog post or forum topic to be about.

Step two:

Research how many people are interested in the subject matter by looking at search volume data for keywords associated with it. This will help determine whether there is a large enough audience for your blog or forum.

Step three:

Set up a website and design it to be user-friendly and visually appealing. This will make visitors more likely to stick around and participate in the discussion.

Step four:

Start publishing content regularly and be sure to respond to comments from readers!

Step five:

Make money! You can do this by selling ad space on your website or using affiliate links for products related to domains. This strategy works best when you have built up some expertise in this area so that people want to listen. In addition, it's also important not too spammy with advertisements because no one wants their reading experience interrupted by ads every few minutes!

Useful Insight:

Start a forum only after doing research around the topic you plan to target using your forums. For example, stack overflow is targeting the programming problems, TripAdvisor is targeting the travel audience. What your forum is focused on?

12.10 Offer Consulting Services

Offering consulting services is another way to make money from domain development. This approach involves providing advice and guidance to people who are interested in starting their website or blog. You can charge a fee for your services, or you can offer them for free in exchange for a link back to your site or blog.

This strategy is ideal for people who have a lot of experience in this area and want to share their knowledge with others. It also has the potential to lead to long-term clients who will continue to use your services over time.

How to get started?

Step one:

The first step is to create a profile on a site like Upwork or Freelancer. This will allow you to showcase your skills and experience to potential clients.

Step two:

Next, start reaching out to people who may be interested in your services. You can do this by sending them an email or posting a message on social media.

Step three:

Once you have a few clients, it's important to establish clear expectations and set deadlines for each project. This will help ensure that both you and your clients are happy with the work that is being done.

12.11 Create a Course

Creating a course is another way to make money from domain development. This approach involves creating a tutorial or training program and selling it on your website or online learning portal such as Udemy, Skill Share etc. You can charge for this course, or you can offer it for free and collect the email of student and build a solid mailing list which you can use in future to promote another course or sell product.

This strategy is ideal for people who want to share their knowledge with others and help them in learning new skill.

How to get started?

Step one: Determine what you want to teach

Before you can create a course, you need to determine what it is that you want to teach. What are the steps involved in starting and running a website or blog? What are the most important things people need to know? Once you have a general idea of what you want to cover, start outlining the specifics.

Step two: Create a course outline

Once you have a general idea of what you want to teach, it's time to start outlining the specifics. What topics will you cover in your course? What order should they be presented in? How much detail will each topic include? The more detailed your outline is, the easier it will be to create the actual course.

Step three: Create your course material

Once you have a detailed outline, it's time to start creating the actual content for your course. This can include written material, videos, or audio recordings. If you're creating a video or audio course, be sure to include transcripts so that people who prefer to read can follow along.

Step four: Publish your course

Once your course is complete, it's time to publish it online. This can be done through a variety of platforms, such as Udemy, Teachable, coursera or skillshare. Be sure to promote your course on social media and through other channels to help get the word out.

Useful Insight:

Research about the course topic, demand of this in market, and your passion and knowledge around the topic is the key to get success in this business. When all these three meets i.e., there is high demand of the course you are offering, you are very knowledgeable and passionate about it and you did research about existing courses, online learning platform etc., only then you can expect significant results.

12.12 Write an E-Book

Writing an e-book is another way to make money from domain development. This approach involves writing a book that covers the topic of domains in detail. You can charge for this book, or you can offer it for free in exchange for a link back to your site or blog. You can make an audience of loyal reader who trust you and your work. Later, you can monetize by recommending product and getting commission or promoting follow author books and charge them based on your audience count.

How to get started?

Step one:

Decide on a topic for your e-book. It should be related to your domain name, and you should have enough knowledge about it. For example, you could write about how to choose an ideal name for your website or blog so that people will remember it more easily and find it faster in search engines like Google.

Step two:

Research the topic you have chosen. This is important, as you want to make sure that your book is packed with information that people will find useful. You can do this by reading other e-books on the subject, conducting online research, or interviewing experts in the field.

Step three:

Write a rough draft of your book in Microsoft Word or any other word processing program. This will help you to get all of your ideas down on paper before committing them permanently through typing up into an e-book format such as PDF, eBook Reader, or Kindle editions (eBooks can be published electronically via Amazon's self-publishing service).

Step four:

Find a graphic designer to help you with the cover of your book. This is important, as people will often judge a book by its cover. Make sure that the design is eye-catching and professional-looking.

Step five:

Upload your e-book to Amazon's Kindle Direct Publishing service and set a price for it. You can also choose to make it available for free.

Step six:

Promote your e-book through social media and other online channels. This is important, as you want to ensure that as many people as possible know about it and can purchase or download it.

Useful Insight:

There are several marketplaces available today to share and sell your eBooks and it can be around any topic you are interested in. Yu can write anywhere between 3000 to 80,000 words. Amazon kindle is great marketplace for eBooks to start with.

1. **Start a Podcast**

Starting a podcast is another way to make money from domain development. This approach involves recording an audio file that covers the topic in detail. You can charge for this file, or you can offer it for free in exchange for a link back to your site or blog.

How to get started?

Step one:

Decide on the topic of your podcast. You can choose to focus on domain development, or anything related to it such as SEO and keyword research. Always select a particular niche and try to remain in them. It will help in long term as people start believing you as a subject matter expert in that specific niche and you can make a loyal audience. In any business, if you have a loyal audience, there are hundreds different ways to monetize it later.

Step two:

Start recording an audio file that covers the topic of your podcast from beginning to end. Make sure you have a clear voice with no background noise so listeners can hear what you're saying.

Step three:

Upload your podcast to a site like iTunes, SoundCloud etc. This will make it easier for people to find and download. Include link of your website in the description so that people can find you if they want to know more about you.

Step four:

Create a page on your website that promotes your podcast. Include information about the topics covered, as well as how people can access them.

Step five:

Start promoting your podcast. You can share it on social media or use paid advertising like Facebook Ads to get more exposure for your podcast and improve its chances of being found by potential listeners.

Step six:

Make money by getting sponsorship from brands related to your podcast topic. You can recommend product, courses, books, or anything related to your topic in your podcast. For example, if someone buys a product because they heard about it on your podcast, you can receive a commission for referring them in your podcast. The amount you make here depends on how much following you have, how many people are listening to your podcast, what product you are promoting etc.

Step seven:

Continue producing new episodes regularly so people have a reason to keep coming back. This will help you build a following and increase your chances of making money in the long run.

12.13 Start a YouTube Channel

Starting a YouTube channel is another way to make money from domain development. This approach involves creating videos that cover the topic of domains in detail.

How to get started?

Step one:

Create a YouTube channel which is relevant to your domain name. create a webpage to move traffic from your YouTube video to your webpage. Remember, all these strategies works only if your domain name and your niche are relevant to each other, and you have knowledge about the topic you are choosing to make video.

Step two:

Start creating videos. If you are new to this, then create a series of short videos that explain the basics of topic you choose and provide some tips on how to do so effectively. Make sure that each video is easy to understand and follow along with, as well as informative enough for your audience to want more.

Step three:

Promote your videos. This can be done in several ways, including social media, blog posts, and even paid advertisement.

Step four:

Wait for the views to come in. Once you have started creating content and promoting it, you will need to give it some time to start generating traffic and views. This can take anywhere from a few days to several months depending on how much content you have created and how popular it is with your target audience. In the meantime, continue to create more video around you niche.

Step five:

Repeat the process. Once you have started generating some income from your videos, then repeat this process over again with new content on your other domain name. This will take some time, but it can be done if you are determined enough!

12.14 Start a Coupon-Based business

One way to make some extra money is to start a coupon-based business. This could involve setting up a website or blog where people can find coupons for local businesses.

How to get started?

To get started, you'll need to follow these simple steps

Step one: Create a logo:

Create a unique logo for your coupon site. If you are not great with graphic design, then consider hiring someone on Elance or oDesk to create the logo.

Step two: Register a domain name and hosting service:

Go ahead and register a domain name to protect your brand. You'll also need some web hosting services to get started. You can usually get hosting for less than $10 per month.

Step three: Build the site:

Now comes the fun part! Make your website look unique and professional by hiring a web developer. Remember, this business is all about coupons, so make sure you include updated coupons on the page. Make the coupons easy to find and organize them by category.

Step four: Promote your coupon site:

Now comes the hardest part of all. You'll want to promote your site so that people can find it. If you are not good at web marketing, then consider hiring someone on Elance or oDesk to help you promote your domain development business.

12.15 Tip for Making Money from Domain Development

One of the most important things to remember is that it takes a lot of hard work and dedication to be successful. Here are a few tips for making money from domain development:

- **Focus on quality:**

To make money from domain development, it is important to focus on creating high-quality websites. This means ensuring that your sites are well designed, user friendly, and optimized for search engine ranking.

- **Research your keywords:**

To ensure that your website traffic is targeted and relevant, you need to do your research and find the right keywords to target.

- **Create valuable content:**

To keep people coming back to your site, you need to provide high-quality, relevant, and engaging content. This could include articles, blog posts, images, or videos.

- **Promote your site:**

Once your website is up and running, you need to start promoting it. This can be done through online marketing channels such as social media, search engine optimization, and Pay-Per-Click advertising.

12.16 Hiring a Freelancer to make Money from Domain Development

If you don't want to spent time in developing your domain name or lacking the skill needed, a freelancer can be hired to help with the creation and promotion of your website. This could include tasks such as designing the website, creating content, and conducting online marketing campaigns. Many freelancers specialize in these areas, so it should be easy to find someone who can help you get your website up and running.

Both Fiverr and Upwork are great platforms for finding freelancers who can help with website creation and promotion. To find a freelancer on Fiverr, simply type in the keyword such as "domain development", "content writer", or "web developer" into the search bar and you will be presented with a list of freelancers who offer these services.

On Upwork, there are many more freelancers to choose from. You can filter your search results by location, skills, and hourly rate to find the perfect freelancer for your project. Once you have found a freelancer that you would like to hire, send them a proposal outlining the details of the project. If they are interested, they will accept your proposal and you can then move on to the next step of developing your domain name.

13.

USEFUL RESOURCES

" All the resources we need are in mind."

-Theodore Roosevelt

This chapter serves as a comprehensive guide to the essential tools, websites, and organizations that can empower domain investors with valuable information and assistance throughout their journey in the domain industry.

From domain history resources to marketplaces for buying and selling, from domain appraisal tools to domain research platforms, this chapter covers an array of valuable resources that cater to various aspects of domain investing. Whether you are a seasoned domain investor or just starting, these resources will prove invaluable in enhancing your domain portfolio management, conducting thorough domain research, and staying up to date with the latest trends and developments in the domain market.

As you explore the different sections of this chapter, you will find detailed descriptions and insights into each resource's functionalities and benefits. We have handpicked these resources based on their reliability, usability, and reputation within the domain community, ensuring that you have access to the best tools available.

Remember that the domain industry is dynamic, with new tools and platforms emerging regularly. Therefore, we encourage you to keep an open mind and continually explore and experiment with different resources to find the ones that best suit your unique domain investment goals and preferences.

Whether you are seeking historical data to assess domain trends, conducting domain appraisals for accurate valuation, or searching for reputable marketplaces to buy or sell domains, the "Useful Resources" chapter equips you with the knowledge and tools to make well-informed decisions and thrive as a domain investor.

Harness the power of these resources to unlock the full potential of your domain portfolio, expand your domain investment strategies, and build a strong foundation for success in the dynamic and exciting world of domain investing.

Domain name history resources

Domain research for traffic analysis

Expired domain name resources

Domain appraisal resources

Domain marketplace for buying & selling

Domain brainstorming

Domain investing updates

Other useful resources

13.1 Domain name history resources

When you plan to register a domain name, there are three possibilities:

No history: The name is not used by anyone before, and you are registering it first time and it usually available at cheapest price.

Bad history: That means the domain name may have some malicious code or sensitive data before or it is blacklisted by search engine such as google, yahoo. It is difficult to rank this domain name in search engine and from SEO standpoint of view, you should stay away from these domain name with bad history.

Good history: This usually means that these domain name have good backlinks from reputed websites, have high domain authority and in the past, these domain names have great ranking in search engine. This usually a good sign and you should go for these domain name. But due to competition in market, these domain names are difficult to find as domain investor register these names as soon as they are available. These names are little expensive than usual price.

So, domain history is very important when registering a domain name, we must check it before registering any domain name. Here I am providing a list of resources which you can use to check domain history:

WhoIs (free): It is a free tool to track the history of domain name and it provides a lot of information about the domain name such as ownership details, statistics, name server information, registration and expiry dates, and registrar data You can search based on domain name or even using an IP address.

URL: https://who.is/

HosterStats (free): This is another free tool which is helpful in tracking the history of domain name using their historical DNS database. HosterStats is in business from 2000 and claims to hold a database of more than 600 million domain names.

URL: http://hosterstats.com/

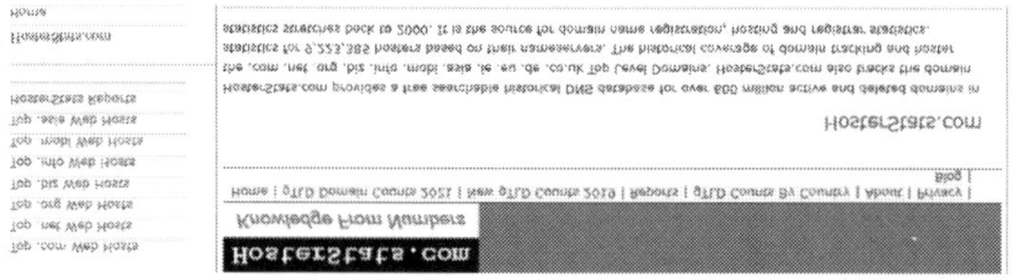

Norton Safe Web (free): This tool is provided by Norton Security to scan the domain name for any history of malicious behavior or unsafe code. You can check the domain name on this website whether it is blacklisted in past or not. This tools is not a typically history checker like other in this list, but you can use it to check the malware or any malicious code hosted on this domain name in past.

URL: https://safeweb.norton.com/

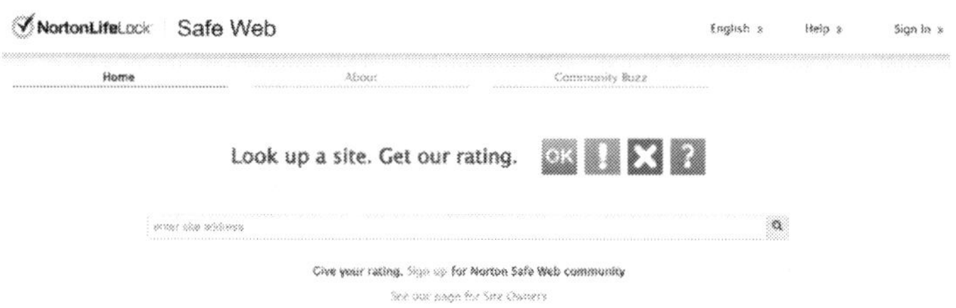

Internet archive wayback machine (free): This is a great tool to check how a website look like in past at specific date. It helps you to capture, manage and search complete information about websites or domain names. The best thing about archive wayback machine is you don't need any technical knowledge or coding skill to use this system and it is free to use.

URL: https://archive.org/web/

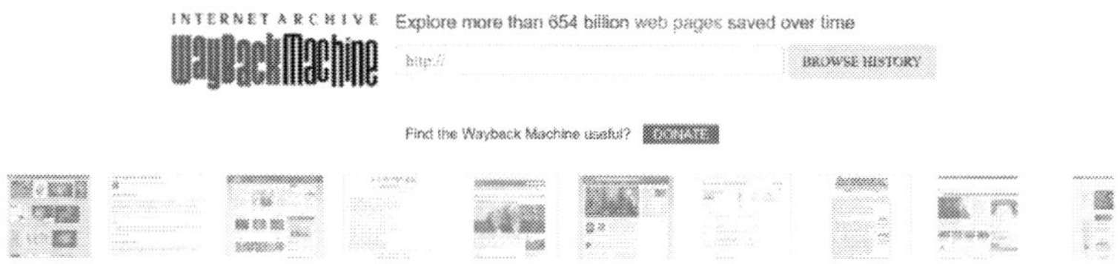

Domain tools (paid): It provides a in-depth information, statistics and previous owner information about the domain name. But it come at a cost of $99 per month. I don't recommend to spent anything on this service when you already have access to other competitive free tools. If you are investing a heavy amount in domain names, you can consider subscribing their service.

URL: https://research.domaintools.com/research/whois-history/

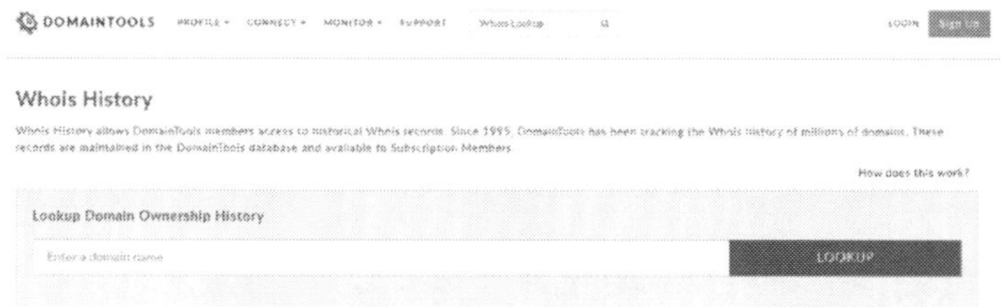

Besides these, there are many other great tool available such as WhoIsXMLApi (https://whois-history.whoisxmlapi.com/lookup), ICANN Lookup (https://lookup.icann.org/), WhoIsRequest (https://whoisrequest.com/) etc.

13.2 Domain name sale history

To make an informed decision on domain flipping, you should know the previous sale/purchase price of the domain name or related or similar name. It is very important to make profit in this market that you should have sale history information. For example, if a domain name with domain extension of ".net" is selling for $500 then corresponding ".com" domain name has much higher price. Here is some great tool for researching the sale history of similar domain name:

DNPric.es (free): It maintain a database of more than 2 million domain sales and continuously adding data of recent sales in database. It is very helpful in getting the sale price of similar domain names.

URL: http://dnpric.es/

NameBio (paid): It is another great tool to get historical domain name sales information.

URL: https://namebio.com/

13.3 Domain research for traffic analysis

If you know the traffic history, SEO ranking, domain authority and search engine ranking of a domain name, you can take an informed decision while selling or buying it. To analyze traffic, keyword research, and tracking keyword ranking, we can use the following tools:

SEMRush (paid): It is one of the best website traffic research tools. You can get the number of unique visitors, number of pageviews, bounce rate, average time spent in a session and much more details.

URL: https://www.semrush.com/

https://majestic.com/

https://ahrefs.com/

https://web.archive.org/

https://www.domcop.com/

https://inbackorder.com/

13.4 Expired domain name resources

Here is the list of some very useful expired domain name resources with their description:

1. ExpiredDomains.net
    - Description: ExpiredDomains.net is a comprehensive and user-friendly platform that provides a wide range of expired domain data. It offers an extensive list of expiring, expired, and dropped domain names from various domain extensions, along with useful metrics such as Domain Authority (DA), Page Authority (PA), and backlink count.
    - Link: https://www.expireddomains.net/
    - Cost: Free (Some advanced features may require registration or subscription).
2. NameJet
    - Description: NameJet is a popular domain auction platform that specializes in expired and deleting domain names. It offers a vast inventory of high-quality domain names from various TLDs that are about to expire or have already expired.
    - Link: https://www.namejet.com/
    - Cost: Free to browse, but participation in domain auctions requires registration and potential bidding fees.
3. GoDaddy Auctions
    - Description: GoDaddy Auctions is a well-known marketplace for buying and selling domain names, including expired domains. It features a wide selection of expired domain names that have been previously registered but not renewed by their owners.
    - Link: https://auctions.godaddy.com/

- Cost: Free to browse, but participation in domain auctions requires registration and potential bidding fees.

4. Dropping.com

   - Description: Dropping.com is a domain name research tool that provides information about expiring and expired domain names. It offers valuable insights into domain auctions, drop lists, and domain statistics to help domain investors make informed decisions.
   - Link: https://www.dropping.com/
   - Cost: Free to access domain drop lists and basic domain statistics. Premium features may require a subscription.

5. Expireddomains.co

   - Description: Expireddomains.co is a website that aggregates data from various sources to provide a list of recently expired domain names. It offers sorting and filtering options based on domain metrics and TLDs.
   - Link: https://expireddomains.co/
   - Cost: Free to use, with optional premium features available.

6. FreshDrop

   - Description: FreshDrop is a domain search engine that allows users to find expired and dropping domain names. It offers advanced filtering options to discover valuable domain names based on metrics, keyword relevance, and other criteria.
   - Link: https://www.freshdrop.com/
   - Cost: Requires registration, with free and paid membership options.

7. DomCop

   - Description: DomCop is a powerful expired domain search platform that provides access to thousands of expired domains. It offers detailed domain metrics, backlink data, and various filtering options to facilitate domain research.

- Link: https://www.domcop.com/
- Cost: Offers both free and premium membership plans with varying levels of access and features.

8. ExpiredDomains.io

- Description: ExpiredDomains.io is a domain research tool that offers a database of expired and expiring domain names. It provides valuable data such as Alexa Rank, Moz metrics, and Majestic Trust Flow to help identify valuable domain opportunities.
- Link: https://expireddomains.io/
- Cost: Offers free basic access, with additional features available through subscription plans.

These expired domain name resources serve as valuable tools for domain investors, providing insights into valuable domain opportunities that can be acquired and repurposed for various purposes. Whether you're seeking to enhance your domain portfolio, find domains with strong backlink profiles, or discover high-authority expired domains, these platforms offer a wealth of information to support your domain investment strategies. Remember to explore their features and offerings to determine the best fit for your domain investing needs.

13.5 Domain appraisal resources

Here is the list of some very useful domain appraisal resources with their description:

EstiBot

- Description: EstiBot is a widely recognized domain appraisal tool that uses artificial intelligence and machine learning algorithms to estimate the value of a domain name. It provides a comprehensive appraisal report, considering various factors such as domain length, keyword popularity, search volume, and comparable sales data.
- Link: https://www.estibot.com/
- Cost: Both free and paid appraisal options available. The free version provides limited data, while the paid version offers more detailed reports.

2. GoDaddy Domain Appraisal

   - Description: GoDaddy Domain Appraisal is a service provided by GoDaddy, one of the largest domain registrars in the world. It offers domain owners a quick and straightforward appraisal of their domain's estimated value based on market trends and historical sales data.

   - Link: https://www.godaddy.com/domain-value-appraisal

   - Cost: Free appraisal service.

3. NameBio

   - Description: NameBio is a domain sales and data platform that aggregates historical domain sales data. While not a direct appraisal tool, NameBio is valuable for domain investors to analyze past sales of similar domain names, providing insights into potential values for comparable domains.

   - Link: https://namebio.com/

   - Cost: Free to use for domain sales research.

4. Free Valuator

   - Description: Free Valuator is a domain valuation platform that provides an estimated value for a domain based on factors such as keyword popularity, domain length, and TLD extension. It offers users a basic appraisal to understand a domain's potential worth in the market.

   - Link: https://www.freevaluator.com/

   - Cost: Free appraisal service.

5. Valuate.com

   - Description: Valuate.com is a domain appraisal tool developed by Epik, offering automated domain valuations using statistical analysis and comparable sales data. It provides users with an estimation of a domain's value and supporting metrics to assess its potential market worth.

   - Link: https://valuate.com/

   - Cost: Free appraisal service.

6. Website Outlook

    - Description: Website Outlook is a multifunctional platform that offers a domain appraisal feature alongside other website analysis tools. It provides users with estimated domain values based on factors like website traffic, domain age, and search engine rankings.
    - Link: https://www.websiteoutlook.com/
    - Cost: Free appraisal service.

7. ValuableDomains

    - Description: ValuableDomains is an online domain appraisal service that evaluates domains based on a combination of machine learning and manual review. It provides domain owners with comprehensive appraisal reports, including comparable sales and domain-specific insights.
    - Link: https://valuabledomains.com/
    - Cost: Paid appraisal service with various pricing options based on the level of detail and data provided in the report.

These domain appraisal resources serve as valuable tools for domain investors to assess the potential value of their domain names or domains they are interested in acquiring. While automated appraisals can provide quick estimates, it's essential to remember that the true value of a domain is subjective and may vary depending on various market factors. As such, consulting multiple appraisal resources and conducting thorough research can lead to a more informed appraisal and better understanding of a domain's market potential.

13.6 Domain marketplace for buying & selling

If you love writing books then you should definitely use this easy to use yet professionally formatted book layout for your next book. The heading above this paragraph is "Level 3" heading.

13.7 Domain brainstorming resources

If you love writing books then you should definitely use this easy to use yet professionally formatted book layout for your next book. The heading above this paragraph is "Level 3" heading.

13.8 Domain investing updates

If you love writing books then you should definitely use this easy to use yet professionally formatted book layout for your next book. The heading above this paragraph is "Level 3" heading.

13.9 Other useful resources

If you love writing books then you should definitely use this easy to use yet professionally formatted book layout for your next book. The heading above this paragraph is "Level 3" heading.

Domain research for traffic analysis

https://majestic.com/

https://ahrefs.com/

https://web.archive.org/

https://www.domcop.com/

https://inbackorder.com/

Expired domain name resources

https://www.expireddomains.net/

Afterleaf

FreshDrop.com

1. auctions.godaddy.com – an annual subscription of $4.99

2. www.namejet.com – a free service

3. www.snapnames.com – a free service

4. www.pool.com – a free service

Paid

https://www.spamzilla.io/pricing/

Domain appraisal resources

Godaddy appraisal

Estibot.com

Mxtoolbox.com/domain

Estibot.com and Valuate.com

Domain marketplace for buying & selling

https://www.namepros.com/

https://sedo.com/us/

https://www.dynadot.com/

Domain brainstorming

Domain Investing Updates

DomainSherpa.com,

DomainInvesting.com

TheDomains.com

DomainNameWire.com

and DNJournal.com.

ChineseLandrush.com

Other useful resources

Whois.net

Domainhole.com

Namemesh.com

14.

GLOSSARY

I try to cover in-depth information about all the topic related to domain investing and flipping in this book. Here I am providing the common terms related to domain name investing for your understanding. The glossary given below will cover all the frequently used vocabulary in domain industry.

A

- **A Record**: A record is a specific piece of information in a domain name system (DNS) database. For example, an A record tells the browser where to find the web server associated with a given website.
- **Acquisition**: The process of purchasing or obtaining domain names for investment purposes.
- **Appraisal**: The evaluation and estimation of the value of a domain name, taking into account factors such as market demand, domain metrics, and comparable sales.
- **Auction**: A competitive bidding process for the sale of domain names, where the highest bidder wins the domain.
- **A-Label**: An "A-Label" in domain naming terminology refers to an ASCII representation of an Internationalized Domain Name (IDN), which allows non-ASCII characters such as accented letters or non-Latin script characters to be included within domain names. An IDN's A-label provides compatibility with existing DNS infrastructure by being encoded ASCII version of an IDN name.
- **Add Grace Period (AGP):** The Add Grace Period allows domain registrars an extended grace period after registering a domain name, during which time they can cancel it without incurring full registration cost and receive a refund from their registry. This window gives registrars time to correct registration mistakes without paying full cost of registration again.

- **Advisory Committee**: An advisory committee in the domain industry refers to a group of individuals or representatives from different stakeholder organizations who provide advice and recommendations regarding policy matters, regulations for domain name use and any industry issues that need attention.

- **AfriNIC**: AfriNIC (African Network Information Centre) is one of the Regional Internet Registries (RIRs), responsible for allocating and managing Internet number resources such as IP addresses and Autonomous System Numbers in Africa.

- **After-market**: In the domain industry, an aftermarket is defined as the secondary marketplace where already registered domains can be bought and sold between investors or end users, meaning these domains no longer available through primary registration processes.

- **Applicant**: For domain names, an applicant refers to any individual or organization who submits an application in order to secure new generic top-level domain (gTLDs), domain services and related provisions.

- **Applicant Guidebook**: This document from ICANN (Internet Corporation for Assigned Names and Numbers) details all the rules, procedures and requirements necessary for applying to operate a new gTLD.

- **Applications**: Applications in the domain industry refers to formal submissions submitted by individuals or entities seeking a new gTLD domain extension or additional domain services.

- **Application forms**: An application form serves as the main interface through which applicants provide all of the pertinent details and information when applying for new gTLD or domain related services.

- **Application Round**: An application round refers to a defined period during which applicants can submit applications for new gTLDs and related domain-related services as established by ICANN.

- **Applied-for gTLD**: An applied-for gTLD string refers to any proposed or requested string for a generic top-level domain (gTLD), submitted as part of an applicant's application process for creating new generic top-level domains (gTLDs).

- **ARIN**: ARIN stands for American Registry for Internet Numbers and serves as one of the Regional Internet Registries (RIRs), responsible for allocating and managing Internet resources such as IP addresses and Autonomous System Numbers in North America, parts of the Caribbean, and sub-Saharan Africa.

- **ARPANET**: ARPANET was an early form of packet switching network and precursor to today's internet, created in the late 1960s by ARPA. Now managed by U.S. Department of Defense Advanced Research Projects Agency, this pioneer network laid down foundation for today's interconnected global web of interlinked systems.

- **ASO (Address Supporting Organization)**: One of three supporting organizations under ICANN, ASO is charged with representing the interests of Regional Internet Registries (RIRs) on policy matters related to managing and allocating IP addresses.

- **Auction**: An auction in terms of domain names refers to a competitive bidding process where multiple parties vie to acquire one specific domain name at auction; ultimately the highest bidder wins their desired domain.

- **Auction Round**: An auction round refers to an area within a domain name auction process where bidders may place bids on available domain names and place bids accordingly.

- **Auction Sniping**: Auction sniping is a strategy used in domain name auctions where bidders wait until the very last moments to place an aggressive high bid, hoping to outbid other participants and secure the domain name they seek.

- **AXFR**: AXFR (Authoritative Transfer) is a DNS protocol used for moving entire DNS zone files between DNS servers during updates or transfers between DNS servers.

B

- **Broker**: A domain broker acts as an intermediary between domain sellers and buyers, facilitating domain sales and negotiations.

C

- **Country Code Top-Level Domain (ccTLD):** A country code top-level domain (ccTLD) is a TLD that corresponds to a specific country.

- **Cybersquatting**: Cybersquatting refers to registering an existing trademarked domain name in order to sell it to the trademark owner.

D

- **Domain**: A unique and human-readable name used to identify a website on the internet.
- **Domain Flipping**: The practice of buying domains at a lower price and then selling them for a profit, usually after a short holding period.
- **Domain Name Registrar**: A company or organization authorized to sell and manage domain names on behalf of domain registries.
- **Domain Parking**: Monetizing a domain by placing advertisements on a parked page when the domain is not in use.
- **Domain Portfolio**: A collection of domain names owned by an individual or entity for investment purposes.
- **Domain Registry**: The authoritative database that maintains domain name registrations for specific top-level domains (TLDs).
- **Domain Transfer**: The process of moving a domain name from one registrar to another.
- **Domain Valuation**: The process of determining the monetary worth of a domain name based on various factors.
- **Domain Name System (DNS):** The Domain Name System (DNS) is a hierarchical naming system used by Internet services in order to convert human-readable domain names into numeric IP addresses.

E

- **Expire Domain**: A domain name that has not been renewed by the owner and has entered the grace period before being released for registration by others.
- **Early Access Program (EAP)**: An Early Access Program (EAP) is an exciting phase of domain launch where interested parties may register domains before general availability to the general public. EAP typically lasts several days and

includes tiered pricing that rewards early registration with higher fees but lower costs over time.

- **End User**: When discussing domain names, an "End User" refers to any consumer or customer who utilizes one for websites, email accounts or any other internet-based services.
- **EPP Code**: An Extensible Provisioning Protocol (EPP) code, commonly referred to as an authorization code or transfer code, must be acquired from your current domain registrar in order to transfer a domain name registration to another registrar.
- **ERDRP**: The Emergency Response Domain Name Registration Policy (ERDRP), established by ICANN, allows rapid registration and activation of domain names linked to disasters, crises or emergencies to support emergency response efforts.
- **Escrow**: Domain name escrow is an alternative financial arrangement where a trustworthy third-party service securely holds payment from both buyers and sellers during domain sales transactions, providing for an equitable exchange. Once transaction terms have been fulfilled, this escrow service releases both payments and domain to their respective parties.
- **Evaluation Fee**: The evaluation fee is a non-refundable charge paid by applicants during the new gTLD application process and used to review initial applications to ensure only serious applicants advance to further stages of evaluation.
- **Evaluator**: An evaluator is defined as any individual or entity responsible for reviewing new generic Top-Level Domain (gTLD) applications to assess and verify they satisfy ICANN's set criteria and regulations for new gTLD registration applications.
- **Existing TLD**: Established top-level domains (such as.com,.org and.net) that have been around since the dawn of internet use constitute existing TLDs.
- **Extended Evaluation**: Extended Evaluation is an additional phase in the new gTLD application process that occurs when an application encounters challenges that require further examination and allows applicants to address identified issues before final decision on their application is reached.

- **Extended Evaluation period**: The Extended Evaluation period provides applicants with time to respond to extended evaluation questions and address any deficiencies found in their applications for new gTLDs.

F

- **Flipping**: The act of buying and selling domains for profit, usually in a short period.

G

- **Generic Top-Level Domain (gTLD)**: A generic top-level domain (gTLD) is a TLD that has been approved by the Internet Corporation for Assigned Names and Numbers (ICANN).
- **Grace Period**: The grace period is a set amount of time in which an expired domain name can be renewed for the original registration fee.
- **GTLDs**: A registry for generic top-level domains (gTLDs).

I

- **Investor**: An individual or entity engaged in the business of acquiring, holding, and selling domain names for investment purposes.
- **ICANN**: The Internet Corporation for Assigned Names and Numbers (ICANN) is responsible for managing the domain name system root zone, coordinating unique global identifiers, and managing policies regarding internationalized domain names.

L

- **Leasing**: Allowing another party to use a domain for a specified period in exchange for periodic lease payments.

N

- **New gTLD**: Generic top-level domains introduced after the expansion of domain extensions, such as .app, .blog, and .shop.

P

- **Portfolio Management**: The strategic planning, tracking, and optimization of a domain investor's collection of domain names.
- **Parking**: Parking refers to displaying advertisements on parked domain names.
- **PDP**: PDP stands for Policy Development Process and is used by ICANN as part of their systematic approach for creating, amending and retiring policies that govern different aspects of domain name system operation and internet use. ICANN utilizes multiple phases involving community input, analysis and consensus-building for this process to ensure an equitable policy development process that ensures equitable decision-making outcomes.
- **Phishing**: Phishing is a fraudulent practice in which attackers attempt to deceive users into giving away sensitive data such as login credentials, credit card numbers or personal data by impersonating trustworthy organizations through deceptive emails, websites or messages.
- **Policy Process Steering Committee (PPSC):** ICANN established the Policy Process Steering Committee (PPSC) as part of their policy development process to monitor and support it, making sure it adheres to established procedures while offering all interested stakeholders equal participation opportunities in policy creation and review.
- **PDDRP**: Post-Delegation Dispute Resolution Procedure (PDDRP) is an arbitration system devised by ICANN to resolve disputes related to the operation or management of TLDs once delegated to registry operators. Third parties have access to PDDRP for raising concerns over compliance issues with contractual agreements by registry operatorss.
- **Pre-delegation test**: New gTLD applicants must go through an evaluation process known as Pre-delegation before being delegated a top-level domain by registry operators. It assesses both their technical and operational readiness to operate their top-level domain successfully.
- **Premium Domain Name**: A premium domain name refers to any name considered highly valuable due to factors like length, keyword relevance, brandability or market demand. Registry operators often charge higher registration or renewal fees for premium domains.

- **Premium Letters**: Premium letters refer to letters that are considered highly valued for domain name selection due to their rarity, memorability or linguistic relevance; these can often be associated with high-value keywords or acronyms.

- **Primary Contact**: A Primary Contact is defined as an individual or entity who serves as the point-of-contact between domain registrar and domain owner/registrant.

- **Principal Place of Business (PPB)**: A primary place of business refers to where an organization or business conducts most of their primary operations and activities.

- **Push**: In domain terminology, "push" refers to the process of moving domain names within one registrar without initiating formal transfer procedures - often for domain sales or account changes between users of that registrar. This term can also refer to sub registrar transfers within an organization registrar as opposed to using various different ones for various domains registrars.

R

- **Renewal**: The process of extending the registration period for a domain name beyond its expiration date.

- **Redemption Period**: The redemption period is a set amount of time in which an expired domain name can be renewed for the original registration fee plus a penalty.

- **Reverse Domain Hijacking**: Reverse domain hijacking is a type of cybersquatting in which a trademarked domain name is acquired and then offered back to the trademark owner at a vastly inflated price.

S

- **Second-Level Domain (SLD)**: The part of a domain name that appears to the left of the dot, such as "example" in example.com.

- **Subdomain**: A subdomain is a section of a domain name, such as "www" in the domain name www.example.com.

T

- **Top-Level Domain (TLD)**: The highest level in the hierarchical domain naming system, such as .com, .net, or .org.
- **Trademark**: A legally registered symbol, name, or logo used to identify and distinguish goods or services of one company from others.

U

- **URL**: Uniform Resource Locator, a web address used to access specific resources on the internet.
- **U-Label**: U-Label or Unicode Label refers to an internationalized domain name (IDN). IDNs permit domain names incorporating non-ASCII characters (such as accented letters or non-Latin script characters) while still adhering to standard ASCII characters; its representation as U-Label encoded Unicode preserves these international character sets in domain names.
- **UDRP**: UDRP (Uniform Domain-Name Dispute-Resolution Policy) was devised by ICANN as an approach for settling disputes over domain names between trademark owners and domain registrants. The policy offers trademark holders a cost-effective yet efficient means for challenging the registration or use of domain names that resemble or confuse with their trademarks, providing trademark holders an avenue of legal recourse and cost savings against similar domain names registered or used without authorisation by trademark registrars or domain name registration companies.
- **Unicode**: Unicode is an international character encoding standard designed to represent every character found across writing systems worldwide, making possible the use of numerous languages, symbols and scripts including non-Latin characters in computing and internet applications.
- **Uniform Rapid Suspension (URS):** Introduced by ICANN to provide faster and cheaper resolution to domain dispute matters, the Uniform Rapid Suspension policy offers temporary suspension of domain ownership rather than transfer in cases involving trademark infringement or abuse of domain registrations.
- **usDRP**: The United States Dispute Resolution Policy is an alternative dispute resolution (ADR) policy specific to.us country-code top-level domain (ccTLD). It serves as a method for settling trademark holders' and domain registrants' disputes over domain registration in that ccTLD.

- **usNDP (United States Nexus Dispute Policy)**: This policy addresses nexus requirements for registration under the.us ccTLD and sets forth eligibility criteria and dispute resolution processes to govern those with connections to America seeking to register domain names under that ccTLD.

V

- **Variant characters**: Variant characters refer to alternate forms or representations of one character that could potentially create visual similarity among domain names in IDNs. Variant characters could lead to potential confusion and visual similarity among names due to domain registration similarities or conflicts in translation systems.

- **Variant TLDs**: Variant top-level domains contain letters with differing lengths in their labels that might cause visual similarity issues, leading to visual similarity concerns. ICANN has adopted a framework designed to mitigate such challenges and ensure accurate and secure resolution of domain name registrations.

W

- **W3C (World Wide Web Consortium)**: W3C is an international community dedicated to improving and expanding accessibility of the World Wide Web for generations of internet users worldwide. Their standards promote compatibility among various web technologies while encouraging long-term growth of this crucial internet medium.

- **WHOIS**: WHOIS is a public database providing registration and ownership details about domain names. Users are able to search this database to quickly gain information regarding domain registrants' contact info as well as registration dates.

- **WIPO**: The World Intellectual Property Organization (WIPO), an intergovernmental agency of the UN dedicated to intellectual property issues, offers dispute resolution services for domain name disputes through its Arbitration and Mediation Center.

Z

- **Zero Click Monetization**: Zero Click is a form of domain traffic monetization in which internet users are directed directly to particular content or advertisements without having to click through links first. It aims to maximize advertising revenues by serving relevant information directly as they type domain names into browsers.

AFTERWORD: NAVIGATING TOMORROW'S DIGITAL GOLDMINE

As we reach the end of *A Complete Guide to Domain Investing: Buy, Sell & Profit*, it's time to step back and contemplate the road we've traveled. This book has been your companion through the intricate maze of domain names, from their basic anatomy to the high-stakes art of flipping and portfolio building. But an afterword is not merely a farewell; it's a bridge to the future, a space for reflection, inspiration, and forward-thinking strategy. In these pages, I've poured over a decade of personal experience, blending lessons from triumphs—like selling a tech niche domain for six figures—and setbacks, such as navigating market crashes that wiped out speculative holdings. The domain industry, as of August 2025, is booming, signaling a resilient and expanding market. Yet, this growth is fueled by rapid technological shifts, making adaptability essential. In this detailed afterword, we'll revisit key insights, explore emerging trends, dissect recent sales for lessons, and chart a path forward. Whether you're holding your first domain or managing hundreds, the principles here will help you thrive in an era where domains are increasingly viewed as a powerful asset class, rivaling stocks or real estate in potential returns.

Domain investing isn't just about buying low and selling high; it's about understanding the digital ecosystem's pulse. As the internet becomes more embedded in daily life—with over 5 billion users worldwide—the demand for memorable, brandable web addresses surges. This book has equipped you with the tools to capitalize on that demand, but the real magic happens when you apply them. Let's start by recapping the core elements that form the foundation of successful domaining.

Recapping the Journey: Essential Takeaways from the Book

The structure of this guide was designed to build your expertise layer by layer, from novice concepts to advanced tactics. Here are the pivotal takeaways, organized by major themes, to reinforce your learning and serve as a quick reference for future endeavors:

- **Foundational Knowledge on Domain Basics**:
  - Grasp the structure: TLDs (e.g., .com, .io) are the extension, SLDs the unique label—together forming a domain's identity. Understand that you don't "own" a domain outright; it's a renewable registration, emphasizing the importance of timely renewals to avoid expiration cycles.

  - Differentiate roles: Registrars (like GoDaddy) handle sales, registries manage TLD databases, and registrants (you) are the end-users. Resellers add another layer for bulk deals, while WHOIS privacy shields your data from spammers.
- **Selecting and Securing Your Gateway: Registrars**:
  - Prioritize honest pricing, free WHOIS protection, and flexible timeframes. Top picks like Namecheap and NameSilo excel in customer support and TLD variety, while avoiding hidden fees in renewals can save hundreds annually.
  - Master transfers: A step-by-step process involving authorization codes and lock removals ensures smooth migrations, minimizing downtime risks.
- **Core Domaining Concepts and Strategies**:
  - Define your approach: Investing for long-term appreciation, flipping for quick profits, or parking for passive revenue. The lifecycle—registration, active use, expiration, deletion—offers entry points, with appraisals factoring in length, keywords, and traffic.
  - Avoid scams: Red flags include unsolicited high valuations or pressure sales; always use reputable tools like GoValue for accurate estimates.
- **Research and Buying Tactics**:
  - Value drivers: Short, memorable names in trending niches (e.g., AI, health) command premiums. Avoid hyphens or numbers unless niche-specific.
  - Methods: Hand registrations for new ideas, auctions for premiums, direct buys via outreach, or drop-catching expired domains using tools like DropCatch.
- **Selling and Monetization Mastery**:
  - Find buyers through marketplaces like Sedo or Flippa, negotiate with data-backed pricing, and close via escrow for security.
  - Beyond sales: Develop with blogs, affiliate marketing, or leasing—turning a $10 domain into $100/month passive income.
- **Portfolio and Financial Management**:
  - Set goals: Aim for diversification across 10-20 TLDs to mitigate risks. Use software for tracking acquisitions, sales, and expenses, ensuring positive cash flow.
  - Budget wisely: Allocate for renewals (5-10% of portfolio value) and taxes on profits.
- **Development and Resources**:
  - Strategies: Create content sites, sell ad space, or launch e-books/courses. Hire freelancers via Upwork for scaling.
  - Essential tools: DNJournal for sales history, ExpiredDomains.net for opportunities, and communities like NamePros for networking.

These takeaways encapsulate the book's essence: Knowledge empowers action, and consistent application yields results. Many readers have shared stories of their first profitable flip after applying these principles—proof that domaining is accessible to all.

The Pulse of 2025: Current Trends Shaping Domain Investing

Mid-2025 finds the domain market in a state of vibrant evolution, driven by technological innovations and shifting consumer behaviors. Collaborative industry reports highlight key developments, including TLD diversification and aftermarket growth. Registrations are up, but the real story is in quality over quantity—premium domains are fetching higher prices amid demand for brandable assets.

AI is the undisputed game-changer. AI-driven tools are automating domain discovery, valuation, and even prediction of future trends, allowing investors to scan thousands of options instantly. For instance, SaaS platforms now use machine learning to suggest undervalued names based on search volume and industry buzz, reducing manual labor and increasing accuracy. This democratization lowers barriers for beginners but raises the bar for pros, who must combine AI with human insight to spot creative opportunities like domain hacks (e.g., del.icio.us style).

Blockchain and decentralized domains are another frontier. Extensions like .crypto or .eth offer true ownership via blockchain, immune to central failures, and integrate with Web3 wallets for NFTs or DAOs. As blockchain adoption accelerates—projected to hit 1 billion users by 2030—these domains could appreciate exponentially, especially in crypto, gaming, and metaverse niches. Investors should allocate a small portion of portfolios here, balancing with traditional TLDs.

The .ai TLD's surge exemplifies trend-driven value. Registrations exploded in late 2024 to early 2025, fueled by the AI boom, with .ai now among the top extensions by count. In 2024, a significant portion of top sales were .ai, a pattern continuing as businesses rebrand for AI relevance. Similarly, eco-related domains (.green, "sustainable" keywords) are rising with global sustainability pushes, while voice-optimized names—short, phonetic—gain from smart device proliferation.

Cybersecurity is non-negotiable. With rising threats, domains with enhanced DNSSEC and privacy features command premiums. Regulatory shifts, like expanded data protection laws, may mandate better WHOIS handling, favoring compliant registrars.

Short, brandable domains remain king. Businesses prioritize memorability for branding, leading to a premium on single-word or creative hacks. ccTLDs like .io (tech) and .co (general) are widespread, offering affordability in saturated markets.

- **Niche Trends to Capitalize On**:
  - **AI/Tech**: Keywords like "quantum" or "bot"—pair with .ai for max value.

- **Sustainability**: "Eco" or "renewable" in .earth; align with green initiatives.
- **Health/Wellness**: Telehealth domains post-pandemic.
- **Web3/Metaverse**: .vr or blockchain for virtual real estate.
- **Local Markets**: ccTLDs for emerging economies, e.g., .in for India.

Overall, 2025's market is up, with sales volume jumping significantly in the first half of the year. This momentum suggests continued growth.

Lessons from Recent Sales: Case Studies in Profit Potential

Sales data provides concrete lessons. In 2024, Rocket.com sold for $14 million to a space startup, showcasing aspirational keywords' appeal in booming sectors like aerospace. Gold.com at $8.515 million went to a commodities firm, proving evergreen terms' stability. Shift.com ($1.365 million) highlighted versatility for business pivots.

In 2025, Bagels.com fetched $500,000, illustrating everyday food keywords' value in e-commerce. Solutions.com at $415,000 underscores generic terms' broad appeal. Peace.com (around $350,000) tied to social causes, showing emotional resonance boosts prices.

These cases teach: Align with trends, hold for appreciation, and market strategically.

- **Key Lessons from Sales**:
  - Timing: Sell during industry booms (e.g., AI surge for .ai).
  - Branding: Short, intuitive names win.
  - Diversification: Mix high-risk (trend) with low-risk (generic).
  - Negotiation: Use data to justify prices.

Future-Proofing Strategies: Adapting to Tomorrow's Market

To endure, evolve your approach. Integrate AI for research, diversifying into blockchain and new TLDs. Develop domains for passive income, using leasing or affiliates to weather slow sales.

Monitor regulations and cybersecurity; use secure registrars. Build community ties for insights.

- **Practical Steps**:
  - Quarterly audits: Refresh portfolio with trend names.
  - Experiment: Acquire one .ai monthly.
  - Automate alerts for drops.
  - Scale ethically, avoiding trademarks.

Personal Reflections and Parting Wisdom

Domaining has taught me resilience and creativity. It's not quick riches but steady building. As domains become prime assets, your potential is limitless.

Call to Action: Launch Your Domain Legacy

Act today—register, list, network. The future is yours; invest boldly.

Expanding Your Toolkit: Advanced Techniques for 2025 and Beyond

To push your domaining journey further, let's delve into advanced techniques that complement the book's strategies. These build on the foundational knowledge, offering nuanced approaches for scaling success in a competitive market.

Leveraging AI Beyond Basic Tools

While AI-driven platforms streamline research, advanced investors can take it further by customizing algorithms. For instance, create scripts to monitor Google Trends for emerging keywords, then cross-reference with TLD availability. This isn't just about speed; it's about precision—spotting a niche like "quantumhealth" before it trends globally. Collaborate with developers on platforms like GitHub to build bespoke tools, or subscribe to premium services offering predictive analytics.

Blockchain Domains: A Deep Dive

Blockchain domains are more than a fad; they're a paradigm shift. Unlike traditional domains, they reside on decentralized ledgers, offering permanent ownership without annual renewals. However, they require crypto wallets, and their market is volatile. Start small with a single .crypto domain, perhaps in a niche like "defifinance," and list it on OpenSea alongside traditional marketplaces. Monitor adoption rates—currently, only 0.1% of domains are blockchain-based, but growth is exponential.

Voice Search Optimization

Voice search, driven by devices like Alexa, demands domains that are short, phonetic, and natural. For example, "EasyRecipes.io" outperforms "Easy-Recipes-4U.com" in voice queries. Test your portfolio names by saying them aloud; if they're clunky, they're less likely to sell in this niche. Pair with SEO strategies to boost organic traffic, increasing passive income potential.

Geo-Specific Strategies

Emerging markets like India, Nigeria, and Brazil are digital goldmines. ccTLDs like .in or .ng are affordable yet high-potential due to local business growth. Research local industries—e.g., fintech in Lagos—and secure domains like "LagosPay.ng" for targeted flips. Partner with local entrepreneurs via LinkedIn for direct sales.

- **Advanced Techniques Checklist**:
    - Develop one AI tool monthly, even if basic, to automate niche discovery.
    - Allocate 5% of budget to blockchain domains for speculative growth.
    - Test all domains for voice compatibility; prioritize single-word or two-word names.
    - Target one emerging market per quarter, securing 2-3 ccTLDs per region.
    - Use analytics like Google Search Console to track domain traffic pre-sale.

Overcoming Common Pitfalls: A Deeper Look

The book highlighted scams and risks, but let's explore deeper traps and how to sidestep them. Overconfidence is a silent killer—buying too many domains without research can drain budgets. Set a strict limit, like 10 new registrations monthly, and validate each with appraisal tools. Another pitfall is emotional attachment; falling in love with a domain can prevent selling at peak value. Schedule regular portfolio reviews to stay objective.

Market volatility is another hurdle. Economic downturns can suppress demand, but they also unearth opportunities in distressed assets. During the 2020 crash, savvy investors snapped up expired domains from failed startups, flipping them post-recovery. Stay liquid to seize such moments.

Legal risks, like UDRP disputes, loom large. A reader once shared how they lost a domain resembling a brand name to a trademark claim. Always check USPTO and WIPO databases before buying, and avoid names too close to established brands.

- **Pitfall Avoidance Strategies**:
    - Cap monthly spending at 10% of liquid assets.
    - Sell domains reaching 80% of appraised value to avoid holding losses.
    - Use trademark search tools before every purchase.
    - Maintain a cash reserve for opportunistic buys during market dips.
    - Document all transactions to defend against disputes.

Real-World Success Stories: Inspiration for Your Journey

Let's ground these concepts with stories from domainers who applied similar principles. Sarah, a freelance writer, started with a $100 budget, buying "GreenTech.io" for $12. She developed a blog on sustainable tech, earning $30/month via ads, then sold it for $3,000 to a startup. Her key? Researching green trends and leveraging parking for interim income.

Mike, a corporate analyst, built a 50-domain portfolio focused on health tech. He leased "TeleDoc.health" for $200/month to a clinic, netting $2,400 annually while holding for a $10,000 sale. His strategy: Targeting niche TLDs and direct outreach to businesses.

Then there's Priya, a student who flipped "StudyAI.app" for $1,500 after buying it for $15. She used free tools like ExpiredDomains.net to find it and marketed it on social media, showcasing the power of low-budget starts.

- **Lessons from Success Stories**:
  - Start small but think big: Even $10 domains can yield 100x returns.
  - Combine monetization: Use parking or leasing while awaiting sales.
  - Market actively: Social media and forums amplify buyer reach.
  - Focus on niches: Align with personal expertise for better picks.
  - Persist: Initial failures are learning steps to bigger wins.

The Psychological Edge: Mastering the Mindset of a Domainer

Domaining isn't just technical; it's mental. Patience is critical—some domains take years to appreciate. Combat frustration by celebrating small wins, like a $100 flip. Fear of loss can paralyze; counter it with data-driven decisions, not gut instincts. Greed is another trap—holding out for unrealistic prices can lead to missed opportunities. Set clear exit strategies, like selling at 5x purchase price.

Community engagement boosts morale. Join NamePros or Reddit's r/Domains to share wins and learn from losses. One domainer I mentored doubled their portfolio value after forum advice led them to .ai domains during the 2024 boom.

- **Mindset Tips**:
  - Set realistic goals: Aim for 20% annual ROI initially.
  - Celebrate milestones: First sale, first $1,000 profit.
  - Stay disciplined: Limit speculative buys to 10% of budget.
  - Engage weekly: Post or comment in communities for perspective.
  - Reflect monthly: Review progress to stay motivated.

Building a Legacy: Domaining as a Long-Term Pursuit

Domaining isn't a sprint; it's a marathon with compounding rewards. A single domain can spark a business empire—think Amazon.com's humble start. Your portfolio could fund retirement, launch startups, or support philanthropy. One reader used profits from a $5,000 flip to fund a coding bootcamp, transitioning to a tech career.

Consider long-term trends: By 2030, the internet will likely host 2 billion websites, with domains central to digital identity. Position yourself now by securing names in nascent fields like quantum computing or space tourism.

- **Legacy-Building Steps**:
    - Reinvest 50% of profits into new domains or development.
    - Mentor others: Share knowledge to build industry goodwill.
    - Diversify income: Use domains for e-commerce or consulting.
    - Plan 5-10 years out: Target future industries like biotech.
    - Document your journey: Inspire others with a blog or book.

Final Call to Action: Your Domain Empire Awaits

This book has given you the map; now, it's time to explore. Register a domain today—perhaps a .ai name tied to an emerging tech. List an existing one on Sedo. Join a forum to learn one new tip weekly. The domain market rewards action, and your first step could lead to thousands in profit or a lifelong passion.

Thank you for trusting this guide. As domains evolve into digital gold, your potential is limitless. Invest wisely, learn continuously, and build boldly—your legacy starts now.

ONE LAST THING

Dear Reader,

I hope you enjoyed reading the book and learn some valuable information about domain name investing. I will be grateful if you post a short review about the book. Your support really does make a difference and I read all the reviews personally so I can get your feedback and make this book even better. Your feedback is very important for me.

If you'd like to leave a review, then all you need to do is click the review link on this book's page on Amazon.

Thanks again for your kind support!

Made in United States
Troutdale, OR
11/03/2026

56845401R00137